GOING FIRST CLASS?

New Approaches to Privileged Travel and Movement

Edited by

Vered Amit

Berghahn Books

New York • Oxford

First published in 2007 by

Berghahn Books
www.berghahnbooks.com

© 2007 Vered Amit

Library of Congress Cataloging-in-Publication Data

Going first class? : new approaches to privileged travel and movement /
edited by Vered Amit. -- 1st hardback ed.
  p. cm. — (EASA series ; v. 7)
  Includes bibliographical references and index.
  ISBN 1-84545-196-1 (hardcover : alk. paper) 1. Emigration and immigration—Social aspects—Case studies. 2. Transnationalism—Social aspects—Case studies. 3. Travel—Social aspects—Case studies. 4. Elite
(Social sciences)—Travel—Case studies.
I. Amit, Vered, 1955-

JV6225.G65 2006
304.8—dc22   2006100466

British Library Cataloguing in Publication Data
A catalogue record for this book is available from the British Library.

Printed in the United States on acid-free paper

Contents

1

Structures and Dispositions of Travel and Movement

Vered Amit

By design, the title of this collection of essays; *Going First Class? New Approaches to Privileged Travel and Movement* prompts the question of the type and scope of the "privileges" that should generally be addressed in comparative studies of spatial mobility and, in particular, by the present case studies. To note in response that privilege is relative is to invoke at one and the same time a tired truism and an open-ended set of analytical complications. Thus one of the central emphases in much of the anthropological literature on "elites" has concerned the importance of relating the issue of relative advantage and power to particular social and political contexts. As a result, anthropological writings on elites have featured situations that when compared to each other appear to be highly divergent in terms of relative resources, influence, power, and scale. Thus Carol Greenhouse's (1983) analysis of elite status concepts among local Baptist, business, and professional networks in a small Georgia suburban town is included in the same anthology as George Marcus's (1983) study of extremely wealthy American family dynasties. Similarly, the cases included in Shore and Nugent's compilation (2002) range from *mestizo* traders in a small rural Peruvian town (Harvey 2002) to the PRI political party machine that governed Mexico for seventy-one years (Gledhill 2002). In other words, anthropologists have dealt with the comparative problems of assessing the general concept of elite by calling upon a flexible notion of the "local" stretched to accommodate a wide range of organizational levels ranging from villages to nations.

Whatever one might generally make of such an accommodation in a discipline that over the last twenty-five years has made increasing efforts to problematize the "local," it is immediately complicated by an ethnographic focus on travel and movement. After all, the mandate of travel, and especially the kind of long-distance travel with which this volume is concerned, is the movement between different "locals." Accordingly, many of the chapters in this volume are concerned with the tensions between different hierarchies and criteria of status and privilege as travelers move from one context to another. Highly mobile British cinematographers who work on location around the world bristle at the suggestion that the "visual" expertise of their French, Polish, or Czech counterparts can provide a more innovative and distinctive product for British producers and directors looking to hone their own competitive advantage (Greenhalgh, this volume). Brazilians arriving in Portugal believed that their professional skills and cultural knowledge could ensure their integration into the Portuguese middle class, but to their surprise they discovered that their influence as well as professional and entrepreneurial success often provoked resentment rather than admiration (Torresan, this volume). The members of a middle-class Jamaican family who had immigrated to the United States worked hard to distinguish themselves from the masses of lower-class Caribbean emigrants with whom they were often identified by members of the receiving society (Olwig, this volume). In Indonesia, their common status as "Westerners" brings expatriates together with people from a wide variety of socioeconomic backgrounds, people with whom they would not normally have socialized in their home countries. And while Western status unifies as well as segregates, it has not eliminated the significance that still continues to be accorded to distinctions in corporate rank among these expatriates. (Fechter, this volume)

The chapters in this volume deal with very different types of voyaging: occupational journeys, migration, corporate-sponsored expatriacy, life-cycle transition. But they feature certain commonalities of privilege that may well point to broader developments in the global scapes of travel and movement. First, all of the chapters deal with instances of voluntary movement and with people who have the resources -variously of money, time, or credentials—to undertake these journeys. Second, if on a global scale the availability of these resources may demarcate these people as among the world's relatively affluent, they could not be described as members of its most powerful elites. They surely do not command the kind of resources or influence of the extremely wealthy ethnic Chinese entrepreneurial "astronauts" participating in the "Pacific Shuttle" described by Aihwa Ong (1999). Micklethwait and Wooldridge have contended that globalization has encouraged the formation of a "cosmocrat" ruling elite, although their description of a densely networked set of corporate executives with an almost "pathological need to remain in touch," hopping around the world, consuming sea bass from Chile, reading magazines like *Wallpaper* or *Condé Nast Traveler* (Micklethwait and Wooldridge 2000: 232–33), seems to owe more to the overworked caricatures promoted by these kinds of popular media outlets than to a rigorous analysis of global economics. In any event, not only do the travelers described in this book not participate in these kinds of lifestyles or occupy these types of socio-economic positions, but also their more modestly prosperous situations likely reflect a much broader reorientation of global long-distance travel and movement around middle-class rather than either very affluent or very poor voyagers.

There are various impetuses for this reorientation that are as much about the strengthening of existing trends as about entirely new developments. On the one hand, as Angela Torresan notes in her chapter, migration out-flows have always tended to select for people with access to the kind of resources and skills that would facilitate their mobility, whether these are personal network connections, financial resources, youth, education, and so on. Thus even those migrants who may appear relatively disadvantaged in respect to the hierarchies of their destination countries possess "above-average levels of education and occupational skills in comparison with their homeland population" (Portes and Rumbaut as cited in Torresan, p 106). Voluntary migrants are not usually drawn from among the poorest and most destitute sending populations. As industrialized countries have reoriented their economies (or at least their economic aspirations) toward knowledge-based industries, their immigration policies have featured an increased emphasis on recruiting highly skilled and well-educated new-comers, even as their sources of recruitment have shifted from the global North to the South.

On the other hand, as Sawa Kurotani's chapter illustrates, an intensifi-cation of global competition has forced many corporations to reorganize the nature of their overseas job assignments away from the elite cosmo-crats described by Micklethwait and Wooldridge. Facing American trade restrictions, the Japanese firms with which Kurotani is concerned moved their production sites to the United States and, subsequently recruited a wider variety of less elite company workers. To cut the cost of these for-eign assignments, Japanese companies have identified a specific group of workers as generic, longer term, overseas specialists and redefined these kinds of assignments from "prestige" to "routine," thereby allowing them to reduce the salary and special benefits that had previously been granted these expatriates. Along similar lines, a recent "how to" guide (Malewski 2005) for young expatriate workers notes that the efforts of corporations to reduce the costs of maintaining dispersed transnational operations has led to a greater tendency to recruit younger, more junior and hence cheaper workers for foreign assignments. Another corporate tactic noted by Malewski has been to formally redefine these assignments as "local" rather than overseas, thus eliminating the requirement to pay out the spe-cial benefits previously accorded "expat" professionals.

Leisure travel has always been and continues to be the province of the world's relatively affluent, those people with sufficient disposable income to expend on these discretionary diversions. But over the course of the second half of the twentieth century and now into the twenty-first, as tourist opportunities and venues have diversified, the numbers and strata of people who are involved as both consumers and purveyors of these services have dramatically expanded, forming the largest industry in the world (Sheller and Urry 2004: 3).

> Internationally there are over 700 million legal passenger arrivals each year (compared with 25 million in 1950) with a predicted 1 billion by 2010; there are 4 million air passengers each day; at any one time 300,000 passengers are in flight above the United States, equivalent to a substantial city; one-half of British adults took a flight during 2001 . . . (Ibid.)

By the time we reach this scale of mobility, we are dealing with many active participants whose wealth may be relatively modest. Thus, all of the Canadian travel enthusiasts included in Julia Harrison's study were working or had worked at professional or managerial jobs and most had some postsecondary education, but their annual incomes ranged from about $20,000 to well over $180,000 (2003: 8–9). As Harrison notes:

> The frequency and variety of the travels they took was imagined at one time to fall only within the grasp of the upper classes, those of established, money backgrounds. . . . For some of these travel enthusiasts, their ability even in retirement to bite at the heels of those in the social strata above them was the source of many a wry smile. As Neil said "We are living proof that you do not have to be rich to travel." (2003: 11)

Along with the augmentation of who can afford to travel for leisure at all, and who can afford to tour frequently, there has also been an interesting shift in who can afford to travel for longer. As Rodman's chapter in this volume illustrates, the increase in the numbers of people who can embark on extended travel, away from their usual places of residence, has been achieved through a blurring of the boundaries between leisure and work. The "resident volunteers" in the Kalani Oceanside Retreat on the big island of Hawaii, paid a maximum of $500 a month for their stay, as opposed to the $1,500 paid by guests. In return for these reduced charges, they worked 30 hours a week for at least a three month period. Their visits occurred on the margin between the categories of guest and staff who also stayed at this spiritual-education retreat, a boundary that was regularly blurred through shared participation in daily activities as well as the movement of people between these categories. "Some who came as guests went on to become resident volunteers and then paid staff; former staff and volunteers have returned to visit as guests" (Rodman, p 146).

Similarly, there is now a significant global workforce of young travelers, many voyaging as a break before or after completing postsecondary studies, who are supporting journeys of several months, occasionally even years, by working at the destinations they are visiting. Ironically, many of these young adventurers are supporting their own tourism by working in service industries serving other tourists. Thus, today, a tourist visiting a

London café or pub during the summer might well be served by a young traveler from his or her own country even as young Britons themselves leave their country for "gap year" sojourns abroad.

Overlapping Categories of Travel

This kind of overlap between different categories of spatial mobility is hardly a novel innovation. The transnational dispersal of the two family networks on which Karen Fog Olwig's chapter focuses, was formed through an initial stream of emigration from the Caribbean in the 1940s. Among the sets of siblings who were the progenitors of these networks, their respective departures from Jamaica and Dominica were initially prompted by a desire to pursue postsecondary educational opportunities abroad with an expectation of an eventual return in order to practice their acquired profession in their homeland. While some of these siblings did in due course return to their country of origin where they pursued successful careers, others settled abroad.

The immigration and border controls of most countries have traditionally stipulated a strict legal distinction between different categories of visitors, between migrants, tourists, students, temporary workers, and so on. But nonetheless the siblings with whom Olwig is concerned will hardly have been the first and certainly are not the last travelers to embark on temporary sojourns in one capacity only to end up staying in another. More generally, the overlap between different categories of travelers has been a significant aspect in the formation of unofficial migration channels. And most countries have always allowed some movement between these different statuses, offering amnesty to unofficial migrants, extending new visas to former students, converting temporary work permits into more permanent immigration standing, and so on.

What is more novel is the implementation of official categories of visitors that explicitly and intentionally incorporate an overlap between different forms of movement. Hence a number of countries now extend "working/holidaymaker" visas to young travelers, usually stipulating either an age restriction or student status. At the same time, international student exchanges may incorporate "co-op" work-study programs or internships, as well as opportunities for simple tourism. Thus three previously distinct statuses—guest worker, tourist, and visiting student—are now converged through visa programs underpinned by international agreements between governments, educational institutions, and travel consortia. An increasingly important segment of "guest" workers, a status once identified with relatively disadvantaged migrants, is thus now ironically comprised of middle-class Western youths who can at one and the same time be wooed as tourists and serve as cheap, compliant, and temporary labor.

At the other end of the life cycle we find a parallel development that also complicates the distinctions between categories of movement, in this case between migration and tourism. Caroline Oliver's chapter focuses on one segment of the burgeoning numbers of middle-class older people in Western countries who view retirement as a "a sphere of new opportunities, increasingly exploited through travel, marking a de-differentiation of tourism into retirement" (Oliver, p. 130). Accordingly, the seaside resorts of Spain, Florida, or Mexico, along with other sunny, coastal climes, have become the venues for an eclectic mix of short-stay tourists, long-term retirement residents, and so-called "snowbirds," retirees who divide their year between winters in warmer locales and summers in their less temperate countries of origin. So significant are these movements of retirees that the government of Canada recently made special efforts to encourage and enable their snowbird citizens to cast absentee votes during the January 2006 federal elections.

It is important to note that in all three types of situations identified above—the "resident volunteers" (Rodman, this volume), the "working holidaymakers," and the retiree migrants and tourists (Oliver, this volume)—geographic mobility has been initiated, in major part, as a vehicle for engaging with a significant life-cycle transition. While, as I will argue below and as others have also noted (Harrison 2003: 11), scholarly literature on tourism has sometimes exaggerated its transformative potential, I would like to suggest that the much more particular instances of life-cycle transition being pursued by a variety of contemporary travelers, while distinct, share a convergence between three different strategic opportunities for repositioning and affiliation.

Travel has a long-standing cachet of cultivated tastes; that is to say, it has been one of the grounds for demarcating or claiming, first, elite status (as in the European Grand Tour of the nineteenth century) and, more recently, middle-class standing (Harrison 2003: 11). This association has been further heightened by the elaboration of a public discourse within many industrialized countries that trumpets the importance of "international experience" within a globalizing economy. The importance of this source of status enhancement is heightened during a period of life-cycle transition in which other sources of cultural capital might well be jeopardized. People on the verge of retirement are losing one of the most critical indicators of social status, namely, a work identity, and are in most cases facing the diminishment of their financial resources. On the other hand, young people leaving home to pursue educational or career opportunities are shifting from the comfortable if secondhand affiliation of their parents' class position and resources to the much more precarious path of establishing their own claims for status and independent incomes. Finally, many of the volunteer residents seeking an educational retreat at Kalani were facing the uncertainties associated with leaving secure if unsatisfying jobs. In these circumstances, extended travel can both offer an escape from situations of potentially jeopardized status and provide its own source of cultural capital. It may well be more prestigious to be a retiree in a Spanish costal village than in Bolton. Similarly, a fairly mundane service occupation can be invested with more cosmopolitan overtones if it is represented as part of an exotic "coming of age" journey.

Second, the overlap between traveler statuses, which occurs in all three types of journeys, provides practical economic advantages. Many of the "snowbird" circuits involve a move to destinations with cheaper costs of housing, land, food, and other services from more expensive locales. In other words, the movements of retirees can serve to stretch further pensions accrued and paid out in one country, thus achieving a higher standard of living in another locale. As I have already noted above, working tourism, whether oriented toward youths or older voyagers, allows people to spend an extended stay away from their usual homes with a relatively small initial commitment of resources. In the case of the "resident volunteers" in the Kalani resort, it was likely cheaper to live in this educational retreat than "at home."

Third, as Caroline Oliver has noted in her chapter in this volume, this kind of "aspirational" movement offers the possibility of constructing new identities. But it combines the potential vested in a "blank slate" of initial anonymity with the comfort of relatively familiar companionability. Many of the snowbirds are moving to expatriate and tourist settlements set up to provide services for migratory retirees. Young travelers are moving through circuits of movements that are increasingly institutionalized and organized to attract and service mobile Western youths. By definition and design, the Kalani retreat offers an organized framework for sociability. This kind of movement therefore offers the possibility of change and self-development, but it encapsulates this potential within a structural bubble of people in similar circumstances. Thus the deliberate convergence between previously officially separate categories of travel has created new, sharply demarcated circuits of travel rather than simply creating a more fluid array of multiple possibilities for movement.

As the numbers and varieties of travelers traversing the globe expands, and as the distinctions between different forms of movement are deliberately blurred, it would be easy to succumb to the presumption that the whole world is in motion and to presume that different forms of mobility are but variations on a modern existential theme of displacement (Clifford 1997: 2). "The mobilities of people comprise tourists, migrants, design professionals, asylum seekers, backpackers, business and professional travelers, students and other young people 'travelling the world' for the OE (overseas experience)" (Urry 2004: 205). But the difficulty with this kind of enumeration is not only that it may minimize crucial differences between situation/experiences or that it can stretch the range of an expansive term like "travel" past the point of comparative utility (Clifford 1997:

11), but that it can also obscure a key impetus and ground for long-distance mobility in various forms.

What link various forms of contemporary travel are not global convergences but a host of asymmetries. For all the hundreds of millions of contemporary passages across regional and international borders, the majority of the world's population is either not moving at all or not moving far. Those who do travel head to destinations because they offer something—landscape, food, exotica, institutions, networks—that other places, their homes most especially, do not have. On the other hand, those who move are able to do so because they have access to resources that other people do not. They travel because the value of their income stretches farther in one site than other. They travel because they have the time to do so when others do not. They move because their skills and expertise are better recompensed in one locale than another. They travel because their activities "away" impart cultural capital—"overseas experience"- when the same tasks carried out locally would be construed as mundane drudgery. They move because there are jobs in one locale and not in another. What drive all forms of movement are the potentialities unleashed by expectations and experiences of asymmetrical distinction.

Structures of Travel and Cosmopolitan Capacities

So is the asymmetry underlying movement the source of the cosmopolitanism that has so often been attributed to travel both in popular and scholarly accounts? Does the pursuit and exploitation of disparity and unevenness necessarily or even likely produce a greater openness to difference, to new ways of being and doing?

In a recent book on *Conceiving Cosmopolitanism*, Steven Vertovec and Robin Cohen define cosmopolitanism as:

> . . . something that simultaneously: (a) transcends the seemingly exhausted nation state model; (b) is able to mediate actions and ideals oriented both to the universal and the particular, the global and the local; (c) is culturally anti-essentialist; and (d) is capable of representing variously complex repertoires of allegiance, identity and interest. In these ways, cosmopolitanism seems to offer a mode of managing cultural and political multiplicities. (2002: 4)

The difficulty with this effort at comprehensiveness is that it encompasses criteria that are by no means automatically or necessarily associated. Affiliations and networks can transcend the nation-state model and still be culturally essentialist. Anti-essentialism can be associated with ideals of universality identified with national citizenship. Complex repertoires of allegiance, identity, and interest may be intensely local.

The further difficulty of locating this concept socially rather than rhetorically is illustrated by Vertovec and Cohen's subsequent effort at identifying its practitioners. They note that cosmopolitanism has often been criticized as available only to an elite with the "resources necessary to travel, learn other languages and absorb other cultures" (2002: 5). But while they acknowledge that historically this has been true, they argue that the omnipresence of cultural and linguistic diversity has now made cosmopolitanism a mundane aspect of everyday life. Brought together by travel and immigration, diverse peoples have been forced to interact with each other at work, recreation, markets, neighborhoods, and so on. In contrast, the authors suggest that the class of highly mobile elites more commonly identified as cosmopolitan—the kind of financial experts, corporate personnel, and the like that Micklethwait and Wooldridge identified as "cosmocrats"—"are marked by a specialized—paradoxically—rather homogenous transnational culture, a limited interest in engaging 'the Other, ' and a rather restricted corridor of physical movement between defined spaces in global cities" (2002: 7). So, it seems, the local diversities disseminated by contemporary forms of mobility have rendered cosmopolitanism an "ordinary" aspect of contemporary modern life. Yet the elites once so identified with it, while still highly mobile, are not, it would appear, very cosmopolitan after all. Is cosmopolitanism then a product of movement in itself or a product of what happens when people stop moving and must therefore contend with one another?

Many of the forms of movements encompassed in this volume reach beyond global cities like London or New York. And, as I noted above, the kinds of people being observed in these case studies occupy a more varied range of situations than the corporate financial elites more commonly associated with notions of a transnational capitalist class or cosmocrats. But most of these situations also feature many aspects of the social encapsulation and specialization identified by Vertovec and Cohen with cosmocrats. And it is interesting to note that this encapsulation appears to be most marked among those people who regard themselves as being on the move, that is as only temporarily present in a locale.

European and North American corporate expatriates and their families who are posted by their companies to Indonesia for periods of one to five years use metaphors like "bubble," "bunker," or "hothouse" to describe their encapsulation within Jakarta. Sheltering from the "local chaos," the noise, fumes, heat, and humidity of Jakarta in fenced villas or high-rise apartments, making their way through the intense traffic of the city in chauffeur-driven cars or taxis, they send their children to private "international" schools and participate in voluntary national associations. It is a "ghetto" some of these expatriates characterize as unreal, floating, a space so bounded and strange that one British woman explained that she "didn't suffer from culture shock with Indonesia. But I had culture shock entering the expat community" (Fechter, this volume, p 45)

While Japanese expatriate workers in the United States live in homes that are externally indistinguishable from their middle-class American neighbors, their wives accept the responsibility of ensuring a domestic bulwark against the foreign *soto* outside, cooking Japanese food and ensuring that their children receive a dual education in both local American as well as supplementary Japanese-language schools. Here too the temporary sojourn is imbued with a suspension of reality, " a long vacation" that must in due course end when they go back to the real world of Japan (Kurotani, this volume, p 26).

It is hardly surprising to discover that geographic mobility does not override and may even exaggerate status distinctions of class, gender, nationality, or race. After all, the stratifications vested in other venerable forms of movement from colonial passages to labor migration have provided considerable previous documentation of the ways in which the disparities that propel travel can also shape attendant sojourns and settlements. But here I want to point to the ways in which these socioeconomic distinctions further interact with the variable purposes, circumstances, and structures of travel. Thus a Euro American development consultant making a site visit of only several weeks to a locale such as Jakarta is likely to engage with different sets of people and services than an "expatriate" consultant of the same nationality who has accepted a longer term assignment of a year or two in the same place. By the same token, a Euro American tourist who can claim comparable educational qualifications and financial resources will engage with still other people and services.

The development consultants with whom my own contribution to this volume is concerned are part of a larger transnational circuit of professionals who advise on various aspects of infrastructure development in the global South. While resident in Canada, they spend a large portion of their year traveling to projects located in diverse locales. Each successive project involves them in a new team of local and international specialists. The transience of these teams and the diverse nature of the projects on which these professionals consecutively work mean that many of the occupational relationships established at any one locale were not maintained over the longer term. Nor was there much opportunity in these relatively short and intense work trips to meet and form relationships with longer-term expatriates. And because time overseas involved intense and long workdays and weeks, these traveling consultants were rarely accompanied by their families on their project journeys.

As Cathy Greenhalgh relates in this volume, the radical restructuring of the old Hollywood studio system has meant that the larger global film industry is now almost entirely project based and draws on networks of freelance employees. As a result, film production is much more dispersed than it once was, occurring at various studio bases as well as on locations around the world. Film crews are constantly reconstituted from project to project. While many crewmembers working at these dispersed sites are hired locally, feature film cinematographers are among the mobile personnel who travel widely, working at a multitude of locales across the world.

Yet the reputation of cinematographers depends not only on their individual talents but also on their ability to organize and deploy a good crew. Hence there is a tension between the shifting structure of teams from location to location and the efforts of cinematographers to retain key personnel between their various projects. But whether working with new or familiar crewmembers, the travels of these cinematographers are largely bringing them into intense if transient contact with the personnel of a dispersed transnational film industry.

The movement of hundreds of millions of people around the world has given rise to specialized structures that accommodate but also canalize the different circumstances, networks, and resources engaged in these various forms of travel. The ubiquitous list of contemporary travelers that is regularly trotted out by scholars to enumerate contemporary forms of movement—the tourists, backpackers, business travelers, expatriates, migrants, students, refugee claimants, working holidaymaker, etc.—is thus not just one featuring variants on a common theme of mobility. These travelers' voyages are critically implicated in the development of differentiated circuits of travel that encapsulate even as they facilitate movement. As a result, travelers moving through these specialized circuits are most likely to encounter other travelers like themselves. By now, backpackers trying to avoid the beaten path trodden by other tourists make use of an almost equally well developed circuit of specialized hostels, tour providers, locales, internet sites, and blogs. Indeed, a transnational industry of agencies has developed that specifically focuses on and competes for youthful clients. As a result, backpackers are most likely to meet and make their most frequent contacts with other backpackers. Retirees relocating—whether for part or all of the year—to centers that have arisen to meet their specific needs are most likely to meet other retirees, often from the same country or region. Cinematographers traveling to work at a temporary film location will have their most intense interaction with film crew members with whom they may well have already worked in a dizzying range of locations around the globe. Development consultants moving from the global North to a diverse range of locales in the South largely engage with industry colleagues—other international and counterpart consultants, multilateral and national agency officials- involved in the same sector. Euro American expatriates in Jakarta make use of a set of institutions, associations, and networks geared to other short-term corporate expatriates like themselves. In short travel, heralded as the most important vehicle for the cultivation of a cosmopolitan orientation and a competence to deal with divergent cultural experiences (Hannerz 1996: 103), is systematically shaped by structures that channel voyagers into contact with others like themselves. As Fechter's chapter indicates, some travelers and temporary sojourners actively erect barriers against the strangeness of the locales they are visiting and purposefully search out people of similar backgrounds, thus accentuating or even exaggerating existing status differences. But other travelers voyage far, in an enthusiastic effort to engage with the "Other" only to find that the circuits through which they are journeying are occupied by other people much like themselves, engaged in similar missions. Hence the image of the "bubble" floats through many of the cases encompassed in this volume.

On the Other Hand: Settling Down and Liminality

Nonetheless, in noting the frequently encapsulating structure of contemporary circuits of travel, I am not arguing that these channels are prisons. Travel that has been initiated to meet particular resources and aims can be transformed in the course of journeys into other pursuits, in the process sometimes radically shifting the terms of social engagement. Nor do all forms of movement entail the same types or extents of enclosure. Thus, among the case studies in this volume we can find instances of two other kinds of postures that seek to mediate, if only partially, the bounded structures of movement.

Two of the case studies (Torresan; Olwig) deal with the most straightforward counter to the circumscription that is often an inescapable entailment of transience; namely, instances of immigration and settlement. The Brazilians immigrating to Portugal, or the Dominicans and Jamaicans who eventually chose to stay in North America and Britain, were seeking to further middle-class aspirations by settling in, rather than passing through their adopted countries. Their aspirations for advancement depended on integration into these new socioeconomic contexts; that is, for the most part, their quests for jobs, clients, recognition, lifestyles, and status depended on local *acceptance,* not separation.

A somewhat different posture is offered by two case studies (Oliver; Rodman) that explore the liminalities of aspirational movement. In certain respects, both of these situations, respectively of a retirement settlement and an educational retreat, exemplify the kinds of encapsulated circuits of mobility I have discussed above, since they involve spatially and socially circumscribed holiday enclaves. But the radical break that participants had made from their previous work roles and involvements, and the sense of holiday relations in these enclaves, generated a state of fecund liminality. And as in Victor Turner's (1969) seminal rendering of this state of "betweenness," in both these situations liminality was invested with communitas as well as the potentialities of self transformation. But as Turner also reminded us, liminality and its attendant sense of communitas cannot comfortably be sustained over the longer term. Retirees in Tocina resentfully found themselves pressed to depart from the anonymity "of being who one wants to be" and to release details about themselves they had not necessarily wished to divulge. In the face of the constant turnover at the

Hawaiian retreat of Kalani, people found it hard, after a time, to maintain a state of openness to new friendships; most moved on within a year.

If people operating within a safely circumscribed field of relations with others largely sharing their aspirations for "community" and self-fulfillment still found it difficult to indefinitely maintain the sense of openness and engagement with new people and possibilities commonly identified with cosmopolitanism, then it is not difficult to understand why in journeys through more uncertain and unfamiliar terrain many travelers would be unwilling to relinquish the advantages and comfort of remaining within a moving convoy. It may therefore be that rather than searching for cosmopolitan transformations among the often regimented and bounded circuits of contemporary travel, we are more likely to find an engagement with diversity among people more modestly in search of satisfying—in terms of livelihood, status, recognition—places to set down. These prospective settlers may not be seeking to ride cosmopolitan waves of international mobility, but in their efforts to win space for themselves in new places, their unavoidable mundane encounters with "others" may well effect more or less subtle changes in perspective and organization.

References

Clifford, James. 1997. *Travel and Translation in the Late Twentieth Century.* Cambridge, MA and London: Harvard University Press.

Gledhill, John. 2002. "The Powers Behind the Masks: Mexico's Political Class and Social Elites at the end of the Millennium." In *Elite Cultures: Anthropological Perspectives,* eds. Cris Shore and Stephen Nugent. London and New York: Routledge. pp. 39–60.

Greenhouse, Carol. 1983. "Being and Doing: Competing Concepts of Elite Status in an American Suburb." In *Elites: Ethnographic Issues,* ed. George Marcus. Albuquerque, NM: University of New Mexico Press. pp.113–140

Hannerz, Ulf. 1996. *Transnational Connections: Culture, People, Places.* London and New York: Routledge.

Harrison, Julia. 2003. *Being a Tourist: Finding Meaning in Pleasure Travel.* Vancouver and Toronto: UBC Press.

Harvey, Penelope. 2002. "Elites on the Margins: *Mestizo* Traders in the Southern Peruvian Andes." in *Elite Cultures: Anthropological Perspectives,* eds. Cris Shore and Stephen Nugent. London and New York: Routledge. pp. 74–90.

Malewski, Margaret. 2005. *GENXPAT: The Young Professional's Guide to Making a Successful Life Abroad.* Yarmouth, ME, Boston and London: Intercultural Press.

Marcus, George E. 1983. "The Fiduciary Role in American Family Dynasties and Their Institutional Legacy: From the Law of Trusts to Trust in the Establishment." In *Elites: Ethnographic Issues,* ed. George Marcus. Albuquerque, NM: University of New Mexico Press. pp. 221–256.

Micklethwait, John and Adrian Wooldridge. 2000. *A Future Perfect: The Challenge and Hidden Promise of Globalization.* New York: Crown Business.

Ong, Aihwa. 1999. *Flexible Citizenship: the Cultural Logics of Transnationality.* Durham, NC and London: Duke University Press.

Sheller, Mimi and John Urry. 2004. "Places to Play, Places in Play." In *Tourism Mobilities: Places to Play, Places in Play,* eds. Mimi Sheller and John Urry. London and New York: Routledge. pp. 1–10.

Shore, Cris and Stephen Nugent. eds. 2002. *Elite Cultures: Anthropological Perspectives.* London and New York: Routledge.

Turner, Victor W. 1969. *The Ritual Process: Structure and Anti-Structure.* Ithaca, NY: Cornell University Press.

Urry, John. 2004. "Death in Venice." In *Tourism Mobilities: Places to Play, Places in Play,* eds. Mimi Sheller and John Urry. London and New York: Routledge. pp. 205–233.

Vertovec, Steven and Robin Cohen. 2002. "Introduction: Conceiving Cosmopolitanism," In *Conceiving Cosmopolitanism: Theory, Context and Practice,* eds. Steven Vertovec and Robin Cohen. Oxford and New York: Oxford University Press. pp. 1–22.

2

Middle-Class Japanese Housewives and the Experience of Transnational Mobility

Sawa Kurotani

The otherwise abstract notion of *gurobaruka*, or "globalization," often becomes concrete reality to middle-class Japanese families in the form of a job assignment in the United States and other foreign locations. Almost all Japanese workers and managers who are sent out on these foreign assignments are men; therefore, when middle-class Japanese women talk about a possibility of temporary migration to a foreign country "on a job assignment," they are usually referring to their husbands.[1] But they also know that, as wives and mothers, they are expected to play a major role during this corporate-driven migration: to create and maintain "Japanese" homes away from home and make a foreign country a livable place for their families. This domestic work of expatriate Japanese wives in the context of Japanese transnational capitalism is the focus of my current discussion. I aim to contribute to the growing body of anthropological literature on global movement and travel in three particular areas. First, I focus on the families of highly mobile transnational professionals whose transnational experiences have received relatively little anthropological attention thus far (cf., Hannerz 1998; Ribeiro 1994; White 1992; Wulff 1998). If the experience of transnationality is class-specific, the mobility practices of those who are relatively affluent and privileged are expected to differ significantly from those who are not—labor migrants and refugees, for example (Friedman 1999). Their mobility practices are often flexible and wide-ranging, utilizing the material resources and privilege granted to many in this category of sojourner/migrants, which defy easy categorization. Somewhere between "sojourning" and "migrating," the study of transnationally mobile Japanese corporate families will shed new light on the increasingly flexible mobility practices and identity formation in the late capitalist world.

Secondly, the critical importance of the domestic—an insight explicated by feminist anthropologists and in theories on modern power—has not been fully explored in the context of transnational mobility, as existing studies have tended to focus on the "public" domain, such as paid labor, consumption, and popular culture (e.g., Appadurai and Breckenridge 1990; Ong 1999; Pinches 1999; but cf., Rapport and Dawson 1998; Sen and Stivens 1998). By contrast, the interconnection between the domestic arena and the "public" interest of transnational capitalism is at the heart of my study. While the transnational migration and homemaking of expatriate Japanese wives are driven by the specific and often contradictory demands of Japanese capitalism, the home of Japanese transnational migrants is a novel ethnographic site in which to examine the connection between the domestic space and larger social and economic systems.

Finally, I will examine the ambivalent outcomes that the global-local articulation generates, and consider how the results of my ethnographic study speak to the recent theoretical development regarding modern power and resistance. Despite the conservative social positioning of middle-class Japanese women as domestic managers, the experience of transnational homemaking has unexpected effects on these women's relationships to their family members, their conception of "home," and their own gender and cultural identity. Varied outcomes of corporate-driven transnational migration indicate that intersecting identities of gender, class, and national culture complicate the individual subject's experience of global processes, and that the consciousness of transnational subjects always remains split and ambivalent.

Transnational Mobility of Japanese Corporate Workers

Kaigai Chuuzai, or the assignment of experienced workers and managers to foreign locations, has been a key transnational strategy for many Japanese corporations (Hamada 1992). The importance of the United States to the Japanese economy is directly reflected in the changing significance of *Amerika chuuzai,* or the job assignment in the United States. In the early postwar period, when the United States was, by far, the most important consumer market for Japanese products, it was considered a rare and prestigious opportunity, reserved for elite corporate workers in international commerce and banking, and promised a fast-track career and a higher standard of living both during and after the assignment. The changes in the relative strength of the U.S. and Japanese economies through the 1970s and 1980s, however, resulted in major shifts in Japanese corporate interests and strategies in the United States. The U.S. government began to tighten trade restrictions against Japanese products to reduce the widening trade imbalance between the two nations, and Japanese manufacturers responded by moving their production sites to the United States.

This "localization" effort initially affected only major manufacturers of consumer end products—or the products that are ready to be sold in the consumer market—but quickly spread to the "second-tier" subcontractors who manufacture parts and components for these major corporations. In the late 1980s, Japanese direct investment in the United States further increased and diversified, as the post-Fordist development and booming economy encouraged Japanese corporations to move research and development functions overseas and invest in technology-intensive transnational ventures (MITI 1996).

Changing economic interests of Japanese corporations in the United States have had several consequences in the patterns of *kaigai chuuzai.* First, it spread the locations of U.S. assignment from a handful of coastal metropolitan cities to midsize and small cities in the Midwest, Southeast, and Southwest, where Japanese corporations found inexpensive land, non-unionized labor, tax incentives, and other advantages for manufacturing operation (Kim 1995). Secondly, it made *kaigai chuuzai* a realistic possibility for a larger number of Japanese workers in diverse occupational categories. Unlike banking or sales activities that a handful of expatriate representatives could manage out of a small branch office, large manufacturing plants required, at least initially, a large number of expatriate workers with technical expertise and managerial skills. Thus, the number of expatriate Japanese more than doubled in the 1980s during the period of increased localization in the manufacturing industries (MITI 1996), and the types of corporate workers who would not have expected a foreign assignment twenty years ago—a plant technician from an automobile parts manufacturer in a rural town, for instance—now expect a foreign assignment or two just about anywhere in the world in their lifelong corporate careers.

Furthermore, increased global competition has motivated many Japanese corporations to manage their expatriate work force on the cheap. The cost of foreign language and international training is substantial, and the expatriate workers have traditionally been compensated with a higher salary and special benefits during and after their foreign assignment.[2] Therefore, one of the immediate strategies to cut the cost of *kaigai chuuzai* is to recycle their expatriate workers, namely, identifying a specific group of workers as generic "overseas specialists," who are given longer and/or repeated foreign assignments and spend ten or more years of their corporate careers overseas. As transnational mobility affects an ever larger portion of their work force, companies are also redefining foreign assignments from "prestige" to "routine," thus justifying the reduction of special benefits for *kaigai chuuzaiin* (expatriate employees) and their family members. In the past, there was also a general assumption that successful *kaigai chuuzai* returnees ought to be rewarded with promotion upon their return to headquarters, which no longer holds true in most Japanese companies.

If a globalizing Japanese economy generates the need for a transnational workforce, the strategy with which Japanese corporations seek to achieve their goals is closely tied to the construction of Japaneseness and corporate-centered subjectivity in the Japanese world of work. Japanese companies often encourage their workers to recognize the collective goals as their own (Kondo 1990; Rohlen 1974), while belonging to the tight-knit corporate community affirms the masculinity of their male core workers (Allison 1994). This corporate solidarity is, then, implicitly understood as the source of productivity, as well as a uniquely "Japanese" advantage in the world of late capitalism (Harootunian 1993). This essentialized connection between corporate solidarity, Japaneseness and productivity, in turn, results in a seemingly contradictory reaction to globalization. Japanese corporations, while situating "globalization" at the center of their agenda, often assign their handpicked Japanese employees to manage their overseas subsidiaries, and consolidate the decision-making power in their Japanese headquarters. These expatriate Japanese workers and managers are fully socialized in the Japanese world of work, and are expected to transplant "homegrown" efficiency to their operation outside Japan (also see Kim 1995; Mannari and Befu 1983; but cf., Milkman 1991). With more and more corporate workers spending longer and longer time on *kaigai chuuzai*, the level of anxiety about the dual requirements of going global yet remaining Japanese are increasingly high. Japanese corporations take advantage of women's domestic labor as a means of labor reproduction abroad, and "Japanese" domestic space becomes a primary location of identity maintenance for corporate workers and their children, where the complex relationship with the foreign other is managed, and the integrity of their "Japaneseness" is protected.

Homemaking away from Home

On the outside, most expatriate Japanese homes in the United States are indistinguishable from other homes in their middle- to upper middle-class neighborhoods; once inside, however, these homes are marked by distinctively "Japanese" aesthetics and conventions (cf., Cieraad 1999).[3] A Japanese home is an experience of comforting chaos, and the homes of expatriate Japanese families are no exception. It is a telltale sign of a space in which informality and physical comfort have priority over orderliness, the signature of an *uchi*/home/in-group where no outsiders are expected. This is particularly important to Japanese homemakers abroad, who often contrast their *uchi*/home against the foreign *soto* (literally, "outside"; metaphorically, a strange place). As they take off their shoes at the entrance and stretch out on the floor, the occupants of this domestic space release a sigh of relief (*hottosuru*). It is the ultimate aim of their domestic work in the United States to make their home a place where their husbands and children can relax and recover from a long day in bicultural workplaces or in foreign schools.

The work of creating and maintaining this domestic space, in turn, becomes an important building block of feminine identity for expatriate Japanese wives, who recognize their homemaking in the United States as their *shigoto* (job) and *yakume* (responsibility). How much and what kind of work is then involved in maintaining this Japanese domestic space in the United States? The daily schedule and the overall amount of housework differ significantly among expatriate Japanese housewives, depending on the children's ages, the husband's job types and ranks, and the particular location of assignment. A busy husband who is in the management rank, who travels frequently, and who brings many guests to home, can add additional burdens to his wife's responsibilities. At the same time, there are some common patterns. When it comes to the tasks directly linked to the physical maintenance of the home, such as cleaning, washing, yard work and light maintenance, women's workload lessens in the United States. Better appliances make household chores less time-consuming; American homes are designed for easy cleaning and require less straightening up than Japanese ones, thanks to abundant storage space and private rooms for individual family members.

What consumes an expatriate Japanese wife's day are other household chores that she distinguishes from home maintenance in the strict sense. First of all, cooking for and feeding one's family recognizably "Japanese" food, for instance, becomes the focal point of transnational homemaking, because eating Japanese also means being at home, being in one's own element, and being relaxed, as opposed to eating foreign food, which signifies a foreign environment, tension, and work. In Japan, one may eat "Japanese" anywhere—at home, in restaurants, even at a company or school cafeteria. Thus, the home-food association is not as strong. In the United States, one usually has to eat "American" away from home, and to eat almost exclusively "Japanese" at home. The conceptual distinction between *uchi*/Japan/home and *soto*/America/foreignness thus becomes synonymous with eating Japanese food, and makes cooking Japanese food the most important homemaking task for expatriate wives and mothers. But cooking "Japanese" is made particularly burdensome, as Japanese women have to go shopping, as part of their everyday routine, for specialty food items at multiple stores scattered around the city.

Chauffeuring children, a familiar chore for an American suburban mother, is an unexpectedly burdensome task to most Japanese mothers. In Japan, children, from the first grade on, walk to and from school with their friends, and some, as young as ten years old, may take public transportation on their own. In the United States, Japanese children often depend on their parents for transportation until they are in college, because their parents, fearing crimes and accidents, would not allow their children to drive or go out on their own. Women with children also take care of most other responsibilities related to child care and education, such as visits to doctors, volunteer work at children's schools, attending parent-teacher conference, supervising homework, finding tutors, and researching educational options.[4] There are two particularly significant factors that affect the experience of Japanese mothers in the United States: the burden of dual education and the effects of biculturalism on their children. Most expatriate Japanese children around the United States attend local public schools during the week and go to supplemental Japanese-language schools (*nihongo hoshuko*) on Saturdays. This caused conflict in some communities, where the local school system was overburdened by Japanese children, who often came without speaking a word of English, took advantage of their ESL (English-as-Second-Language) and/or bilingual education programs, and went home to Japan after a few years. For mothers, too, this means the double duty of managing their children's lives in American schools and in supplementary Japanese schools. Dealing with tasks related to American schools is made difficult for them owing to a lack of English skills and familiarity with the way U.S. schools are operated. Even an otherwise simple task of reading a written instruction about an upcoming school event can take them hours, because most of the Japanese mothers have to sit down with a dictionary trying to make sense of it. They may need to call other mothers or wait for their husbands to come home to discuss a particularly confusing passage; if all else fails, they might even have to go to school and speak to their children's teacher face-to-face to make sure that they understand the information correctly.[5] Navigating between the educational systems of Japan and the United States also poses a considerable challenge to expatriate Japanese mothers as well, who spend a great deal of time dealing with school bureaucracies on both sides, trying to map out the most appropriate path for their children throughout the period of transnational mobility.

Many expatriate wives in their late forties to fifties, whose children are old enough to manage on their own or be left with relatives in Japan, escape most of these tedious daily activities of child care. However, they may have different kinds of work to take up that are just as consuming of their time and energy. In this age group, many of the husbands are overworked and stressed managers and executives who are prone to many health issues. I encountered several cases in which middle-aged expatriate workers fell seriously ill during their U.S. assignments and their wives had to nurse them back to health in an unfamiliar place, away from families and friends in Japan who would have provided support in such times of need. Their aging parents in Japan may also become ill or otherwise require periodical visits. I even heard of an extreme situation in which one family was scattered between the United States, Europe, and Japan, with the wife traveling between three countries where her husband, children, and parents separately lived (also see Osawa 1986).[6]

Most important, the critical component of their homemaking work is the emotional labor to help fulfill the changing needs of their family members, so that they remain productive in the foreign environment.

"Being there" and "providing support" are themes that were repeated to characterize the nature of domestic work that these women performed, and these concerns permeated their every decision and every task performance of the everyday. These notions are understood to be both metaphoric and literal. For instance, mothers insisted that they "had to be there" in person when their children returned from school, and also to avoid any activities that will keep them from giving their children the fullest attention, including talking with friends on the phone or being interviewed by an anthropologist. "Providing support" can also mean anything and everything that "helps" their husbands and children do well at work and school, from cooking nutritious meals, to making sure that their shirts are pressed, to patiently listening to their gripes. Thus, in every domestic task they perform, Japanese wives and mothers have to filter out and temper the often inhospitable reality of the foreign environment right outside the door of their homes, and negotiate the boundary between their Japanese *uchi* and the foreign *soto*. In doing so, they themselves become the buffer zone that separates the familiar from the foreign, the self from the other.

While expatriate Japanese wives' sense of duty comes through clearly and strongly in their words and daily activities, tension also emerges during *kaigai chuuzai*. To most Japanese corporate wives, *kaigai chuuzai* means disruption or difficulty in this process of self-fulfillment outside the home, which is increasingly important to Japanese women (Rosenberger 2000). While the irony hardly escaped my female informants that more (geographical) mobility meant more (domestic) fixity, they often seemed resigned that this was simply unavoidable, or *shikataganai,* because it is part of their "job" as a middle-class housewife and mother. The degrees of dissatisfaction about their life abroad depend largely on the life experience of each woman prior to *kaigai chuuzai.* It is practically impossible for an accompanying Japanese wife to obtain a paid job in the United States. First, they are not legally permitted to work in the United States as the "dependent" of their husbands. Second, Japanese employers strongly discourage, or even prohibit, their expatriate employees' wives to work outside the home, to "protect" them from neglecting their domestic duties. Finally, even without such legal and corporate limits, their shortcomings in language and cultural competency severely curtail their chance of finding a job. Many women, who were accustomed to working outside the home, told me that they were just not interested in domestic work as much as others, and found it "boring" to have to stay home. Some women also sacrificed their own professional and personal interests outside the domestic sphere to accompany their husbands to the United States. A few of my informants left their professional jobs, knowing that there was little chance of resuming their career after *kaigai chuuzai.* While explaining their own career setback as "necessary," they struggled with an undeniable sense of loss and frustration.

Kaigai Chuuzai as Vacation

While Japanese corporate wives' experience of transnational mobility is often frustrating and even alienating, there is also an escapist aspect in *kaigai chuuzai,* as expressed in the metaphor of "a long vacation" that temporarily removes the traveler from her everyday life and allows her to indulge in otherwise impermissible pleasures (MacCannell 1976, 1992). To many of my informants, *kaigai chuuzai* offered a temporary relief from their strained relationships with their in-laws; to some, a break from part-time work that they hated but found necessary to make ends meet in Japan. To others, it was a pure pleasure of material abundance. Most expatriate Japanese families can afford to live in much larger homes and take many more vacations while in the United States. Many wives enjoy shopping for brand-name clothes and accessories, playing golf and tennis, and frequenting theaters and concerts, all made possible by relatively affordable leisure activities and higher standard of living that are beyond the means of an "ordinary" middle-class Japanese family. In this environment of affluence, they indulge in the "feeling of richness" (*ricchi na kibun*), even though it is theirs only for a limited time.

However, material consumption is also about buying into "the mythology of the American way of life" (Clammer 1997: 96). Whenever my female informants spoke of material wealth, their thoughts turned quickly to a more psychological "wealth" (*yutakasa*) and "leisureliness" (*yutori*) of middle-class America, vis-à-vis the "poverty" (*mazushisa*) of their Japanese lifestyle. *Amerika* was, my informants often told me, the country of freedom, wealth, and individual happiness, where they and their family members could have a more human-like or humane lifestyle (*ningen rashii ikikata*) (cf., Kelsky 2001). Such a ready opposition between the self and the other is overly simplistic, and I also suspect that my informants' utopian notion of *Amerika* is tied to the role of the United States in postwar Japan as the purveyor of democracy and modernity (Dower 1999). Yet, the expatriate Japanese interpretation of the life of "ordinary Americans" as "more human-like" is often based on their own daily observations in this foreign country. Inamura-san, who lived in a middle-class neighborhood in Centerville, told me about her next-door neighbor who came home from work promptly at 5:30 p.m. every day, played with his kids, mowed the lawn, and lit up the grill to cook dinner for the whole family. "How is it possible," she asked, "for a man to have a full-time job to support his family, *and* come home early to do all that?" Kudo-san, a veteran expatriate wife from New York, told me at length about the local school that treated her three children warmly and fairly. Shimura-san, who lived in New York for a little over two years, found during her latest visit back to Japan that people ignored one another in crowded public places, bumped into others without saying "excuse me," and let the door go in front of a woman with small children, violating—to her own surprise—the sense of common courtesy that she had acquired in the United States.

To these middle-class Japanese women, the lived experience of *Amerika* as a utopian Other embodies an alternative possibility to their life-as-usual in Japan, with overworked husbands who are never home, the school system that rejects all but impeccably "Japanese" children, and people who are too busy to show courtesy to one another. These concrete practices that they witness and eventually adopt in their "temporary" lives are both the result and the source of the "humanness" that they find in middle-class American life, made possible by the seemingly "bottomless" material wealth that American society—in my Japanese informants' views—promises and delivers to its citizens. This is not to say that these expatriate Japanese want to become "American." Most of them are quite conscious of their own "Japanese" roots, and realize that, having come to this country as adults, they would never become American in the true sense of the word, no matter how long they stay in this country. However, *Amerika* provides them a space outside Japan from which to reflect on and critique their *uchi,* whose integrity is maintained at the cost of their very humanness.

Transforming *Uchi*

After a few years in the United States, many things, large and small, can change in the life of an expatriate Japanese wife. She may learn to get around in the local area with little trouble, celebrate Halloween, Thanksgiving, and Christmas at her own home or the homes of her husband's American colleagues, and exchange some cooking recipes with her neighbor. Domestic management and childcare require interaction with the world outside her home, and she may create many points of connection with the "foreign" surroundings around her. While the networking with other expatriate Japanese wives is critical, she will also have found American neighbors to whom she can go with questions about local schools or neighborhood rules, and have hired an American woman as her English tutor, who can also give her advice about local customs and cultural events. At her children's school, she may become friends with other American mothers through volunteer work. Communicating with these "foreigners" through the barriers of language and cultural differences is hard; yet there are also delightful moments—when she finally gathers up the courage to join the group of women from the neighborhood for a sidewalk chat, when she manages to negotiate prices with American customers at her garage sale, or when she finds out that her *origami* lessons are very popular with her children's classmates. These community-based contacts can also lead to other activities outside the domestic space, as the experiences of some of my informants indicate. For example, one of my key informants in Centerville became a community liaison for a local U.S.-Japan organization, and as a result got to know more people in the local American community than her husband, whose daily life was limited to his workplace. Another found many of her American neighbors more generous and supportive than their expatriate Japanese friends when her husband had fallen seriously ill in Centerville. By the time we met, she and her husband had so many friends in the neighborhood that they could not take their daily walk without being stopped for a chat.

If these are all part of the constantly changing lives of expatriate corporate families, the biggest and most fundamental change in their domestic life often happens in the family relations, particularly between the husband and wife. In Japan, it is the assumption of both men and women that everybody's husband comes home late at night and everybody's wife takes care of all the family matters. Once in the United States, they realize that what they thought of as "ordinary" (*atarimae*) is not so in another cultural context. Such an awareness can be so powerful that it may result in serious marital difficulties and even divorce (*Yomiuri America* 4/18/1998). In my own fieldwork experience, divorce between expatriate Japanese wives and husbands were extremely rare. My female informants, instead, encouraged, urged, and coerced their husbands into taking more interest in domestic life; and it was often through everyday practices in and around their homes that they began to renegotiate their domestic relationships. It might start with something small—helping with yard work, going to grocery shopping together, cleaning after dinner, or taking trash out, perhaps. Many husbands/fathers also become more involved in financial management and educational decision making for children. Japanese wives, who are used to making household purchasing decisions and supervising their children's education on their own, often depend on their husbands in the United States, particularly in the beginning, because their communication skills and local knowledge are insufficient to enable them to do these tasks by themselves. However, domestic task sharing seemed to take hold in many households, and became more or less a permanent practice, even after the wives became more familiar with the local surroundings. These practical changes seem to have had a subtle yet definite impact on the Japanese wives' perception of their relationship with their husbands. Domestic management, previously the sole responsibility of the wife, became a joint responsibility of both the husband and the wife, and many of my informants commented that they welcomed the increased presence of their husbands at home, and enjoyed the sense of closeness and egalitarian partnership as a result of shared family responsibilities. In addition, the parent-child relationships grew stronger and much more egalitarian, as they shared difficult experiences together as a "family," in which the father's increased presence was also identified as a critical factor.

At the same time, wives also become involved in their husbands' work more heavily than in Japan, and begin to understand the corporate world

of work better than they could ever imagine in Japan. Corporate enter-
taining is, for example, an added burden to the expatriate Japanese wife's
domestic workload as I pointed out above; yet, it also gives her an opportunity to meet her husband's colleagues and clients, to overhear busi-
ness-related discussions, and to feel a sense of connection to his work.
At times, the organization of work at the *chuuzai* location also makes
it necessary for wives to stand in as a secretaries for their husbands, as
was the case for Mrs. Kumagai, a veteran expatriate wife in New York.
Her husband traveled extensively, and in the meantime, Mrs. Kumagai
took business calls in both Japanese and English and sorted out faxes in
his absence. "At first, it was scary (to have so much responsibility), but
once I got used to it, it became kind of fun. I know many of the people
my husband works with, and I know some of his major projects." As the
separation of work and home is more complete in Japan (both because
of the distance between business centers and suburbs, and because the
organization of work rarely spills over to domestic spaces), these women
might not have found out anything about their husbands' work, even
after years of marriage and coresidence.

Another important factor in the changing husband-wife relationship is
the distance from the interpersonal networks and social activities in Japan
that kept married couples apart from each other for most of their waking
hours. The social lives of married Japanese men and women are largely
gender-segregated, and a husband and a wife (except perhaps during the
honeymoon period) rarely spend their leisure time together as a "couple."
In times of need, they often turn first to their homosocial networks outside the marriage—extended families, corporate socialization groups, and
long-term friends—for support, encouragement and advice. *Kaigai chuuzai* pulls a Japanese husband and wife out of their respective, and largely
independent, webs of human relationships, and puts them together in a
strange place with little external support. I heard a practically identical
line from different informants in different *chuuzai* circumstances: *Koko-
deha, otagaishika tayoreru aitega inai* ("here in the United States, we only
have each other to rely on"). To many of my informants, this was "the
best thing" that happened to them during *kaigai chuuzai.*

The connection between corporate interests and women's homemaking
labor also becomes clearer than ever during corporate-driven migration,
and women begin to speak up against their husbands' corporate employers. Often this is done through their husbands, but sometimes wives will
act more directly to protest imposition by corporate employers. The critique of *kaigai chuuzai* practices may also be publicly voiced under the
disguise of a personal narrative. Many of the published memoirs of former
corporate wives reveal, through the details of everyday life both abroad
and back in Japan, the negative effects of displacement and the difficulty of
homecoming after *kaigai chuuzai.* As male Japanese workers spend more
time at home with their families, they often find themselves enjoying their

expanded roles at home and depending more than ever on their wives' support. At the same time, the division of labor between a husband and a wife
that seemed clear and unchangeable in Japan is blurred as the wives are
called on to assume the role not only of a supportive spouse but also of a
job partner. While corporations make these modifications in the name of
economic interest, they inadvertently blur the boundaries between productive male work and reproductive female work, and cause the Japanese
husband and wife to rework their relationships.

When the Vacation Ends

The majority of Japanese corporate families go home to Japan at the end
of their *kaigai chuuzai* in the United States, and they expect that they will
have to slip back into their old niche in the world of middle-class Japanese.
After all, their life in *Amerika* was a "long vacation," and all vacations
have to come to an end. A good example is Kawagoe-san, who personally
enjoyed living in the United States and saw no particular reason to return
to Japan. In fact, four years after *kaigai chuuzai,* she often finds herself
"wanting to go back" (*kaeritai*) to the United States, and she laughs at
herself for such a "confused" state of mind. At the same time, she says, she
knew it was best for her family to return to Japan, and as a member of this
family unit, it was also the best decision for *her.* Such choices therefore
seem to contradict the awareness by these Japanese expatriate women of
the alternatives outside Japan, and to indicate that they tend to fall right
back into the role of dutiful wives and mothers, despite their desire for
change. Accounting for this seeming gap between their consciousness and
action is my final task.

At the same time, a small but increasing number of Japanese corporate
families are considering the alternative of turning their "vacation" into
real life. *Yomiuri America,* the most widely circulated Japanese newspa-
per in the United States, reported in its feature article on March 28, 1998,
that an increasing number of expatriate corporate Japanese were looking
at permanent residence in the United States as an alternative to returning to Japan after *kaigai chuuzai.* Those who chose "freedom over wage"
traded the secure yet constraining life with a Japanese corporation for a
more fulfilling career and family life in the United States. The possibility
of permanent immigration becomes real enough for only a few expatriate Japanese families whose breadwinners have a marketable skill in the
United States. In New York, international financial analysts were said to
have many opportunities to move to a U.S. bank or securities company;
in North Carolina, workers in the computer industry found themselves
in a de-territorialized job market where major multinationals routinely
recruited skilled employees from around the world. Interestingly enough,
the specificity of manufacturing know-how and inadequate language

skills of most expatriate workers in Centerville radically reduced their job prospects outside Japan. It is difficult to quantify this "exodus" phenomenon partially because of the general absence of statistical information on expatriate Japanese. Even Japanese consulates and embassies do not have accurate figures on how many Japanese are living in their administrative territories in the United States, and the number of expatriate corporate Japanese is even harder to come by. Furthermore, many cases of permanent migration happen under less clear-cut circumstances. Some of my male informants told me that it would "look bad" to just quit their jobs while on a foreign assignment; therefore, they would have to first return to Japan, and then come back to the United States permanently. In several cases, my informants were semi-permanently stationed in the United States, and thus remained "expatriate corporate Japanese" while they had already made the decision to make the United States their home—or at least one of their homes. Overall, I estimate that approximately 10 percent of my informants became (semi-) permanent migrants.[7]

In addition to the professional flexibility of the husbands, two familial concerns often weigh heavily on the decision of expatriate Japanese families whether to remain in the United States. Children's educational achievement and future success are obviously very important factors in the decision of expatriate Japanese couples to go back to Japan or to permanently live in the United States. Some of my informants made a conscious decision to remain in the United States to give their children the best educational opportunities. Aging parents in Japan constitute another family-related concern. The care of the elderly has traditionally been in the hands of family members in Japan, and in the lingering norm of primogeniture, the eldest son is expected to take on the responsibility of parental care. In reality, however, this has meant that the daily care of the aging parents fell on the shoulders of the sons' wives. The increased longevity and shrinking number of offspring have made the care of the elderly one of the most pressing concerns in contemporary Japan, and both government policies and societal expectations have naturalized the increased burden of parental care on married women in their middle age as part of their "domestic" responsibility (Lock 1993).

Homemaking as Resistance

Hegemonic power, as Gramsci theorizes, works quietly and thus insidiously so that subjects will "make it spontaneously their own and bear it around with them as a principle inseparable from their identities" (Eagleton 1991: 116). The ideology of feminine domesticity permeates Japanese women's sense of self to such an extent that it may first appear that women have incorporated that notion of self as their own. James Scott, however, cautions that a disparity between behavior and consciousness is typical of the oppressed, and that "[much] of what passes as deference" must be interpreted carefully in the context of sociocultural, economic and political "constraints" at work (Scott 1976: 232). We can expand Scott's insight to understand the seemingly contradictory choices of middle-class Japanese women (also see Kondo 1990; Lock 1993). The most significant constraint at work is cultural as well as economic, where women are primarily defined in their roles as homemakers and caretakers. For the majority of these full-time housewives, to ignore and/or overtly transgress this cultural dictate is to lose their subjecthood as well as their *livelihood* under current social conditions in Japan that leave very little room for divorced women to achieve economic independence (Brinton 1993). Most Japanese corporate wives with whom I worked were keenly aware of their positions as their husbands' dependents, and some were also quite vocal about the clear and definite boundary within which they could exercise their own choices. It did not seem to me that they "made their own" the "good wife and wise mother" ideology that had defined Japanese femininity throughout Japan's modern history.

Rather, they appeared fully aware of its function as *tatemae*, or officialese, quite apart from their own *honne*, or honest sentiment,[8] and sought to make the best of their opportunities within their sanctioned realm, the domestic. De Certeau's thesis on the practice of everyday life outlines a possible mechanism in which the hegemonic is actively challenged and transformed in the most trivial, "minor" practices and choices of everyday living. De Certeau considers the everyday life of "the anonymous crowd" as an opportunity for "microresistances" and "minitransgressions" (de Certeau et al. 1998: xxi). His emphasis on the "everyday-ness" of resistance resonates with the experience of middle-class Japanese women who as wives and mothers are in charge of everyday life away from Japan. Furthermore, de Certeau points out that ordinary people may feign obedience on the surface to the dominant power while cunningly scattering their actions of disobedience throughout their ordinary daily activities (de Certeau 1984: General Introduction). This recognition of duality allows us to accommodate the discord between consciousness and action that I observed so often among Japanese corporate wives.

The process through which the notion of *uchi* is challenged during *kaigai chuuzai* suggests that as it is politicized, the domestic becomes an important location of identity negotiation. Everyday-ness loses its appearance of innocence and stability, when the routine homemaking practices become more intentional, when the "everyday" becomes not so everyday and the "mundane" takes on a new significance. While the corporate practice of *kaigai chuuzai* makes explicit the relationship between the global and the domestic, the shift of domestic responsibilities in expatriate Japanese households also blurs the naturalized division between male work and female work. As an expatriate Japanese husband and wife actively participate in each other's "work," their conjugal relationship also begins to change into a more egalitarian partnership. At this moment, expatriate Japanese wives come to recognize, to varying degrees, the problematics of *uchi* as a closed space of cultural reproduction, and begin to question the ideological underpinnings of their own femaleness based on domestic labor. Thus, this location of subjectivity-making can—if only fleetingly— also become a space for unexpected change and subversion. In some of the cases I have described, the experience of transnational migration opens up otherwise unavailable avenues of self-expression, the possibility of the transformation of family relations and cultural identities, and leads ulti- mately to a new life course in a place that women originally thought of as "foreign." In other words, when the global comes into the home, the home can also become the space of reworking the global.

Acknowledgements

Findings discussed in this article are based on field research funded by the Na- tional Science Foundation Dissertation Improvement Grant, Rockefeller Post- doctoral Fellowship, and the University of Colorado Graduate School Dean's small grant. The views expressed in this paper do not represent those of the funding organizations.

Notes

1. The Japanese corporate world of work is still dominated by men, despite the outcry of feminist and other critics. Although legal measures exist to promote equality among workers, there are many informal mechanisms that continue to keep separate male and female employees in Japanese workplaces (for fur- ther discussion, see Brinton 1993, Lam 1992, Ogasawara 1998).
2. In the 1990s, a typical *kaigai chuuzai* benefit package included a temporary salary raise (of up to 100 percent), additional health care coverage, housing subsidy, language training and/or educational allowance for family mem- bers, and travel allowance. Other benefits might be added in accordance with the specific circumstance of the assignment, such as a chauffeured car in some Third World countries. These special benefits for expatriate families vary greatly from one corporation to another, but as a rule, larger corpora- tions with a heavier emphasis on overseas operation tend to reward their ex- patriate workers with more generous and wide-ranging benefits than smaller companies.
3. Japanese corporate families often rent houses and apartments in the United States, because they assume their residency there to be temporary. They may decide to purchase homes that are ready to move in, if there is no appropri- ate rental property in the area of their assignment, but very few have time or money to invest in custom-built homes. As a result, they mostly lived in

cookie-cutter suburban homes with typical "American" floor plans and dimensions. Some of my informants also told me that they tried to keep the outside appearance of their homes indistinct in order not to be "singled out" as a foreign family.

4. Detailed and well-documented accounts of the educational conditions of expatriate Japanese children in the United States (and particularly in greater New York) can be found in Okada (1993) and Osawa (1986).

5. In a Japanese educational setting, particularly in kindergarten and elementary school, it is considered the responsibility of the mother to attentively follow every instruction from teachers. Mothers quickly find out that the failure of compliance raises serious questions about their commitment to the ascribed role (Allison 2000).

6. Many mothers of teenage children, who are going through the period of *juken jigoku*, or the "hellish" time of preparation for rigorous high school or college entrance exams, opt to stay in Japan, and let their husbands go abroad on *tanshin funin*, or "single transfer."

7. This estimate is most likely inflated by my "snow ball" sampling method. In general, those who are (potential) permanent migrants were more open to discussing their *kaigai chuuzai* experience, and were thus more likely to participate in my research. In the general population, the percentage of expatriate corporate workers who remain in the United States on a (semi-)permanent basis may be significantly lower than my estimate.

8. For further discussion on the significance of *honne* and *tatemae* in Japanese society, see Doi (1973) and Nakane (1967).

References

Allison, Anne. 1994. *Nightwork: Sexuality, Pleasure and Corporate Masculinity in a Tokyo Hostess Club.* Chicago: University of Chicago Press.

———. 2000. *Permitted and Prohibited Desires: Mothers, Comics and Censorship in Japan.* Berkeley: University of California Press.

Appadurai, Arjun and Carol Breckenridge. 1990. "Why Public Culture?," *Public Culture* 1 (1): 5–10.

Bammer, Angelica, ed. 1994. *Displacements: Cultural Identities in Question,* Indianapolis: University of Indiana Press.

Brinton, Mary. 1993. *Women and the Economic Miracle: Gender and Work in Postwar Japan.* Berkeley: University of California Press.

Cieraad, Irene, ed. 1999. *At Home: An Anthropology of Domestic Space.* Syracuse: Syracuse University Press.

Clammer, John. 1997. *Contemporary Urban Japan: A Sociology of Consumption.* Oxford: Oxford University Press.

Clifford, James. 1997. *Routes: Travel and Translation in the Late Twentieth Century.* Cambridge, MA.: Harvard University Press.

de Certeau, Michel. 1984. *The Practice of Everyday Life,* trans. Steven Rendall. Berkeley: University of California Press.

de Certeau, Michel, Luce Giard, and Pierre Mayol. 1998. *The Practice of Everyday Life,* vol. 2: *Living and Cooking.* Minneapolis: University of Minnesota Press.

Doi, Takeo. 1973. *Anatomy of Dependence,* trans. John Bester. Tokyo: Kodansha International.

Dower, John. 1999. *Embracing Defeat: Japan in the Wake of World War II.* New York: Northon.

Eagleton, Terry. 1991. *Ideology.* London: Verso.

Friedman, Jonathan. 1999. "Class Formation, Hybridity and Ethnification in Declining Global Hegemonies," In *Globalization and the Asia-Pacific,* eds. Kris Olds, Peter Dicken, Philip Kelly, Lily Kong and Henry Wai-chung Yeung. London: Routledge.

Hamada, Tomoko. 1992. "Under the Silk Banner: The Japanese Company and Its Overseas Managers," In *Japanese Social Organization,* ed. Takie Sugiyama Lebra. Honolulu: University of Hawaii Press.

Hannerz, Ulf. 1996. *Transnational Connections.* New York and London: Routledge.

———. 1998. "Reporting from Jerusalem," *Cultural Anthropology* 13 (4): 548–574.

Harootunian, H. D. 1993. "America's Japan/Japan's Japan." In *Japan in the World,* eds. Masao Miyoshi and H. D. Harootunian. Durham, NC: Duke University Press.

Kelsky, Karen. 2001. *Women on the Verge.* Durham, NC: Duke University Press.

Kim, Choong Soon. 1995. *Japanese Industry in the American South.* New York: Routledge.

Kinoshita, Ritsuko. 1983. *Oukoku no Tsumatachi: Kigyou Joukamachi nite* [the wives of the kingdom: at corporate castle towns]. Tokyo: Komichi Shobou.

Kondo, Dorinne. 1990. *Crafting Selves.* Chicago: University of Chicago Press.

Koyama, Shizuko. 1994. "The 'Good Wife and Wise Mother' Ideology in Post-World War I Japan," *U.S.-Japan Women's Journal, English Supplement* 7: 31–52.

Lam, Alice. 1992. *Women and Japanese Management: Discrimination and Reform.* London: Routledge.

Lebra, Takie Sugiyama. 1984. *Japanese Women.* Honolulu: University of Hawaii Press.

Levitt, Peggy. 2001. *Transnational Villagers.* Berkeley: University of California Press.

Lock, Margaret. 1993. *Encounters with Aging: Mythologies of Menopause in Japan and North America.* Berkeley: University of California Press.

MacCannell, Dean. 1976. *The Tourist: A New Theory of the Leisure Class.* New York: Schocken.

———. 1992. *Empty Meeting Grounds.* New York: Routledge.

Mannari, Hiroshi and Harumi Befu, eds. 1983. *Challenge of Japan's Internationalisation: Organization and Culture.* Tokyo: Kodansha International.

Milkman, Ruth. 1991. *Japan's California Factories: Labor Relations and Economic Globalization,* Monograph and Research Series 55. Los Angeles: University of California, Los Angeles.

Ministry of International Trade and Industry of Japan (MITI). 1996. *Summary of "The Survey of Trends in Overseas Business Activities of Japanese Companies,"* International Business Affairs Division, MITI.

Mori, Rie and Hibari Saike. 1997. *Chuuzaiin Fujin no Deepu na Sekai* [the profound world of expatriate wives]. Tokyo: Media Factory.

Nakane, Chie. 1967. *Tate Shakai no Ningen Kankei* [Human relations in vertical society]. Tokyo: Kotanda.

Ogasawara, Yuko. 1998. *Office Ladies and Salaried Men: Power, Gender and Work in Japanese Companies.* Berkeley: University of California Press.

Okada, Mitsuyo. 1993. *Nyuu Yoku Nihonjin Kyoiku Jijo* [the circumstances of the education of Japanese in New York]. Tokyo: Kenkyusha.

Okifuji, Noriko. 1986. *Tenkinzoku no Tsumatachi* [the wives of the corporate transfer tribe]. Osaka: Sougensha.

Ong, Aihwa. 1999. *Flexible Citizenship: the Cultural Logics of Transnationality.* Durham, NC: Duke University Press.

Osawa, Chikako. 1986. *Tatta Hitotsu no Aoi Sora: Kaigai Kikoku Shijo ha Gendai no Sutego ka* [The one and only blue sky: are overseas returnee children the orphans of the contemporary era?]. Tokyo: Bungei Shunju.

Pinches, Michael, ed. 1999. *Culture and Privilege in Capitalist Asia.* London: Routledge.

Rapport, Nigel and Andrew Dawson, eds. 1998. *Migrants of Identity: Perceptions of Home in a World of Movement.* Syracuse: Syracuse University Press.

Ribeiro, Gustavo. 1994. *Transnational Capitalism and Hydropolitics in Argentina.* Gainsville, FL: University Press of Florida.

Rohlen, Thomas. 1974. *For Harmony and Strength: Japanese White-Collar Organization in Anthropological Perspective.* Berkeley: University of California Press.

Rosenberger, Nancy. 2000. *Gambling with Virtue: Japanese Women and the Search for Self in a Changing Nation.* Honolulu: University of Hawaii Press.

Scott, James. 1976. *The Moral Economy of the Peasant.* New Haven, NJ: Yale University Press.

Sen, Krishan and Maila Stivens, eds. 1998. *Gender and Power in Affluent Asia.* London: Routledge.

White, Merry. 1992. *The Japanese Overseas: Can They Go Home Again?* Princeton, NJ: Princeton University Press.

Wulff, Helena. 1998. *Ballet across Borders.* Oxford: Oxford University Press.

Yomiuri Amerika. 1998. *New York Local Edition.* 28 March.

———. 1998. 18 April.

3

Living in a Bubble

Expatriates' Transnational Spaces

Meike Fechter

It is a cage, cocoon and cradle.
—Former diplomat's spouse on her life abroad
with the British Diplomatic Service

Global flows and boundaries

The introductory quote brings to mind the experiences of a group often overlooked in migration discourses: those of privileged mobile professionals such as diplomats or corporate expatriates. It evokes the peculiar spaces that they create and inhabit during their time abroad, which are expressed in metaphors like the "cocoon" or "bubble." In this chapter, I want to explore these spaces and the associated senses of boundedness that often pervade their lives, and consider its implications for notions of transnational spaces more generally.

As the majority of migration studies have concentrated on non-privileged migrants, discussions of affluent movers from Western societies have not only been less prominent but often rather speculative. This is apparent in the loosely constructed categories in which globally mobile professionals are placed: Castells, for example, in his work on the "network society," simply regards them as "professional transients" (Castells 2000), while Sklair positions them in the framework of a "transnational capitalist class" (Sklair 2001). Friedman, in his theory on class formation, locates them at the top of a global hierarchy, and regards them as members of a "transnational elite" (Friedman 1999). Without considering the particulars of these different models here, it is significant that all of them embrace what could be called a "paradigm of flows." A key aspect of globalisation and transnationalism, they suggest, is the mobility of people, objects, and ideas, as well as a fluidity of lifestyles and working practices. National borders or other boundaries such as those defining social, cultural, or ethnic groups, are seen as being increasingly irrelevant, particularly for affluent movers. As Favell fittingly observes, "internationally mobile 'elites' are often pointed to as the embodiment of the new transnational world" (2003: 399).

Such discourses of fluidity have been questioned on various grounds. On a general level, it has been noted that much of the literature on globalization, while producing wide-ranging claims about the nature of a "global transnational elite," is marked by a comparative lack of substantive empirical data. It is therefore uncertain to what extent the assumption of the borderless existences of these people is grounded in social realities. In addition, Conradson and Latham point out that these global narratives provide little sense of the "everyday texture of the globalizing places we inhabit" (Conradson and Latham 2005: 228). In contrast, this essay aims to provide a more fine-grained ethnographic analysis of the social and material practices of such privileged migrants.

Meyer and Geschiere have warned that "the notion [of flux] can be easily equated with the disappearance of boundaries" (Meyer and Geschiere 1999: 5). Whether this assumption is adequate, though, is rather questionable. One case to the contrary is presented in Favell's work on mobile professionals within the European Union (Favell 2003). Favell strongly criticises the notion that such professionals lead "borderless lives," and contends that they do not represent "culturally interchangeable 'citizens of the world'" who are "unproblematically converging on a form of life which incarnates a privileged 'global society'" (Favell 2003: 402). Instead, he claims that their lives are significantly affected by boundaries, those determining access to housing markets or education, health and pension systems, for instance.

Meyer and Geschiere (1999) further probe this apparent persistence of boundaries in the midst of "global flows." In their introduction to *Globalisation and Identity,* they argue that global flows and boundaries are interdependent insofar as "global flows actually appear to entice the construction of new boundaries as much as the reaffirmation of old ones" (Meyer and Geschiere 1999: 5). In particular, they identify a tension between "globalisation and identity, between 'flow' and 'closure'"(1999: 2). Globalization and transnationalism thus not only incorporate both flows and closures, but these concepts are inherently contingent on each other. Following both Meyer and Geschiere (1999) and Favell (2003), I argue that the case of corporate expatriates further undermines assumptions that they, as members of a "transnational elite," exist in global spaces that are solely configured by flows.

The fact that borders and boundaries continue to matter in a globalizing world has been discussed comprehensively in relation to non-privileged groups (Smith and Guarnizo 1998; Kearney 2004; Cunningham 2004). While their continuing relevance for these groups may be self-evident, the question arises as to why boundaries should matter for privileged migrants. A tentative rationale is provided by Meyer and Geschiere in their observation that, given the interrelatedness of flows and boundaries, "people's awareness of being involved in open-ended global flows seems to trigger . . . determined efforts to affirm old and construct new boundaries" (Meyer and Geschiere 1999: 2).

Significantly, this statement emphasises the active role of individuals in producing such boundaries. This aspect is not taken into account by Favell, who considers European professionals rather as victims of such boundaries, which are imposed on them, for example, by a host society or nation-state. He tends to stress how these professionals are subjected to "coercive and assimilatory" national norms of behavior (Favell 2004: 6). Going beyond this, I suggest that expatriates' lives are also fundamentally structured by boundaries that they actively construct, maintain, and negotiate. The boundaries in question here are primarily those of race, nationality, class and gender.

One could argue that emphasising racial and national boundaries among populations living outside their "home country" constitutes a well-established practice that has not recently emerged in the wake of contemporary "global flows." Studies of colonial populations provide ample evidence of such practices, such as among European colonials in Sumatra (Stoler 2002: 22–40). I would argue, though, that these very same practices assume a new significance in the context of current theories of globalization and transnationalism. If expatriates are part of a "global elite" with supposedly fluid lifestyles, then the efforts they expend on the construction of boundaries call into doubt the adequacy of such visions.

I therefore argue that the in the context of expatriates, boundaries rather than flows become the analytically relevant concept. Barth has made this broader point in his seminal text on ethnic boundaries (Barth 1969). He proposes that boundaries themselves should be the site of investigation, rather than the "cultural stuff" enclosed by them. I follow Barth (1969) in asking what kind of boundaries expatriates construct, and explore the practices of making and negotiating them (see Cohen 1985, 1986). I also explore the spaces, however, that are created through the drawing of such boundaries, without reifying the "cultural stuff" that might be placed within. This is complemented by paying close attention to how these boundaries are contested and transgressed. I thus aim to examine the boundaries that matter for expatriates to illuminate the nature of their transnational lives.

Research Context

The material I shall discuss is based on twelve months' fieldwork in Jakarta, and forms part of a wider study focusing on expatriates as transnational migrants (Fechter 2002). It is concerned with European and North American corporate expatriates and their families who are posted to Indonesia by multinational companies for periods between one and five years. They work for manufacturing or oil companies, in banking and consultancy, in the development sector, and for cultural institutions. The term "expatriates" here provides an umbrella for a heterogeneous group, whose members hold a range of motivations and attitudes toward Indonesia. While outlining some broader tendencies, the following discussion acknowledges the diversity of their experiences and practices.

The data on which this essay is based consists of forty in-depth interviews, informal conversations, and participant observation. While informants were both male and female, mostly between thirty and fifty-five years old, the majority of the material presented here relates to the accompanying spouses of male expatriates. Participant observation focused on expatriates' leisure spaces rather than their workplaces, and was conducted in their homes, community spaces, and public venues in Jakarta. The material I will draw on includes quotes from interviews, conversations, and an Internet discussion forum, as well as sketches and anecdotes, all gathered during participant observation at informal gatherings and social events within expatriate communities.

Expatriates' Spaces

To explore the notion of expatriates' spaces, I want to take on Meyer and Geschiere's (1999) suggestion that individuals are prompted to erect boundaries because they feel immersed in "global flows," and try to investigate more specifically the nature of the spaces that these boundaries enclose. One of the key questions concerns how expatriates' spaces relate to concepts of transnational spaces as espoused by current discourses of globalization and transnationalism. Such discourses have generated a range of related definitions of transnational spaces, which I cannot attempt to discuss here (see Pries 2001 for an overview). They include, to name just a few, Appadurai's notion of "global ethnoscapes" (Appadurai 1991), Basch et al.'s "transnational social fields" (Basch et al. 1994), and Ong's concept of "transnational spatial processes" (Ong 1999). Irrespective of their specific features, they all share the assumption that transnational spaces are created by the mobility of people's lives and that this embodies the very essences of transnationalism.

Pries's (2001) definition can be taken as an exemplar here. He writes that, "transnational social spaces can be understood as pluri-local frames of reference which structure everyday practices, social positions, biographical employment prospects, and human identities, and simultaneously exist above and beyond the social contexts of national societies" (Pries 2001: 23). Significantly, what this and similar definitions highlight are the associations between transnational spaces and qualities such as fluidity, openness, and malleability. As Low and Lawrence-Zúñiga observe, there is a tendency to conceive of transnational spaces in terms of "cultural hybridity, multipositional identities, border crossings" (Low and Lawrence-Zúñiga 2003: 27). These qualities starkly contrast with—if not contradict—the tendency of expatriates to refer to their transnational spaces in metaphors of boundedness. I therefore argue that notions of transnational spaces need to be complicated to recognize the multifaceted experiences and practices involved in creating and inhabiting them.

What kind of transnational spaces, then, are produced by corporate expatriates? According to Pries's definition, expatriates' spaces would have "pluri-local frames of reference." While this may be true, I suggest that at the same time, they are externally bounded, as implied by the image of the "bubble," and internally divided. Boundaries not only demarcate expatriates' spaces from the outside, but also produce multiple divisions within them. As mentioned above, it is important to note that expatriates do not simply occupy these spaces, but are actively involved in their creation through erecting and maintaining their boundaries.

Without entering into a detailed discussion, suffice it to say that I assume a constructivist notion of space that regards space as created and continuously modified through individuals' practices. I draw here on Merleau-Ponty's (1962) concept of "anthropological space," which regards space not as a material given but as a multitude of spaces that are constructed and experienced by active subjects (see also Tilley 1994). The arguments discussed here thus apply not only to material space but also to social and symbolic space. In particular, I aim to look at expatriates' housing practices, their national communities, and social networks. It is important to note that I do not consider physical and social spaces as disjunct, but as mutually constitutive and expressive. They represent interlocking dimensions that engender particular social and spatial practices in interaction with each other. It also needs to be stressed that while expatriates' spaces appear to be strongly bounded, they turn out to be permeable in many ways, as there are flows and exchanges of substances, ideas, and people across their boundaries.

Metaphors

One way of teasing out the meanings of expatriates' spaces is through a closer examination of the language metaphors that expatriates employ in interviews or everyday conversation to describe their situation. Such metaphors include living in a "bubble," "bunker," "ghetto," "hothouse," or in a "Disneyland." These highly evocative metaphors can function as heuristic devices to elucidate the nature of expatriates' spaces. Lakoff and Johnson (1980) argue that metaphors not only represent forms of language but forms of thought that play a key role in defining people's everyday realities: "the way we think, what we experience, and what we do every day is very much a matter of metaphor" (1980: 3). Consequently, metaphors have experiential as well as theoretical significance: while they capture expatriates' sentiments, a closer examination of the qualities associated with each of them also provides conceptual insights into the spaces they describe. This is not to suggest that metaphors provide a privileged way of understanding expatriates' spaces, but they present a form of access that is socially salient and not adequately explored in the expatriate context.

While expatriates draw on a whole repertoire of metaphors, I want to focus on a few specific ones that express particular qualities of expatriates' spaces. These are the "bunker" and "Disneyland," which are used in relation to dwelling, and the "ghetto" and "hothouse," which are used to refer to the aspects of community and social life. I will explicate the meanings and connotations attached to each of these metaphors in the contexts in which they occur. The metaphor of the "bubble" holds special significance insofar as it is applied to expatriate life in its entirety. It incorporates features such as boundedness, seclusion from the outside, a certain glamor as well as an artificial atmosphere inside it. Its versatility means that the bubble is an iconic image capable of signifying expatriate life as a whole. This is exemplified in a quote taken from an Internet discussion forum for expatriates:

> Plenty of expats live in the "expat bubble." They spend outrageous prices buying pre-packaged foods like they eat at home. Some do not even learn to speak the language. They live in high-rise apartment buildings, so noise is not a problem. If you live in the "expat bubble" you are pretty safe on a day-to-day basis. (Linkh@bigfoot.com, posted on the "Living in Indonesia" Forum 23/01/2000)[1]

Finally, the "bubble" also includes a quality seemingly at odds with its bounded nature, that is, the apparent permeability of its boundaries. It emerges, though, that such permeability is an integral aspect of expatriates' spaces, as their housing and social lives are subjected to frequent intrusions, transgressions, and transactions across their boundaries.

Housing

One of the metaphors most telling of expatriates' housing practices is that of the "bunker." This metaphor was suggested to me by a British woman in her late sixties who had accompanied her geologist husband working for a large oil company to different postings around the world, including several stints in Southeast Asia. I spoke to her in London a few years after the couple had retired from expatriate life. Recalling her time in Malaysia in the 1970s, she said: "it was like being in a bunker. We stayed in a little settlement for expatriates, and we were very closed off from everything around us. Our whole life revolved around the expat community. It was a very strange atmosphere."

Although she was not referring to contemporary expatriate life, a similar sense of "strangeness" also surfaced in conversations I had with expatriates in Jakarta. Probably more than any other metaphor, a "bunker" embodies the fortified and fundamentally bounded form of expatriate spaces. One could object that the "bunker" is an inappropriate metaphor for expatriates' rather luxurious residences, as it invokes sparse, pared-down, brutal spaces equipped with bare necessities. I would argue, though, that the primary point of comparison here is the seclusion and shelter that a bunker and expatriate housing offer, even if under very different material circumstances. The relevant features of the bunker here are its safety, a protection from the outside world, and a sense of community among the people within it. The metaphor also encapsulates the sense of "strangeness," though, that can characterize spaces that are set apart from the ordinary and cut off from the outside world.

I suggest that a similar marked division between inside and outside is typical of expatriates' housing practices in Jakarta. Expatriates usually rent houses in one of the affluent quarters of South Jakarta, such as Kemang or Pondok Indah, which are known as areas where expatriates as well as wealthy Indonesians live. Generous salaries, and the fact that employers partly or entirely subsidize the rental costs, allow expatriates to settle in urban villa-style houses. These houses are often surrounded by high brick walls or fences; they include a forecourt, garage, staff quarters, and have a spacious layout including several bedrooms, a large lounge, reception area, and often a garden with a swimming pool. The properties are usually staffed by a security guard by day and night. Sometimes, they are part of gated residential compounds where oil companies and foreign embassies provide housing for their employees.

The structure and design of these houses reiterates the contrast between interior and exterior that is connoted in the metaphor of the "bunker." While the interiors are spacious, air-conditioned, and clean, the surroundings are likely to be bustling, hot, and dusty. The interiors often exude an air of order and "Western" tastes, created by the careful arrangement of furniture, bookshelves, sound systems, and artefacts that expatriates have collected on their travels. Being inside one of these houses, one would not necessarily be able to identify it as located in Jakarta. Similar interiors could be found in expatriates' houses in Bangkok or Kuala Lumpur, for example. Stepping outside the gates, however, one would be immediately surrounded by a contrasting environment in the form of rubbish-filled ditches, speeding motorbikes, and street-cart vendors plying their trade—all elements of what many expatriates might consider "disorder." The insides of the houses could thus be seen as a shelter, protecting expatriates physically from unwanted impacts from the outside, but also symbolically shielding them from what expatriates perceive as "local chaos."

The "strangeness" that can sometimes pervade these interiors and the social events held in them are illustrated by an informal "German" gathering in which I participated. Erika, a German expatriate wife in her late forties, had invited some friends to her house for coffee and cake. Coming from a hot, dusty outside, one entered the air-conditioned house, where the lights were dimmed. The hostess had done much to recreate a proper "coffee afternoon" such as would typically take place among families in rural and suburban Germany. Candles had been lit on the carefully laid-out table, which was complete with serviettes and cake forks, and home-baked cake and waffles were served. These were accompanied, as they might be "at home," by jam and freshly whipped cream, but given the heat and humidity, the cream threatened to disintegrate at any moment and therefore had to be taken away by the Indonesian maid immediately after serving. Such a scenario provides one example of the atmosphere created within these houses, which may contribute to the feeling of "unrealness" experienced by some expatriates, which stems not so much from the practices themselves, but from their apparent contrast to the local environment.

Apartment Living

Younger expatriates, particularly unmarried professionals in their thirties, often do not choose to live in villa-styles houses, but rent apartments in high-rise buildings in the town center. I suggest that these housing styles represent another form of "living in the bubble," while also inviting comparison with "Disneyland." They link to the "bubble" insofar as the metaphor entails a certain transparency—it is possible to gaze from the inside out. A key feature of such high-rise apartments, accordingly, are large windows, which offer panoramic views of the city. From such a perspective Jakarta as a cityscape becomes tolerable and even attractive. Removed from the bustling streets below with their noise and fumes, the Indonesian city is experienced as a wide-screen view of landmarks, fly-overs, and high-rise architecture, which becomes even more impressive when illuminated. A related sentiment was expressed by Marc, a young Canadian expatriate, as we were gazing out his apartment windows on the twelfth floor, and he remarked: "this is how I like Jakarta—from the inside, at night, or from above."

While this distance is often experienced as pleasant, it can also create feelings of artificiality. Marc referred to this on one occasion, as we had gone through the marble-floored corridors of his serviced apartment building, entered the elevator with chrome-rimmed mirrors and indirect lighting, and rode to the roof terrace. Standing at the rail of the bar, overlooking the kidney-shaped swimming pool that was glowing turquoise under the night sky and absorbing toned-down jazz music playing in the background, he said, "Look at all this . . . such a Disneyland." The metaphor of "Disneyland" here carries connotations of a theme park, a stage set, a façade—invoking carefully managed fantasy worlds.

As Zukin describes in her study of Disney World, the aim of its planners was to create a "Disney realism," aiming to "program out all the negative, unwanted elements and program in the positive elements" (quoted in Zukin 1991: 222). Doubtlessly, Marc was aware of these dimensions; he knew that when leaving the residence court, he would be confronted with traffic, exhaust fumes, street vendors, Indonesian office workers waiting in clusters for buses in the rush hour, beggars on the pedestrian overpasses, and street children offering to shine shoes. While relieved at not having to pass through this when returning from his office, there may have been a lingering awareness of how "this projection of desire taunts the image of reality" (Zukin 1991: 231). Such an awareness may be reflected in some expatriates' sense of the "unrealness" of their worlds, and their resulting unease with it.

Intrusions

As much as the idea of a sheltering interior might appeal to some expatriates, a closer look at their everyday lives reveals that the metaphor of the "bunker" describes their situation only partially. As the presence of the Indonesian maid described in the coffee afternoon scenario above indicates, expatriates' houses are not free of outside influences; rather, elements of "Indonesia" are present in or intrude into their homes in various forms. On a practical level, many were continuously concerned with keeping outside influences such as dust, cockroaches, or lizards at bay. In the rainy season, this could take the form of leaking roofs or power surges that were damaging electrical equipment. Some were complaining about Indonesians burning rubbish in their back yards, with the resulting smoke wafting across expatriates' gardens and pools.

Such dismay at outside intrusion was, for example, expressed by Tania, a German wife of a medical doctor, as we were standing on the terrace of their house, which overlooked an unusually green area of Jakarta. Replete with banana and palm trees, the roofs of neighboring houses almost disappeared among them. As we took in the view, she said: "Isn't this beautiful! But it's spoilt by the mosques. There are so many in the neighborhood, and they go off three, four times a day. They sound horrible! But you can't escape them, so I go inside when they start." One could object that complaints about offensive smells or sounds may be equally typical for densely populated neighborhoods in Europe. I suggest, though, that it is not just the physical discomfort that matters here, but that these smells and sounds were understood as signs of an ethnic other. The burning of rubbish was frequently cited as an example of the primitive habits of Indonesians, whereas the Muslim call to prayer constituted for many a reminder of the fundamental religious difference of Indonesians, compared to the mostly Christian background of Euro Americans.

As these examples show, expatriates' spaces are not as hermetically sealed-off from the outside as some may wish them to be. "Indonesia" seeps into their spaces in the form of Indonesian staff, or forces of nature such as rain or vermin. As discussed above, the permeability of boundaries is alluded to in the metaphor of the "bubble." Although it implies a clear division between the inside and outside, the bubble also has a membrane—like a cell's membrane, which can be permeable and allow outside fluids to enter the cell's inside.

Movement

As indicated in Marc's characterization of his residence as a "Disneyland," many expatriates' feelings about their spaces are decidedly ambiguous. While there is a desire for seclusion from what is seen as the turmoil of "Indonesian" life, some also seem unhappy about this distance, and remarks such as "we are living in a bubble here" are also expressive of regret or unease about this separateness. Conversations with individuals, especially Germans, who had recently returned from a trip home often touched on how pleasurable it had been to "go for a walk in the forest" and to be "in nature."

Kathrin for example, a German art teacher in her late forties who had given up her job temporarily to accompany her husband to his posting, reflected on her lifestyle in Jakarta with some sadness: "I don't like that I am spending most of my time indoors. I am always under neon lights, in air-conditioned rooms. I so long to get fresh air, just to go for a walk." Like many of her friends, she felt that it was not possible to do that. Annoyed by this indoor lifestyle, one afternoon she decided to walk the short distance from her house to a nearby sports stadium, where her son was practicing with his school team. After a few hundred meters, though, she felt overwhelmed by the heat and the dust, and unnerved by the manifold smells, she gave up the idea and hastily returned home.

Kathrin's experience points to a recurring feature in expatriates' lives: since so much of their time is spent in closed spaces, contact with the outside—for example, walking through streets—is rather limited. Owing partly to the topography of downtown Jakarta, which, due to the scarcity of pedestrian walkways and intense traffic, does not encourage walking, expatriates undertake most of their journeys through the city in chauffeur-driven cars or by taxi. There is a sense that it is "not possible" to use public transport such as buses or trains, since they are seen as overcrowded, dirty, and dangerous. As a result, many expatriates spend their entire days in the city without so much as setting foot on a street surface. On a typical day, one could for example leave the house in the morning by car; the driver would pull up in front of a hotel lobby, where one would enter an air-conditioned interior. On return, the driver would be called from the car park through an intercom, and pick up his client from the entrance. Children were driven to school exclusively by bus or car; husbands were similarly transported to and from the office in this way.

Many expatriates, even if they may have been initially bewildered by these practices, slip rather easily into these convenient routines. Like Kathrin, though, some become dissatisfied with this "indoors" lifestyle and its remoteness from an "outside" world. One way of addressing this lack, one could imagine, would be to engage in outdoor activities. Although much exercise is done in indoor gyms, sports such as golf or tennis are pursued outdoors. Significantly, though, these take place in settings such as golf courses or tennis courts that are fenced off from onlookers or trespassers, and thus replicate the boundedness of expatriates' indoor spaces.

Communities and Sociality

If their dwelling spaces are reminiscent of "bunkers," expatriates' social lives are founded on similar tendencies to erect barricades against various groups defined as "other," whether non-expatriate locals or expatriates of other nationalities. I employ the term "expatriate community" here in two ways: as referring, first, to the group of Euro American expatriates in Jakarta, and, second, to the national communities within this larger Euro American group. This is not to assume fixed divisions between them, but to explore how people conceptualize, maintain, or overcome them. In addition to external boundaries, I argue that these social spaces are also marked by internal divisions along the lines of gender, ethnicity, and class. Both are expressed in the metaphors of a "ghetto" and "hothouse," conjuring up isolated groups and inward-looking attitudes. While such settings may be predicated on similarities among inhabitants, they also accentuate differences.

A key metaphor for expatriates' social spaces is the "ghetto," referring to demarcated areas of settlement for certain ethnic or social groups, both non-privileged and privileged. The "ghetto" connotes a hermetic social world that generates its own "cultures" and specific rules of behavior. A feeling of commonality among the inhabitants is coupled with a sense of mistrust and fear toward outsiders. Such features also characterize some of the social worlds of expatriates in Jakarta, as the following example illustrates.

Elisabeth is a Bavarian in her early forties, whose husband is working for a major German manufacturing firm. She has three children, two of whom are attending the "German International School," while the youngest daughter is still at home. Elisabeth considers herself a pragmatic person and is very active in an organization for German women in Jakarta called Die Bruecke (The Bridge). She takes an active role in the new-comers' committee, which offers support to newly arrived Germans. A meeting for such newcomers was held once at Elisabeth's house in South Jakarta. On entering the house, one could not fail to notice boldly col-ored, rustic Bavarian-style interior decoration, including a wicker basket holding a dried-flower arrangement and an antique wagon wheel that was propped decoratively against a wall. During the meeting, as the conver-sation turned to everyday life in Jakarta, Elisabeth explained to the new arrivals, "In fact, during the course of one day, I can only speak German and only meet with Germans. If I want to, I can spend my whole time in a German world."

What would such a "German world"—or "ghetto"—in Jakarta con-sist of? Elisabeth's morning starts with getting her children ready to be picked up by the bus of the German International School. Her husband is driven to his office, where he would conduct at least part of the day's business speaking German with some of his colleagues. Elisabeth's morn-ings can be taken up by activities related to the German women's asso-ciation, such as organizing a household-goods sale, book exchanges, or newcomers' activities. A German friend might stop by later to pick up some baby equipment that Elisabeth had offered to lend her. In the after-noon, she might attend a meeting of the parent's association of the Ger-man school, where she was an active member. Social outings with her hus-band involved mostly other German couples—for example, in the form of a so-called *Stammtisch*, a once-monthly German pub gathering at a hotel. For Sunday worship, the family occasionally attended a service held by the German Catholic community in a church in South Jakarta. During the summer holidays, Elisabeth and the children would return for several weeks to Germany, staying with relatives, where her husband would join them for a while.

Given such a scenario, it becomes imaginable how the majority of one's social interactions can be conducted in one's native language even in such a comparatively distant location as Jakarta. Notably, such environments would be available not only to Germans but also to French, American, Japanese, or Dutch expatriates. The creation of these "ghettos" in Jakarta is made possible through the relatively high numbers of expatriates of any one nationality. In this context, the importance of newcomers' meetings as mentioned above with their provision of practical and emotional sup-port is not to be underestimated, as they often constitute entry points into these spaces.

Unsurprisingly, not all newcomers become fully signed-up members of national women's associations or their national expatriate community. Af-ter an orientation period, some expatriates purposefully avoid nationally oriented organizations, and create social networks outside of what they perceive as their conventional and stifling social settings. Margarete, for example, a German biologist in her late sixties who had been living in Jakarta for a number of years and spent most of her time working for the Jakarta zoo and its orangutan conservation program, responded emphatically when asked about the German women's association: "Those ladies? Oh, leave me alone. They just drink coffee and gossip all day. I've always stayed away from them!"

What is experienced as supportive and comforting by dedicated members of these groups can appear to others as claustrophobic, resembling a "hothouse," as described by some. The "hothouse" constitutes another pertinent metaphor for expatriates' lives. Like the "ghetto," it implies a bounded space, but also an intensified social climate that demands social accord and is sensitive to trespasses. Newcomers often find that social interactions in expatriate communities can be governed by particular sets of rules regarding social ranking, dress codes, or forms of socializing. As Paula, a British woman, poignantly remarked: "When I came to Jakarta, I didn't suffer from culture shock with Indonesia. But I had culture shock entering the expat community"—thus hinting at the distinctive "culture" that can characterize such communities.

Internal Divisions

While such groups may maintain strong boundaries toward the outside, they are also intersected by multiple internal boundaries, especially those of gender, ethnicity, and class. Sociality, in the overall group of Euro American expatriates, is structured by two seemingly contrastive processes. On the one hand, a diverse assembly of Euro Americans are identified as members of the shared category "expatriates," either through self-ascription or being defined as such by their companies on the basis of their employment status. This can engineer a sense of commonality vis-à-vis a non-expatriate outside world, in this case Indonesia, which can be aligned with racial boundaries. On the other hand, differences within this collective are emphasized more strongly in the context of expatriate living compared to its members' home countries, a situation expressed in the metaphor of the "hothouse." This metaphor represents a closed space, which traps sunlight and raises the temperature inside. Transferred to the expatriate community, the metaphor captures their seclusion from the outside world, leading to a heightened atmosphere within, and signals the intensity with which internal differences and deviations are experienced and judged.

Such internal boundaries manifest themselves in terms of gender. While a number of expatriate women held jobs prior to following their husbands to their postings, they are often unable to work in Indonesia because of legal restrictions and thus become "accompanying wives." Subsequently, expatriate life can become more gender-segregated than it might have been at home as a form of labor division is reinstated that many would view as outdated in their home countries. Women are often assigned the tasks of caregivers, household managers, and generally reproducing the family abroad, while husbands' responsibilities are defined foremost as wage earners. This gender divide is reflected in the creation of women's organizations, such as the British, French, or American women's association in Jakarta.

The fact that women's organizations are structured along national lines points at the same time toward the salience of national or ethnic boundaries within the expatriate community. While grouped together as "Westerners" or "whites" in certain contexts, national divides run more or less visibly through the expatriate community as a whole. The criteria for being part of such national groups can vary. An example is the membership rules of women's organizations. While the German women's association identifies German language proficiency as an entry condition, the American Women's association requires American citizenship to become a member, whereas the British women's group offers non-British citizens an associate membership. The importance of these boundaries becomes apparent through seemingly mundane transgressions. For example, a Swiss woman whom I had come to know through the German women's association was highly embarrassed when I encountered her at an event of the British Women's Association, as if I had witnessed a situation that she would prefer to keep confidential.

Such guardedness could indirectly take on a more racist tone in relation to women of Asian origin who had met and married white expatriate men on other postings, and who had followed them to Jakarta. Although some had acquired British or American citizenship, for example, their claims to belong to the predominantly white expatriate women's associations could be uncertain. It seemed that in the eyes of some white women their status as "Asian females" placed them in closer proximity to Indonesian "bargirls" or even prostitutes as opposed to respectable expatriate spouses. While such boundaries may underpin expatriate groups, they were also contested, for example, through the efforts of "Asian" wives to become proficient in their husbands' languages, to follow dress codes, and to participate in "national" community events.

Apart from gender and ethnicity, differences in class also gain importance. The process of becoming an expatriate brings together individuals from relatively diverse socioeconomic backgrounds in their home countries, such as families of engineers, senior managers, or finance directors. While uniting them as white Westerners in Indonesia, this process brings into socio-spatial proximity individuals who might not have normally socialized with each other in their home countries. Silvia, for example, the wife of a German senior manager, remarked that "at home, we are friends with some of my husband's colleagues, and my colleagues from school, but we certainly wouldn't be socializing with the family of the German ambassador, as we do here." This unifying process, though, engineers its own divisions. I was told that a few years ago, women would be seated at coffee mornings of the German women's association according to the corporate rank of their husbands. I was informed that such practices were less common now, although many were still aware of such differences. The persistent appearance in side remarks and informal conversations underlines the significance of such status divisions in the climate of an expatriate "hothouse."

"Living in a Bubble"

One of the key questions of this paper concerns the nature of the spaces expatriates create. While metaphors such as the "ghetto" and the "hothouse" invoke their seclusion as well as the heated atmosphere inside, another characteristics is the "unrealness" or "artificiality," as contained in the metaphor of a "Disneyland." These sentiments may be fuelled by a range of experiences, which are difficult to pinpoint exactly. The sense of "artificiality" is probably most distinctly expressed in the metaphor of "living in a bubble." I take this metaphor to suggest a colorful, but fragile existence; one that is carefully created like a soap bubble, floating above the ground, and not touching the earth. It gleams and shimmers, displaying an exotic attractiveness, but also an ephemeral nature.

One aspect of expatriates' lives captured by this metaphor is its floating character, untouched by what many know to be a powerful reality outside it. Some expatriates expressed concern that they—and especially their children—were not experiencing what they regarded as a "normal" world anymore. In concrete terms, this meant not feeling able to take public transport, since all journeys were undertaken by private or chauffeur-driven car, or feeling incapable of crossing hectic roads by themselves anymore. Some women in particular found that their life had become "unreal" since most of the housework, even tasks such as laying the table, was taken over by staff. As a response, some women purposely dismissed staff at weekends in order to "get their hands dirty," as one woman put it, and thus regain a feeling of "reality."

The bubble metaphor also implies a suspended, self-contained world with its own microclimate. This relates to expatriates' lives insofar as they are predicated on a double remoteness: geographically distant from their home countries, they are also based on a sense of social and cultural difference from Indonesian society. Expatriates' spaces could therefore be regarded as worlds unto themselves; they are secluded from their surroundings in housing compounds, and floating above the ground almost literally in the rooftop swimming pools on high-rise apartment buildings some inhabit. Although tentative links bind them both to their home and host countries, the spaces they create are neither wholly of one or the other. I will illustrate this in relation to so-called "coffee mornings," a long-standing institution in most women's associations. Such coffee mornings are forums for meetings and exchanges with other members, and can be organized around a theme, an invited speaker, or a performance; they are usually held once a month on a weekday morning in one of the main hotels in central Jakarta.

Taking a coffee morning of the British women's association as an example, starting at 9 a.m. members would arrive at the "Regency" hotel in chauffeur-driven cars and make their way to a large downstairs ballroom. In the ballroom foyer Indonesian vendors set up stalls selling handicrafts, textiles, and jewelry. Expatriate women, all of whom appear carefully dressed and groomed, greet each other before they proceed to the main room, lit by chandeliers, where tables are laid with white cloth and silverware, and people take seats on plush gold-framed chairs. After an official welcome, a buffet of tea and cakes is opened; uniformed waiters serve cups of tea, which are accompanied by miniature-sized muffins and dainty sandwiches. This is followed by a choir performance from an Indonesian orphans' village that the association supports. In a break, copies of the newsletter are distributed, which contains columns such as a "Letter from Middle England," recipes for "British cooking in Jakarta," and information on the upcoming Garden Party for the Queen's birthday. Meanwhile, the women have the chance to browse an English-language bookstall and arrange dates with their tennis or golf partners. As the meeting closes at 12:30, the women proceed to the hotel foyer, have their drivers recalled from the car park, and return home.

A scenario such as this could, with some variations, take place at the American or German women's association. Given its comparatively luxurious venue, attentive staff, and sophisticated food, one might get a sense of an exotic fairytale atmosphere, which contrasts starkly with the grubby surroundings faced by the Indonesian drivers waiting in the underground hotel car park. As one British woman, Laura, remarked: "it is like being in an oriental dream, the hotels, the waiters, the drinks and decorations—it looks so fancy that it is slightly unreal, like it can't last." While the event echoes some "British" practices in terms of sociality and food, it is far removed from comparable coffee mornings held in Britain in their possibly less glamorous settings. I would therefore argue that the spaces constructed by these expatriates are neither "British" as they exist in Britain, nor "Indonesian," but rather constitute a form of "being British abroad." Expatriates' feelings of unrealness could be partly fuelled by a sneaking sense of living in a fairytale world that is removed from many Indonesians' lifeworlds, as well as being a purposefully recreated form of "British life" that has connections with, but is essentially different from, life in Britain.

So far, one could argue that such practices closely resemble those created by other expatriate or migrant communities, and that there is little, if anything, unique about these kinds of spaces. As discussed in the introductory section, though, it is not the practices themselves but the meanings they assume in the context of contemporary discourses on transnational spaces that make a difference here. A key argument outlined at the beginning was that taking the case of expatriates into account leads to a more complex notion of transnational spaces insofar as they do not exhibit openness and fluidity, but seem to reinforce boundaries, reintroduce traditions, and insist on differences instead. From this perspective, expatriates' transnational practices represent not just reenactment of what may be a well-known "cocooning" of expatriate populations, but they question discourses that implicitly assume that contemporary transnational spaces must be progressive ones.

Contact Zones

However much these spaces may seem removed from "Indonesian" surroundings, it would be mistaken to envisage them as entirely separate, as the metaphor of the bubble might imply. Instead, as mentioned earlier, the membranes of the bubble are permeable and allow for exchanges across its boundaries. Expatriates' spaces are thus inevitably marked by their Indonesian setting in some form. The transgression of boundaries, as discussed in relation to housing, can be inadvertent or intentional. In the case of coffee mornings, the presence of Indonesian staff situates these events in Indonesia, while the choice of luxurious venues is related to the entertainment spaces available in a capital city.

A more intentional, if guarded, form of interaction between expatriates and "Indonesia" takes place in what Pratt (1992) has termed "contact zones" (see also Yeoh and Willis 2005). In the context of travel writing, she uses the term to refer to "the space of colonial encounters, the space in which peoples geographically and historically separated come into contact with each other" (Pratt 1992: 6). In the expatriate context, such zones exist in the form of institutionalized encounters between expatriate and Indonesian women in a so-called "Ladies' Club." This club brings together a select group of well-educated elderly Indonesians, some from diplomatic circles, who are often fluent in German, Dutch, or French, with members of the German women's association, who see this as an opportunity to converse with members of Indonesian society in a setting that is not structured by employer-employee relations, as many of their encounters are. Even if these "intercultural" coffee mornings can be rather orchestrated events with well-meant, if stilted, conversations, German participants often express great satisfaction at meeting such "cultured ladies."

Similar contact zones are created by the "Indonesian Heritage Society," an expatriate-led organization that aims to familiarize expatriates with aspects of Indonesian culture. This takes place through cultural tourism trips around Jakarta, voluntary work in the National Museum, and a public lecture series, resonating with Clifford's view of museums as contact zones (Clifford 1997). While the nature of these zones cannot be discussed in detail, the concept significantly complements the notion of expatriates "living in a bubble," as it points to the diffuse fields that can surround boundaries—constituting "border zones" between the sheltered space of the bubble and the outside. It could also be argued that such zones throw into greater relief the otherwise secluded and esoteric nature of expatriates' spaces. Especially in regulated forms such as intercultural coffee mornings, contact zones constitute spaces into which expatriates can foray without fear of unanticipated or unwanted encounters with local worlds.

Conclusion

The starting point for this essay was the question of in what way boundaries matter for privileged mobile professionals. While it has been acknowledged that they significantly affect non-privileged migrants, it is often assumed that affluent movers live in a "borderless world," where boundaries have become irrelevant. Considering the case of corporate expatriates, I argue that although they may be immersed in "global flows," their transnational lives are also characterized by the continuous drawing, maintaining and negotiating of boundaries, such as those of ethnicity, nationality, or gender. I have more specifically tried to identify what kind of spaces these boundaries enclose—in other words, what spaces expatriates create.

The exploration of these spaces was informed by metaphors that are prominent in expatriate discourses, such as the "bubble," "bunker," "ghetto," and "hothouse." The metaphor of the "bubble," in particular, symbolizes an artificial construct, a "fantasy world" floating above the ground, which captures many aspects of expatriates' lives. It resonates strongly with their experiences of their environments as both closed and "unreal," a sentiment also reflected in the image of a "Disneyland." Both the "bunker" and the "ghetto" carry connotations of secluded spaces, offering shelter from an outside world, but also fostering a claustrophobic atmosphere inside. In relation to social lives, the metaphor of the "hothouse" is used to describe the dense, heated climate within these communities, which intensifies distinctions of class and gender.

Despite this fundamental boundedness, however, transgressions and transactions across boundaries occur. One space where such exchanges take place are "contact zones," such as the activities of the "Indonesian

Heritage Society," which potentially enable expatriates to overcome the limits of the "ghetto."

I have here attempted to complicate the notion of transnational spaces as they are conventionally understood in current discourses of globalization and transnationalism. The case of Euro American expatriates in Jakarta suggests that spaces created by transnational migrants are not always "transnational"—as in fluid, malleable and progressive—but that they can be bounded, rigid, and conservative. Furthermore, as discussed above, the emphasis of ethnic, racial, or national boundaries among Europeans living abroad is not a recent phenomenon, but links to practices such as those of colonial populations. It is a reminder not only that "transnationalism" has a history, but also that, despite the rhetoric of social theorists, transnational spaces have probably comprised such contradictory meanings and practices all along.

Notes

1. The "Living in Indonesia" Forum (www.expat.or.id) is a Web site specifically designed for expatriates who are posted to Indonesia and aims to provide information and advice, including an open discussion forum, from which this quote is taken.

References

Appadurai, Arjun. 1991. "Global Ethnoscapes: Notes and Queries for a Transnational Anthropology." In *Recapturing Anthropology: Working in the Present,* ed. R. G. Fox. Santa Fe, NM: School of American Research Press. pp.191–210.

Barth, Frederik. ed. 1969 *Ethnic Groups and Boundaries: The Social Organization of Culture Difference.* Bergen: Universitetsforlaget.

Basch, Linda, Nina Glick Schiller and Christina Szanton Blanc.1994. *Nations Unbound: Transnational Projects, Post-colonial Predicaments and Deterritorialized Nation-States.* Basel: Gordon and Breachs.

Beaverstock, Jonathan V. 2002. "Transnational Elites in Global Cities: British Expatriates in Singapore's Financial District." *Geoforum* 33 (4): 525–538.

Castells, Manuel. 2000. *The Rise of the Network Society.* Oxford: Blackwell.

de Certeau, Michel. 1984. *The Practice of Everyday Life.* Berkeley: University of California Press.

Clifford, James. 1997. *Routes: Travel and Translation in the Late Twentieth Century.* Cambridge and London: Harvard University Press.

Cohen, Anthony P. 1985. *The Symbolic Construction of Community.* London: Routledge.

———ed. 1986. *Symbolising Boundaries: Identity and Diversity in British Cultures.* Manchester: Manchester University Press.

Conradson, David and Alan Latham. 2005. "Transnational Urbanism: Attending to Everyday Practices and Mobilities." *Journal of Ethnic and Migration Studies* 31 (2): 227–233.

Cunningham, Hilary. 2004. " Nations Rebound? Crossing Borders in a Gated Globe." *Identities: Global Studies in Culture and Power* 11: 329–350.

Favell, Adrian. 2003. "Games without frontiers? Questioning the Transnational Social Power of Migrants in Europe." *Archives Europeennes de Sociologie* 44 (3):106–136.

———. 2004. "Eurostars and Eurocities: Free Moving Professionals and the Promise of European Integration." *European Studies Newsletter* 6 (3/4): 1–10.

Fechter, Anne-Meike. 2002. *Transnational Lives and their Boundaries: Expatriates in Jakarta, Indonesia.* Unpublished Ph.D. Thesis, University of Hull.

Friedmann, Jonathan. 1999. "Class formation, Hybridity and Ethnicification in Declining Global Hegemonies." In *Globalisation and the Asia Pacific: Contested Territories,* eds. K. Olds, et al. New York: Routledge.

Kearney, Michael. 2004. "The Classifying and Value-Filtering Missions of Borders." *Anthropological Theory* 4 (2): 131–156.

Lakoff, George and Mark Johnson.1980. *Metaphors We Live By.* Chicago: University of Chicago Press.

Low, Setha and Denise Lawrence-Zúñiga, eds. 2003. *The Anthropology of Space and Place: Locating Culture.* Oxford: Blackwell.

Meyer, Birgit and Peter Geschiere. 1999. *Globalisation and Identity: The Dialectics of Flow and Closure.* Oxford: Blackwell.

Merleau-Ponty, Maurice. 1962. *Phenomenology of Perception.* London: Routledge and Kegan Paul.

Ong, Aihwa. 1999. *Flexible Citizenship: Cultural Logics of Transnationality.* Durham, NC: Duke University Press.

Pratt, Mary. 1992. *Imperial Eyes: Travel Writing and Transculturation.* London: Routledge.

Pries, Ludger. 2001. *New Transnational Social Spaces: International Migration and Transnational Companies in the Early Twenty-First Century.* London and New York: Routledge.

Sklair, Leslie. 2001. *The Transnationalist Capitalist Class.* Oxford: Blackwell.

Smith, Michael Peter and Luis E. Guarnizo. 1998. *Transnationalism From Below.* New Brunswick, NJ: Transaction Publishers.

Stoler, Ann. 2002. *Carnal Knowledge and Imperial Power: Race and the Intimate in Colonial Rule.* Berkeley: University of California Press.

Tilley, Chris. 1994. *A Phenomenology of Landscape.* Oxford: Berg.

Yeoh, Brenda and Katie Willis. 2005. " Singaporean and British Transmigrants in China and the Cultural Politics of 'Contact Zones.'"*Journal of Ethnic and Migration Studies* 31 (2):269–285.

Zukin, Sharon. 1991. *Landscapes of Power: From Detroit to Disney World.* Berkeley: University of California Press.

4

Globalization through "Weak Ties"

A Study of Transnational Networks among Mobile Professionals[1]

Vered Amit

Network Analysis Then and Now

For a discipline such as anthropology that has traditionally anchored its investigations in the observation of day-to-day interactions among small groups, contemporary efforts to examine globalizing processes can pose special problems of definition and scale. But as Alan Smart has noted in a recent article, these are problems that had first been encountered in the early struggles of urban anthropologists to position themselves as ethnographers in large, dense metropolitan settlements (1999: 60). Smart locates these struggles within a primarily methodological challenge of balancing holism and participant observation within these complex urban contexts, a difficulty even more exacerbated when anthropologists had to "cope with the further shock that cities are not themselves contained units, but are parts of regional, national and global systems" (ibid: 61). In response to this methodological problem, Smart proposes the reinvigoration of network analysis, an approach that achieved considerable prominence in the concerted movement between the 1950s and the 1970s to conduct anthropological fieldwork in urban settings.[2] In this essay, I want to take up Alan Smart's call for a return to network analysis both for the general anthropological effort at charting transnational relationships and interactions as well as for my own study of a particular set of peripatetic professionals. However drawing on some useful lessons from the past, I want to reorient this renewal away from network-as-method to network-as-paradigm.

The excitement originally generated by network analysis centered on its promise for dealing with the kind of open-ended situations usually encountered in cities. The relationships of most urbanites could not easily be contained within one social group, activity, or setting. Urban connections more often ramified across a variety of activities, institutions, events, identities, groups, and spaces. And unlike the multiple and overlapping roles encumbered in the social relationships characteristic of smaller rural localities, the wider distribution of metropolitan contacts was also often associated with the compartmentalization of different spheres of interaction. Within a dense urban setting, there was therefore a strong likelihood that many of the people with whom an individual resident was acquainted and interacted would not similarly know each other. Metropolitan fieldwork thus quickly raised questions of how to contend with complex and not easily restricted urban ambits of social interaction.

One response by anthropologists to this quandary, which was noted and criticized by Ulf Hannerz, involved an attempt to shut out much of this urban cacophony by focusing on ethnic enclaves that seemed to approximate the conditions of the contained folk community (1980: 5). But another effort centered on the notion of network analysis and the possibility it seemed to offer for opening up the boundaries of anthropological inquiry without sacrificing its grounded micro perspective. Indeed, now the launching point of the inquiry could be as particular as the individual. Tracing the personal links of an individual allowed the fieldworker the possibility of examining involvements and relationships that cut across enduring groups, institutions, and even beyond the urban locale altogether. A focus on networks thus offered the promise of an analysis that could be both highly grounded and open-ended at the same time, prefiguring the processual concerns of later critiques.

As a technique, however, the analytic utility of networks often seemed to operate inversely to its methodological rigor. Thus, the earlier phase of network analysis eventually reached an impasse in the effort to convert it into systematic morphological calculations, descending into ever more complex but increasingly constrained statistical calculations. The kind of comprehensive enumeration of social links required to carry out statistical measurement of such morphological variables as density, reachability, centrality, and clustering was usually only attainable within very small units (Hannerz 1980; Granovetter 1973). Ironically, therefore, the more technically exacting network analysis became, the less it was able to relate "micro-level interactions" to "macro-level patterns" (Granovetter 1973: 1360), the very sort of bridging capacity that had excited interest in networks in the first place.

In 1980, Ulf Hannerz responded to this methodological stalemate by urging a different direction for network studies. He argued that the promise of this type of analysis was most likely to be realized when "network thinking" became "normalized," and entered the general repertoire of anthropological concepts, "to be used with just that intensity and completeness which the occasion calls for . . ." (Hannerz 1980: 186). In other words, the conceptual promise of networks was most likely to be realized when it was not restricted to one kind of methodological application or setting but instead informed general anthropological conceptions of social ties. Unfortunately, for the most part over the intervening years, this did not happen. Instead until recently, networks gradually receded from the anthropological armature, usually appearing, if at all, as a casual reference rather than as an analytic focus. This development was in marked contrast to the continued salience of network analysis in disciplines such as sociology and geography (for example, Wellman 1999; Dorein and Stokman 1997; Stokowski 1994).

At first glance, the waning of anthropological interest in networks seems surprising because it occurred just at the point when the issues already confronted by anthropologists in cities were now being encountered by ethnographers investigating global and transnational phenomena. These issues included the difficulty in delimiting boundaries, in tracking nesting contexts of increasing scale, and charting translocal connections on the one hand, and fragmented, compartmentalized associations on the other hand, the very issues that had catalyzed interest in the analysis of urban networks. But at second glance, the waning of interest in networks appears to be associated with a familiar retreat to tried and tested social concepts, a retreat reminiscent of the tendency among a previous generation of urban anthropologists to seek out ethnic enclaves. There is, however, a twist in the latest instantiation of this tendency.

In contrast to earlier scholarship, which appears to have been drawn to urban ethnic enclaves as an approximation of a traditional, bounded, and localized anthropological site, today's ethnographers appear willing, even eager to conduct fieldwork in very different kinds of circumstances. This includes a willingness to follow transnationally mobile people across the multiple locales and diffuse relationships with which they maintain an involvement. But, as I have argued elsewhere, anthropologists have tended to anchor such mobility, cross-border connections, and fluidity in familiar ethnic categories (Amit and Rapport 2002).[3]

One framework for this interpretation appears to draw heavily on Benedict Anderson's notion of "imagined community" (1991/1983). Thus, Arjun Appadurai argues that the mass mediated capacity to imagine work and residence in new places as well as an eventual return to the point of origin are a major stimulus for contemporary migration and adaptation (1996: 8). This electronic technology also makes it possible for widely dispersed migrants to imagine themselves as communities, an imaginative capacity that ostensibly carries with it always the potential not only for shared sentiment but for collective action (ibid). A large body of migration literature has linked this notion of imagination to the delineation of intimate links of family and consociation across state borders, links that are in turn viewed as the ground for the formation of new and ongoing transnational collectivities and identities (Basch et al 1994; Guarnizo and Smith 1998). Other anthropologists have joined in the multidisciplinary celebration of diaspora exemplified by the establishment of a journal of *Diaspora Studies.*

In short, this is a literature that has tended to assimilate contemporary forms of migration, communication, even new multi-locale fieldwork modalities under the rubric of long-standing anthropological categories of peoplehood and collective identity, albeit sometimes cloaked in new euphemisms. In so doing, anthropologists have often been able to claim an embrace of fluidity, mobility, and permeability and a transcendence of discredited notions of bounded cultures and places while still locating their ethnographic subjects in the comfortable familiarity of bounded ethnic categories of community and belonging. In 1980, Ulf Hannerz argued that "the flocking of urban anthropologists to the ethnic enclaves of our cities" was an evasion of the full spectrum of ethnographic possibilities offered by the urban environment (pp. 5–6). Twenty-five years later, the rather similar positioning of a large swathe of transnational studies within the rubric of ethnic/ diaspora/ transmigrant collectivities is arguably no less an evasion.[4]

Unlike Alan Smart, I do not think that renewing an anthropological interest in networks is likely to provide a ready methodological prescription for working through relationships, processes, institutions, and systems that are not readily delimited in space and time. Even the most particular of such networks, the personal links of one individual, may not be accessible through direct contact or observation and an arsenal of less direct methods of investigation—interviews, life histories, archival data, electronic communication- might still only yield frustratingly partial information. Attention to networks does not resolve the quandaries of *how* anthropologists conduct research in complex and open-ended contemporary situations, but it can open up the range of social situations and the types of links they can envisage to explore. It allows for a more "open and agnostic attitude" (Smart 1999: 73–74) than an a priori focus on one kind of collectivity or social link. With that open-ended attitude in mind, we also need to resist the current interdisciplinary bandwagon, which has formed around the notion of network as the architecture of institutional links between organizations, cities, states, and technologies, rather than as a conceptualization of social relations (Sassen 2002; Castells 2000). On the one hand, we will be better able to contribute a more distinctively grounded anthropological understanding of these kinds of post-Fordist structures and technologies if we retain a notion of network as a framework for probing the articulation of links between persons. On the other hand, the analytical utility of networks is most likely to be effective if it is not too closely identified, a priori, with any one type of organization, whether transnational ethnic communities or "flexible" corporations/societies.

"Weak Ties"

In this essay I want to consider an example of far-flung professional networks formed on the basis of a different principle of connection than the long-standing, intimate links of family and close friendship or the ideological commitment to communal identity that are so often the focus of migration or diaspora studies. Instead, these are occupational networks that operate within the bureaucratic terms of reference and procedures promulgated by a convergent set of international institutions. These networks take shape through the transnational dispersion of professional reputations and the episodic mobilization of instrumental and frequently transient relationships. In exploring the broader significance of this type of network, I want to return to the venerable concept of "weak ties" proposed by Mark Granovetter in 1973.

Granovetter was interested in probing which kinds of social links were most likely to function as bridges between distinct personal networks. With this question in mind, he argued that relationships that were fairly limited in scope and intensity were most likely to provide that kind of bridging function. By virtue of their restricted quality, these kinds of "weak ties" were not likely to be part of shared and encapsulating personal networks. The parties to such relationships would probably be dependent on other people for many of their social needs and hence to have recourse to distinct networks. However, their relationship could provide a conduit or bridge along which information or influence could pass onto their respective contacts. On the other hand individuals involved in more fully rounded and intense relationships comprised of "strong ties," who were more likely to confide in, and spend a lot of time with each other, were also more likely to have other friends and contacts in common. Thus, the strength of a dyadic tie was likely to be correlated with the degree of overlap in the personal networks of its protagonists, that is, the number of people who are tied to both of these individuals. Given this overlap, this kind of strong link was less likely in itself to act as a conduit to other distinct networks. Granovetter noted that an individual's network could be divided into different parts, one "part made up of strong and nonbridging ties" and another comprised of weaker, more superficial ties (1973:1370). It was this latter part of an individual's relationships that was most likely to provide the bridges for indirect contacts. Thus in conducting a random sample of "professional, technical and managerial job changers living in a Boston suburb," he discovered that often the most useful contacts in the search for a new job were quite marginal links within the individual's network (ibid: 1371). "It is remarkable that people receive crucial information from individuals whose very existence they have forgotten" (1372). These types of marginal ties could therefore provide a source of mobility to the extent that they allowed people to move between networks. Given their bridging qualities, Granovetter argued that weak ties would probably constitute better channels for diffusion than strong ties. If Granovetter's hypothesis is correct or even partially correct, then we can extrapolate that in exploring the extension of personal connections across the globe we must focus more intensively on the establishment and workings of these weak ties.

Traveling Professionals

In terms of each of the indices applied by Granovetter to assess the relative strength of personal relationships, most of the ties that are formed through the occupational networks of the peripatetic consultants under consideration here are "weak." They do not involve a large amount of time spent in ongoing interaction; for the most part, they are formal rather than intimate and therefore do not usually evoke much emotional intensity. The reciprocal services they involve tend to be constrained by the context of particular and often time-limited projects.

My research has focused on consultants who were nominally based in Canada but whose work involved frequent and consecutive projects in various locales situated in the global South. As a result, many of these consultants were away from their place of residence for several months every year, and for some individuals or in some periods this could involve half or more of the year. Most of these consultants worked on various aspects of development infrastructure. Some had worked as independent freelancers. Others were salaried employees of large private corporations, often engineering firms, that might also incorporate an environmental or planning section. A few worked for or were partners in smaller consulting agencies. While my research focused on Canada-based professionals, this group also formed part of a much larger transnational circuit of consultants who advise on various aspects of infrastructure development in southern countries including project planning, implementation, evaluation, human resource development, communications, and so on. Together the people moving and working on this circuit are among the most visible representatives of the broader global privatization of development work.

The projects they worked on were principally funded by national and multilateral aid agencies or development banks such as the Canadian International Development Agency, the World Bank, the Asian Development Bank, and so on. As such, these projects operated within the terms of reference set by the funding agencies. These terms could range from direct organizational control over the recruitment of personnel to less direct enforcement of particular technical standards or procedures. Tanya, who specialized in environmental and urban management, had worked for two large Canadian engineering firms with international projects before eventually moving into freelance international consulting work. She explained the role of the funding agencies thus:

Let's take the World Bank and this may be construed as somewhat of a hard judgment but I think it's accurate in many senses. The World Bank is a bank and they set extremely high standards for loan projects, for loan agreements that they will negotiate with governments, whether it is the quality of the technical proposal, whether it is the standards for environmental review or for again, population resettlement, whether it is the cost–and very often that is least cost. So, they have very high standards. Often you sometimes wonder whether they're totally realistic standards . . . But notwithstanding the bank has those and they won't approve projects if they don't come all the way up to, or close to those standards. That's normally not a major challenge for international firms because we are all used to working to those standards. But for many local counterpart consultants that we work with, and the quality of the work they produce, yes, it is very difficult.

Projects might involve a wide variety of different companies and agencies: the funding agency, the local executing agency, and several consulting agencies and/or independent consultants who might be variously working as joint venture consortiums, subcontractors, or on different aspects of the same project. Since international funding agencies now regularly require that the projects they fund involve a capacity for transfer of knowledge, projects also usually included a mixture of international and local "counterpart" consultants. Thus, even consultants who conducted their work on successive projects as employees of the same large company were still likely to find themselves working with a largely or even entirely new set of colleagues in successive locales, regions, or countries.

As the British anthropologist, R. L. Stirrat observed for a similar pattern of development consultancy in Sri Lanka, teams are likely to bring together

> a very disparate collection of people differentiated in terms of nationality, experience, motivation and background. But for a period of a few weeks members of a team work together in an extremely intensive way and then the group disbands. (2000: 35)

Then it's on to the next project and the next set of workmates. Stirrat argued that what makes it possible for these transient consultancy teams to function is their shared, if sometimes ironic, subscription to what he called a "culture of modernity." In using this term, Stirrat was concerned with delineating particular paradigms of knowledge and rationality as these are used to account for standardized, dis-embedded protocols of evaluation and application. In principle, consultants are important agents of standardization since their work rests on the presumption that certain kinds of expertise are portable. But with the portability of their expertise also goes the portability of the person of the consultant him/herself. And this portability of persons and its concomitant dis-embedding of social relationships is as much an aspect of this culture or paradigm of modernity as the standards these practices are meant to disseminate.

Entailed in the spatial mobility characterizing this form of international consultancy were two particularly important aspects that structured the personal networks of its practitioners. First, as Stirrat's observation indicates, it demanded a continual reconstitution of work groups, and associated with this necessity was the transient nature of many of the occupational relationships in which these specialists participated. Occupational relationships were constantly being shed to make way for new projects and new teams. Over and over again, individuals explained that while they were occasionally able to maintain contact with people they had worked with even after the project in which they met has ended, they were not able to sustain many of these relationships. They worked with far too many people, over far too great distances and diverse locales to sustain contacts with most of them, and this was especially the case for localized contacts whom they were not likely to encounter in other regions.

James explained:

> And it is a challenge to keep in touch and you know, it's sort of like here when you move from Montreal to Vancouver, you might keep in touch with one or two special friends but the rest of the network kind of drops off. It's very much the same thing and most people find it difficult, you know, unless for some reason you stay working in the same region. But I tend to do all kinds of work in all different regions and move from project to project so I think that's challenging.

Daniel, a senior project manager who worked for a for a much larger Montreal engineering firm explained:

> I try to maintain contacts but it's not easy because first you travel, you're not home. And their interests change. You keep contact over one or two years, but then after that . . . Unless you have a chance to go back to the same area. Otherwise, it's hard [to maintain contact].

This is not to argue that there were no continuities or recurrences in the networks established by consultants. Consultants working for firms, rather than as freelancers, might find themselves repeatedly working with a small core of colleagues. If local contacts were for the most part left behind, similarly mobile professionals specializing in development projects in the South might well encounter each other again, even if only at intervals years apart. But even more important than actual repeated face-to-face encounters—and there was considerable variation between different individuals in their appraisal of how common such reencounters were likely to be—was the knowledge people gained of who was working in this global field and what kind of qualifications and experience they were best known for. Even more important, with each successive project these professionals were able to extend their own reputation for particular kinds of expertise or credentials. This expertise was extended through both the roster of projects they could now cite on their curriculum vitae and the larger number of people who, either directly or indirectly, now knew of them, of their formal qualifications, and/or their project experience.

This information was thus circulated both formally and informally within a well-developed, even regimented institutional circuit shaped and managed by the funding agencies and their respective organizational networks of subcontractors. Curricula vitas were solicited and circulated as companies tried to develop teams on paper as part of their submissions for new contracts. When I asked Daniel, who specialized in environmental work, how he organized teams for various projects, he explained:

> And also many of these jobs, we get these jobs by competition. We send in a proposal. So basically you try to get the best c.v. Not the best expert but the one who will make it that you will win. And if you work in Asia, they're going to be keen on the academic level. If you want to get a job in Africa, they will look at your local expertise. "Oh yes, this guy's already been in Senegal so he knows." Even though it's not the same area of expertise but he knows Senegal. In Asia—and basically I think this is coming from the Asian Development Bank—they are very keen on how many Ph.D.s you have on your team. Whereas in Africa, they will never ask you how many Ph.D.s but they'll ask how many people know Senegal or Ivory Coast or whatever.

Daniel explained that the people he recruited to these teams were not always people he had previously worked with:

> We have people who will work with us on several occasions but other people . . . [don't]. We use the best experts in Canada so you can make a few phone calls and someone will tell you this guy's from the University of BC, can you have his phone number and that's how connections are made.

On one occasion, Daniel had been in search of someone with specific expertise in hurricane and disaster control in the Caribbean. He was finally able to identify the "expert" that he hired for this project through a phone call to a Canadian government department dealing with related types of emergencies. And, he had previously identified this government department through an internet search.

Second, alongside the constantly changing composition of work teams, the spatial mobility of these "international consultants" also entailed an acute compartmentalization between work and domestic spheres of relationships as consultants journeyed far afield leaving families and close friends behind. With the exception of longer-term contracts of a year or more, their families rarely accompanied consultants working in this field on their travels. Spouses had jobs they couldn't leave; children had to attend school. But even without these competing responsibilities, the intensity of the schedule of project trips abroad, which usually involved 12- to 13-hour workdays and six-day workweeks left very little time left to spend with accompanying family members. Roland, a specialist in social-economic impact assessment explained why he normally preferred that his wife remain in Montreal rather than accompany him on missions.

> Normally I would prefer her to stay here. Yes. Sometimes she doesn't like that but I try to explain when I go [on] these missions generally, it's, I wouldn't say it's hard work, it's not hard work because I like it. You discover a lot of things, it's very interesting so it's not really hard but it's long days. I start early, finish late because you have a lot of people to meet, a lot of reports to read, very often I work, not all the weekends, but one of the two days. So being with somebody else, it would be hard to manage. And I have to visit strange places. It's hard to be with somebody else who is not a colleague, who is not working. So sometimes she went with me but we tried to make it so she came at the end of the mission, before or after, not too much overlap.

At one point James, a partner in a small consulting firm focusing on training and evaluation, and his wife both held jobs that required frequent travel:

> I really missed the children when they were young and it put increasing pressures on my wife who worked the whole time. And I worked. In fact, at one point, she was traveling and I was traveling and it was very difficult with a three year old and a six year old.

He added:

> We eventually had to have a live-in nanny, because we just couldn't manage the running around and one of us trying to do it alone. And so maybe when we were younger and had more energy, I can't imagine it now, but yeah it was tough. We basically had to hire a lot of support systems to help the children, and I mean, I met my wife overseas, and she's very understanding about the job and its requirements. It just required a tremendous amount of scheduling.

He hadn't been around his children as often as he had wanted and he regretted missing the day-to-day interaction of their childhood.

So consultants like James, Roland, and Tanya regularly left behind family members and friends in order to work intensively with temporary colleagues. And these absences could in turn engender a sense of displacement even at "home." Ian, who worked for the large engineering consulting company that had also, for a time, employed Tanya, explained:

> The curious isolating thing is, even when we are back here, is that we'll go out with friends that we've known for thirty-five, forty years. And as soon as you start talking about overseas, you can quite often see them glaze over, because they don't have the background to understand what you are really talking about.

Similarly Mark, a consultant with a competing engineering firm, who thought his frequent travels had had a beneficial effect on his immediate family, enlarging his children's sense of the world, acknowledged that his traveling had inevitably affected the continuity of his friendships in Montreal where he was based.

> Usually the first week back, I don't know if it's out of guilt or just out of habit now, but just making up with them, and then "oh yeah! You're back, how about getting together next week?" No, I'm gone again. . . .

What did his friends think of his work?

> I think a lot of them don't understand what I do. I know a lot them didn't and I still think a lot of them don't. A lot of them, they think a job is nine to five, you go and sit, you work at a factory, or you do office work and you come home. For me, it's my life; nine to five doesn't matter. I mean, I get up at five in the morning and I'm doing my e-mails to India so I can get an answer from them by the time I get to the office. I don't think they understand the development side of it. I think too many Canadians or North Americans if you want to extrapolate even more, are unaware of what development work really is. And explaining to them is hard. I mean how do I explain to a bunch of ten-year-old girl guides what I do? My kids don't know how to explain. He travels a lot. That's my profession, traveling. Some people have an idea but most of them don't.

And as Tanya and others acknowledged, a social life of frequent absences can get pared down to "a few good and constant friends" while many other relationships fall by the wayside. Keith, whose marriage had endured over many years of frequent absences, noted that it was a lifestyle that

> is hard on marriages I think. I'm probably one of the few people who are working like this who is still married to the same people. We've been married for thirty years now. It tends to be hard on marriages.

Its important to note that there was variation in this regard among the people being interviewed. In a number of instances, the individuals involved felt that other opportunities for involvement at least partly mitigated the impact of their absences. James argued that while his international travels had created domestic stresses, he tried to make up for them whenever he was at home by making more time for his family.

> . . . if I've been away for two weeks, I would then take the next few weeks slower, so my wife could catch up, and I'd work shorter hours, be home in the morning, take the kids to school, pick them up after school. I'd basically say to employers and my colleagues at work: "look I'm an active parent, so yeah I'll do the overseas stuff, but I'm going to want time to be with my family and support my family when I get back." So, I'm not going to be one of these workaholic guys who works twelve hours a day on a mission and when he comes back he's in the office seven days a week. I know people who do that and they make other arrangements with their families. But my choice was no, I'm not that ambitious and I'm

not going to sacrifice my family plans. So I basically take more time when I'm in Canada for family and community. Because, to make up. . . .

Daniel explained that he didn't lose touch with his Montreal friends because his wife whose career was more stationary maintained his connection with a localized network of friendships during his absences. And many of these consultants tried to limit the duration of their overseas trips to relatively short passages of two to four weeks in order to limit the effect on their closest relationships. Thus, over the course of a year they might be gone cumulatively for months but they tried to ensure that they were not gone for more than a few weeks at any one time. Almost everyone noted that improvements in electronic technology, e-mail and cell phones, had made it easier to be in regular touch with distant family and friends.

When I first started describing the peripatetic lifestyles of transnationally mobile consultants to audiences of anthropologists, my presentation was sometimes greeted with a certain bemusement, as an account of an unusual, even aberrant case. The enthusiastic willingness of these consultants to participate in a sector that required repeated disengagement from relationships as well as the concomitant spatial compartmentalization of different sectors of their networks seemed strange to some members of my audiences. And yet these forms of compartmentalization and disengagement simply represent spatially more extended versions of processes of abstraction that have characterized the development of "Western" economic practice since the eighteenth century (Carrier 1998a). These processes of abstraction, which inexorably separated economic activity from other social relationships and activities, became accelerated over the course of the twentieth century (Carrier 1998b), reaching their apex in the mantra of flexibility applied variously to the organization of the corporate supply chain, to the shop floor, or to personal dispositions (ibid; Ong 1999). The concomitant and exponential growth of consultancy across a broad spectrum of services, including development work, has been axiomatic of this orientation toward mobility, specialization, and progressive dis-embedding. After all, consultancy rests on the premise that particular classes of knowledge can be abstracted from the contexts in which they are developed and then consecutively applied in other circumstances. So, it's not really surprising to find that the specialists, on whom my research focused, accepted the transient nature of many of their occupational relationships or related friendships as a pragmatic, necessary aspect of "doing business" as a consultant.

A Model for Transnational Connection?

Hence many of the contacts being mobilized in this occupational network were at least as "weak," and often even more indirect and marginal than those described by Granovetter as key resources amongst Boston job changers. More to the point, this "weakness" is a systematic feature of the global bureaucracy within which these contacts were established and mobilized. That is to say, the limited and transitory nature of these relationships is an inherent aspect of the organization and procedures through which transnational consulting projects, jobs, and grants are structured and allocated. By definition, foreign consultants are being recruited as temporary outsiders. If occasionally some of the professionals operating in this system are able to establish more continuous and intimate connections with people they encounter through their occupational travels, this is more likely to have occurred *in spite of* rather than *because of* the structures though which these links had been formed. And if some of the consultants came to doubt the utility or appropriateness of the kind of development work in which they were involved,[5] nonetheless, the movements of these individuals did serve to extend a set of transnational institutions, protocols, and networks across the globe. And in turn, this extension facilitated the movements of these consultants because it standardized the frameworks within which they worked in otherwise enormously diverse and disparate locales. Each new site might be unfamiliar but the procedures were not. And with the standardization of these procedures, the "expertise" of the professional who applies them was buttressed and legitimized. Thus, the irony of this particular sector of consultancy is that it extends global connections by encouraging the disposability — or, to use Granovetter's term, the "weakness" — of many of the interpersonal relationships it creates.

None of the people who were interviewed had the same view of their intimate relationships with family and close friends, relationships they certainly did *not* view as disposable or temporary. However, as the rueful comments of Ian, Mark, Tanya, and James above indicate, most also acknowledged that their frequent absences could and indeed often did have some attenuating influence even on these connections. Notwithstanding the often considerable efforts they made to mitigate the effects of their absences, the circumstances of their peripatetic work careers ensured that they would be away from their "homes" and intimates for significant portions of every year, accordingly limiting the amount of time they could spend with these associates, the range of services they could provide, the events in which they could participate and the dependability of their presence. It is not difficult to see that the circumstances of this kind of work could constrain or "weaken" even this core of affective links and in some cases sever them altogether. The latter was especially likely to be the case for more casual friendships, which like localized overseas work contacts, often could not be sustained in the face of frequent or long absences. In other words, notwithstanding the very different principle of connections that these professionals attributed to "at home" networks of family, friendship, or local community, nevertheless, over time, these tended to take on some of the structural attributes characterizing dispersed overseas professional connections.

Thus in this case, transnational mobility was facilitated by the extension of "weak" occupational ties across vast geographic spans at the same time as it "weakened" other, more localized relationships of family and friendship. While there are many aspects of this particular sector and career structure that are specific to it or cognate activities, I want to suggest that it is this relationship between mobility, globalizing connections, and "weak" ties that has the most general relevance. And with this suggestion I come full circle to the kind of literature that has dominated anthropological studies of transnational connections.

At first glance, the situation I have described above appears to be almost the inverse of the kinds of relationships and forms of transnational mobility on which anthropological scholarship has generally focused. As I noted at the beginning of this essay, much of this literature has continued the legacy of an older tradition of labor migration and ethnic studies .[6] In exploring the transnational circuits of migration, anthropological studies have tended to emphasize the extension of intimate and communal relationships across space. Thus, in exploring movements between Aguililla in the state of Michoacán and Redwood City in California, two thousand miles apart, Roger Rouse argued that these settlements had become so tightly interwoven in the lives of the migrants regularly moving between them that they had become a single community. "More significantly, they are often able to maintain these spatially extended relationships as effectively as the ties that link them to their neighbors" (Rouse 2002: 162).

Linda Basch described Vincentian and Grenadian family networks that spanned national borders and provided a variety of supports for migration including capital, looking after children and property, providing immigrants with shelter, and assistance in finding a job (Basch et al 1994: 82). And yet, in a family case study that Basch used to illustrate these processes, these kinds of family contacts and assistance were separated by considerable spans of time as well as space:

> Mavis Carrington's aunt, whom she had not seen since she was a baby, encouraged and assisted Mavis' migration to New York, giving her a place to live and aiding her quest for employment, and fifteen years later Mavis provided similar aid to her sister-in-law, Sandra. (Basch et al 1994: 83)

I want to suggest that what makes dispersed family links, such as those described by Rouse or Basch, important resources for migration is not that they remain somehow unchanged by the distances imposed by mobility. Rather, their usefulness is more likely to arise from the opportunities that settlement elsewhere has afforded migrants to transcend these original networks of family and neighborhood and form new contacts abroad. What made a relative like Mavis' aunt such a useful resource were the *new* links and networks she had established over the course of long residence in New York, contacts Mavis herself did not have. In other words, migrant networks become transnationally useful because they begin to take on the "weak" structural attributes described by Granovetter. By necessity migrants can no longer be fully encapsulated—if they ever were—within networks of family, friendship, and neighborhood in their community of origin. To survive or prosper in a new locale they have to form new contacts, and it is precisely access to these indirect contacts that allow pioneer migrants to serve as such valuable bridging resources for those fellow travelers who follow in the pathway they have established.

It is indeed these kinds of bridging contacts that are encompassed in the notion of "winning their affection" that Carla Tamagno described for a Peruvian family whose daughters had migrated to Italy (2002). While the daughters continued to maintain regular contact with their family in Huancayo, it was their capacity to successfully establish new relationships that allowed the family to "move forward":

> To Camila's daughters in Italy, "to win the affection" of their employers means to gain the trust and acceptance of the receiving society, to become a part of its process of interaction. When Rita got a job in the home of the Bocelli family, she was warned that poor Santiago (the elder son of the family) was bad tempered because he was confined to bed and could only move about in a wheelchair. But with her mother's help and advice, her patience and ability for work, Rita "won his affection." Now he is her friend and he has convinced his father to guarantee Rita and Kitty in the negotiations over their soggiorno. (Tamagno 2002: 116)

In turn, Pedro, Rita and Kitty's brother, was now planning to join his sisters in Italy.

> For Pedro, having two sisters in Italy means being linked with the "world." He says that if it were not for them, he would not know anything about Europe or have other news of the world. (Tamagno 2002: 120)

Establishing new contacts and networks in the "world" carries with it the possibility that in time these may supercede distant family connections. Basch, Glick Schiller, and Szanton Blanc contended that the ongoing training and movement of children along transmigrant links was likely to sustain these connections across generations (1994: 242–243). However, other research on similar paths of migration suggests that especially for children growing up outside their parents or grandparents' country of origin, these kinds of transnational links can be superseded by competing local affiliations and identifications.

Karen Fog Olwig conducted life-story interviews with members of three dispersed family networks, originating respectively in Jamaica, Dominica, and Nevis (2003: 221). While the three sibling groups that had originated in these Caribbean islands had been born and raised in these locales, they had resided for many years elsewhere and accordingly many of their descendents had spent all of their lives outside the Caribbean, for the most part in the United States, Canada, or Britain. The 150 persons that Olwig interviewed included 31 children and youths, all but three the grandchildren of the siblings originating in Dominica and Jamaica. Olwig found that rather than identifying with the Caribbean origins of their grandparents, most of the children identified strongly with the local institutions and places of their daily experiences in Canada, Britain, or the United States.

> The local community figured as the most important frame of reference in the children's description of themselves in the life-story interviews. Children described their lives with reference to such local places as the houses where they had lived, the schools they attended and the clubs where they played different kinds of sports. (Olwig 2003: 228)

Olwig noted that these children and youths had limited exposure to the Caribbean and were therefore far more concerned about "sources of belonging that would ground them where they lived" (ibid: 230). Accordingly, Olwig cautioned that the current emphasis in migration studies, and its corresponding echo in state immigration policies, of children as "guardians of identities rooted in a distant ancestral homeland" (219) could end up denying them the right to construct their own far more complex and multiple cultural identities (233).

By the time, therefore, that we reach this level of dispersal, in which contacts with family members scattered across large distances and national borders can be intermittent at best, the structural distinction between the kinds of episodic professional connections being formed by development consultants, and the family and friendship networks linking transmigrants, becomes so thin as to be moot. In spite of the very different principles of connection—bureaucratic professionalism versus intimate sentiments and obligations—animating them, what can sometimes allow both of these types of networks to provide effective connections and bridges for diffusion—whether of institutions, procedures, practices, ideas, or sentiments–is their extension across an expanding repertoire of contacts. While there may be a limit to the number of long-distance contacts, which, albeit new communication technology, any one person can effectively sustain on a one-to-one basis, the breadth of these successive contacts can in some instances create important connections, of knowledge, familiarity, or as conduits to new possibilities and involvements.

The "ethnic" template that has tended to dominate anthropological investigation of transnational mobility and connection, and before that of rural to urban migration, has privileged a focus on emotionally charged links of family and community and on ideologies of identity. As a result, much of the ethnographic focus has been on the retention of strong communal links. This emphasis has more often asserted the enduring strength of these ties rather than actually demonstrating it in terms of ongoing and regular contacts, sometimes appearing to conflate the ideological valence of certain kinds of links with their organizational strength or personal relevance. The result has been that the formation of new contacts as well as breaches among previous contacts and concomitant changes in the networks of mobile people, have often been elided altogether or relegated to a backdrop for those links that are sustained. Rather than focusing on the kinds of cross-cutting links that animated early urban ethnographic interest in the potential of network analysis, recent transmigration research has tended to emphasize those contacts that occur within a particular ethnic category.

The portrait that is thus produced of transnational mobility and connections is not only very partial, it also ignores the formation and organization of those very types of networks and social links that most effectively facilitate globalization. In this essay, I have argued that the absences necessitated by spatial mobility are likely to constrain the scope and intensity of relationships formed across these distances and encourage the formation of alternative sets of social connections. I have also argued that this is not necessarily just a feature of a particular professional context but is likely to be occasioned by more general structural logistics of travel and distance. At the same time, however, the very "weakness" of these ties can enable important bridging functions between locales, institutions, groups, and personal networks. The paradox of globalizing connections is that they are likely to be most effectively facilitated by "weak" rather than "strong" interpersonal links.

Notes

1. This project was made possible by a Standard Research Grant from the Social Sciences and Humanities Research Council of Canada. The interviews being reported in this essay were all conducted between 2002 and 2004. In order to preserve the confidentiality of the identities of respondents, aliases have been used in place of their actual names.
2. The use of network as a model of social relations was actually first used within anthropology by Ian Barnes in respect to Bremnes, a small Norwegian fishing and farming community, but it was Elizabeth Bott's somewhat later application of Barnes's concept to the study of families in London that catalyzed network analysis in cities (Hannerz 1980: 164–168).
3. Alan Smart notes this tendency as well but refers to this as an emphasis on "identity issues" (1999: 63).
4. It is therefore doubly disappointing that one of the relatively rare efforts over the 1990s to systematically use network analysis in anthropological analysis should have contained it yet again within the analysis of urban ethnic groups (Rogers and Vertovec 1995).

5. Roland could not help wondering whether the kind of work he had been doing was too expensive, "too much for the real needs of these countries"; and Peter had often thought that international consultants like himself were "parasites."
6. There are important exceptions to this orientation, among which can be included Ulf Hannerz's multi-locale study of foreign correspondents (2004) or Helena Wulff's study of ballet companies (1998).

References

Amit, Vered and Nigel Rapport. 2002. *The Trouble with Community: Anthropological Reflections on Movement, Identity and Community.* London and Sterling, Virginia: Pluto Press.

Anderson, Benedict. 1983/1991. *Imagined Communities: Reflections on the Origin and Spread of Nationalism.* London and New York: Verso.

Appadurai, Arjun. 1996. *Modernity at Large: Cultural Dimensions of Globalization.* Minneapolis and London: University of Minnesota Press.

Basch, Linda, Nina Glick Schiller and Cristina Szanton Blanc. 1994. *Nations Unbound: Transnational Projects, Postcolonial Predicaments, and Deterritorialized Nation-States.* Basel, Switzerland: Gordon and Breach Publishers.

Carrier, James. 1998a. "Abstraction in Western Economic Practice." In *Virtualism: A New Political Economy,* eds. James G. Carrier and Daniel Miller. Oxford and New York: Berg. pp. 25–47.

Carrier, James. 1998b. "Introduction" to *Virtualism: A New Political Economy,* eds. James G. Carrier and Daniel Miller, pp. 1–24.

Castells, Manuel. 2000. *The Rise of the Network Society.* Oxford and Malden, MA: Blackwell.

Doreian, Patrick and Frans N. Stokman, eds. 1997. *Evolution of Social Networks.* Amsterdam: Gordon and Breach Publishers.

Granovetter, Mark S. 1973. "The Strength of Weak Ties." *American Journal of Sociology* 78 (6): 1360–1380.

Guarnizo, Luis Eduardo and Michael Peter Smith. 1998. "The Locations of Transnationalism." In *Transnationalism from Below,* eds. Michael Peter Smith and Luis Eduardo Guarnizo. New Brunswick, NJ and London: Transaction Publishers. pp. 3–34.

Hannerz, Ulf. 1980. *Exploring the City: Inquiries Toward an Urban Anthropology.* New York: Columbia University Press.

Hannerz, Ulf. 2004. *Foreign News: Exploring the World of Foreign Correspondents.* Chicago and London: University of Chicago Press.

Olwig, Karen Fog. 2003. "Children's Places of Belonging in Immigrant Families of Caribbean Background." In *Children's Places; Cross Cultural Perspectives,* eds. Karen Fog Olwig and Eva Gulløv. London and New York: Routledge. pp. 217–235.

Ong, Aihwa. 1999. *Flexible Citizenship: The Cultural Logics of Transnationality.* Durham and London: Duke University Press.

Rouse, Roger. 2002. "Mexican Migration and the Social Space of Postmodernism." In *The Anthropology of Globalization: A Reader,* eds. Jonathan Xavier Inda and Renato Rosaldo. Oxford: Blackwell. pp. 157–171.

Rogers, Alisdair and Steven Vertovec, eds. 1995 *The Urban Context: Ethnicity, Social Networks and Situational Analysis.* Oxford and Washington D.C.: Berg.

Sassen, Saskia, ed. 2002. *Global Networks, Linked Cities.* New York and London: Routledge.

Smart, Alan. 1999. "Participating in the Global: Transnational Social Networks and Urban Anthropology." *City and Society* 11 (1–2): 59–77.

Stirrat, R. L. 2000. "Cultures of Consultancy." *Critique of Anthropology* 20 (1): 31–46.

Stokowski, Patricia A. 1994. *Leisure in Society: A Network Structural Perspective.* London and New York: Mansell Publishing Limited.

Tamagno, Carla. 2002. "'You Must Win Their Affection . . .': Migrants' Social and Cultural Practices between Peru and Italy." In *Work and Migration: Life and Livelihoods in a Globalizing World,* eds. Ninna Nyberg Sørensen and Karen Fog Olwig. London and New York: Routledge. pp. 106–125.

Wellman, Barry, ed. 1999. *Networks in the Global Village: Life in Contemporary Communities.* Boulder, CO and Oxford: Westview Press.

Wulff, Helena.1998. *Ballet Across Borders: Career and Culture in the World of Dancers.* Oxford and New York: Berg.

5

Traveling Images, Lives on Location
Cinematographers in the Film Industry

Cathy Greenhalgh

Introduction

In this chapter I examine the logistical challenges, identifications, and professional expectations that characterize the lives of highly mobile feature-film cinematographers[1]. The cinematographer, or director of photography, is a key collaborator with the director, (along with the producer, production designer, editor, and sound designer). He or she "choreographs" the crew in the organization of bodies and technology on location or set, framing, lighting, and moving the camera within the director's "vision" of the film.

In focusing on feature-film cinematographers, I am concerned with that segment of the larger film industry that claims for itself the "highest" expression of the art form and also the most challenging and complicated expression in terms of production logistics[2]. Individuals working predominantly on feature films are considered to have achieved the greatest career success as cinematographers and are usually members of elite national professional societies and guilds. Cinematographers working at this level are frequent flyers who travel to "shoot" fiction scripts in a wide range of destinations, cultures, and climates.

Film crews are constantly recomposed from project to project, with a requirement for quick response and willingness to move at a moment's notice. While in many respects unique to the film industry, these work-team flexibilities highlight aspects of new post-Fordist modes, which are required in other fields as well. For example flexible specialization may still allow jobs to be carried out near headquarters of companies, but other production areas can now be wholly outsourced to cheaper labor in another country. Films require both location and studio filming, but shooting at the primary, traditionally used studios has more recently been outsourced, while postproduction activities (editing and visual effects) are carried out at a number of bases. This circumstance affects the type of places cinematographers travel to as well as the amount of time spent there.

In carrying out this research, the extreme mobility of these professionals posed special challenges in locating my fieldwork. In seeking out their sites of activity, it quickly became clear that although I am a London-based researcher, a focus on British cinematographers would not be possible. The film industry characteristically employs individuals on a transnational basis so that films with a production base in the U.K. often involve substantial location work abroad. As a result, most British cinematographers are constantly working outside of the United Kingdom while the main London studios: Pinewood, Leavesham, Shepperton, and Elstree, are often occupied by foreign cinematographers. Accordingly, I conducted interviews at trade venues in London, conducted semi-participant observation on sets in the U.K. (ongoing) as well as at the annual *Camerimage* International Festival of the Art of Cinematography held each December in Lodz, Poland.

Moving Images and Practitioners

The idea that images migrate and travel across cultures and borders more than any language is often cited by cinematographers in explaining their role as the image makers in feature film production. Cinematographers want to produce memorable images, aware that these can usually transcend language and culture barriers once released to the world. The competitive quest for arresting images leads to secrecy about process and content, a secrecy that is maintained until the film is released and is now explicitly enforced in work contracts.

British producers and directors particularly like to hire a so-called "foreign eye," believing that this novel outside perspective will bring added value to a project. For example, a director may believe a foreign cinematographer will be less likely to resort to conventional pictorial and picturesque images of English landscape and hence that the director will achieve a more innovative and marketably unique product through what s/he deems to be the "more visual" expertise of French, Czech, or Polish cinematographic traditions. This presumption provokes a good deal of ambivalence and contentiousness among British cinematographers, who point to the large number of Oscars that have been awarded to British cinematographers for their artistry (often on films shot outside of the U.K.), as well as their expertise on large-scale productions such as the James Bond films.

Like British cinematographers who object to losing work to their counterparts from Europe and the United States, the e-mail discussion list of the Indian Society of Cinematographers has featured similar unhappiness about the number of foreign cinematographers working with Indian directors within India. But as this e-mail debate has also noted, at the same time as foreign cinematographers have been imported to work on Indian productions, Indian cinematographers have recently achieved fame on international productions shooting outside of India. The tension between "local" and "foreign" works both ways in a global market with large diasporic audiences and cofinanced cross-cultural productions in which Bollywood films are also consumed by some U.K. audiences and the Scottish Highlands landscapes are becoming popular backdrop locations for dance numbers.

The extreme mobility associated with creative collaboration in the global film industry is generally only a requirement for the higher echelon of film personnel and crew. Filmmaking is extremely expensive, and employees are hierarchically organized. Most crewmembers are hired locally, while top personnel travel extensively from job to job. The cinematographer has an agent and is hired by the producer, but depends on the reputation s/he has achieved with directors to get work. Cinematographers travel widely, even more so than most producers and directors, because they work on a wider variety of projects and for shorter periods. As a result, elite cinematographers may end up spending more time on "location" at a multitude of sites across the globe than in their official residences.

Chris Doyle, a cinematographer who is Australian born but is a long-time Hong Kong resident, works worldwide, and is best known for his work with director Wong Kar-Wai. Here is how he describes the tensions of being "at home" on location:

> . . . you are from outside, and yet you look for how to be inside . . . That it is about the intimacy and distance. It is about looking at things afresh, but looking at them with a sympathetic eye, or looking at them with an intimate eye . . . coming from somewhere else . . . much is familiar because we have traveled a lot, and yet much has to be seen in a special way in order to make a film interesting. That balance is really basic to the cinematographer's job. You have to be familiar enough in order to be able to spend some time there, or you have to know the culture, or you have to be from that culture, and yet you have to have a distance. On location, doesn't that imply locale? Let's break it down to the really simple . . . locale means *local.* It means "of where you are." So I think if you look at it in that way, to be on location means to be at home . . . for a cinematographer.

This attitude of feeling more at home on location, or of seeing the profession as an art of living as well as working, is part of the cinematographer's mode, a commitment to a much-desired vocation, which recurs in their stories of working life in this field.

When I posed the question "where have you traveled in the last year or two for work" several cinematographers listed a bewildering variety of places, wider perhaps even than for other types of privileged travelers such as businesspeople. For example, Chris Doyle speaks fluent Mandarin, and has agents in Los Angeles, Japan, and Hong Kong. I caught up with him after a talk he gave in 2005 at the National Film Theatre in London.

> I feel more comfortable on planes than I do on the ground. I'm thinking flights. The last twenty days, I've been in the air every single day . . . this makes your de-placement, this trust in, what's the word, "appropriation" and all that kind of stuff. Yeah, China, Mongolia, Kazakhstan, . . . erm, Viet Nam, India, Hong Kong, Singapore, Australia, er . . . Poland, London . . . England, Belgium, France, Finland, Denmark, United States . . . etcetera, etcetera. I mean, how big is your globe, you know!

Similarly, Mexican cinematographer Rodrigo Prieto who lives in Los Angeles had a diverse list of "locations" mainly encountered in recent work with director Oliver Stone.

> My passport is falling apart. I've really lost track a little bit, I would have to look at my agenda and remind myself. . . . With him we visited Kenya, Ethiopia, Sudan, Poland, we were in Germany, in England. For the postproduction for *Alexander,* we were in France. We were moving to Morocco, Thailand then England. Man, ah ha, erm I don't know . . . Cuba, Israel, Palestine . . .

Nina Kellgren, who lives in London, shot the feature *Wondrous Oblivion* in the U.K. during the year before my interview with her, but the travels she listed were mainly related to work on commercials abroad: "I just went to Montreal . . . I shot in Spain and Prague and Iceland . . . oh yeah I went to Italy this year . . . and I was on a panel in South Africa . . . and I've been to Gambia."[3]

These lists were often recounted to me with a sense of breathlessness and humor. My informants knew that, like many of their friends and family members outside the film business, my own life seemed static in comparison. But in their accounts, there was care also taken to emphasize the professional necessity of this travel. Here is cinematographer Phil Meheux's account, which was recorded in December 2003.

> September 2001, I went to Montreal, Namibia, and Thailand for two weeks to scout *Beyond Borders.* At the end of that I came back to London for a week, I went to Los Angeles, where I have an apartment, to spend some time there . . . while I was in Los Angeles they asked me to go to Montreal to start the prep for *Beyond Borders* . . . Came home at Christmas to London. After Christmas went back to Montreal to start shooting *Beyond Borders.* In March . . . Oh . . . in February I went from Montreal to Quebec. From Quebec, in March, I went to Namibia. In April I went from Namibia to Thailand, went to Bangkok, to Chiang Mai, to Chiang Rai, to Chiang Mai, to Bangkok. Then back to . . . via Tokyo to Los Angeles. Then to Canada to do more shots of the mountains in snow. Then went to London to do St. Pauls at dawn. Then got a commercial in New Zealand. On the way back from New Zealand I stopped off in Los Angeles, met

the man who's doing *Around the World in Eighty Days*. Went from Los Angeles to London to Berlin to scout Berlin. Went home to London. Then in January of this year . . . that was 2002. In 2003, January 4th I went to Thailand for a week. Came back and did a commercial in Rome for a week. Went to Berlin for a week. Went to Los Angeles for three weeks to do the final print of *Beyond Borders*. Went to Thailand to start *Beyond Borders*. Went to Berlin in the middle of all of that . . . to finish the movie off in Berlin. Came back to London for two weeks. Then went to Los Angeles to do an extra day's shooting . . . two extra days on *Around the World in Eighty Days*. Came back to London. Went to South Africa for a commercial. Came back to London. Went to New York for the premiere of *Beyond Borders*. Back to London. Went to Hong Kong to do shots of Jackie Chan to fit into the *Around the World in Eighty Days* shoot. Came back from Hong Kong. Went to Spain to do another commercial. Came back from that to London. Then came to Poland (to this festival).

Poland is where I caught up with him. In fact he had not shot a film in the U.K. for a few years, but I knew him by reputation as the current president of the British Society of Cinematographers. While the locations on which Phil works are in very different countries, he continuously passes back and forth through the main headquarters of production, Los Angeles and London, working on a medium-size feature, a blockbuster, and several commercials over an eighteen-month period. He has meetings in both these cities about future projects and attends premieres of completed work.

There is, however, also unabashed pleasure expressed in the experience of frequent travel to such a wide range of locales. British cinematographer Tony Pierce Roberts grew up in Kenya and first traveled with the Central African Film Unit and later the BBC. Remarking on a shoot in Alaska he explained "I like wilderness . . . and that's one thing I like about our business is (that you) still do get to visit places like that." There is a certain overlap therefore between the "traveling capital" featured in cinematographers' accounts of their frequent professional journeys to film "locations" and the more general tourist embrace of travel as a vehicle for developing social and cultural capital that has been described by such tourism scholars as Sheller and Urry (2004) and Harrison (2003).

Yet cinematographers are also experts who are called upon to interpret this succession of landscapes for fictional purposes by drawing on their visual grammar and back catalogue of experiences and images as well as their technological knowledge of shooting in certain environments and light. Cinematographers work both in studios and "on location." When they work in studios they have to light and film actors on sets constructed by production designers to look like parts of real or fantastical places. On the other hand, when cinematographers go "on location," they go to a real place that they must refashion into the fictitious place written in the script. The very concept of "location" therefore inherently involves forms of appropriation. Locations are "reccied" (an army term meaning reconnaissance trip) before shooting to assess the suitability of the terrain for transformation at minimal cost.

In turn, "previsualization" of the script/story by the cinematographer influences the practical decisions made on the recce for the shoot. Locations may not fit story needs. Dawn light called for in the script may not hit the appropriate side of the house location found. Weather changes and seasons may not suit schedules. Visualizing the shots beforehand in an actual location with the director, production designer, and cinematographer determines which exact equipment needs to be brought, how many crew, blocking space for the potential cast, how much rebuilding work, and so on. Visualization involves several stages: photographs and painting references, drawings and video footage from recces aligned to accumulating art department images with notes on textures and coloring, rigging and lighting diagrams, scale models of sets, screen tests for actors, and, finally, possible storyboards and the sequence and shot list made prior to shooting.

Appropriating space is therefore a crucial aspect of the professional duties of the cinematographer, both in the travel involved and in the "cheating" (this is the actual term used) of space, people, props, and tools to achieve the fictional reality in actual space.

Yet even this special appropriative expertise interacts with the augmented technological sophistication now available to tourists seeking to record images. People now can document their travels around the world for friends and family using camcorders, digital cameras, and by sending images via phone and the internet in real time. The form of these "amateur" images are implicitly shaped by the form of images people have viewed in feature films. In turn, knowledge of this audience and its interactivity also affects the ambitions of feature film producers, as well as generating a constant pressure on expanding the limits of the techniques employed by cinematographers and directors.

Production Practices and Milieus

The breakdown and radical restructuring of the Hollywood studio system has led to a situation where the larger transnational film industry is now almost entirely project based, drawing on flexible freelance labor. The old vertically integrated studio firms like MGM and Warner Brothers made a formula product that was passed through departments like an assembly line with large numbers of staff, actor stars, teams of writers, directors, cinematographers, and so on. The accumulated expertise dispersed when the system disintegrated as government rulings forced a split between studio distribution of films and their production and as the new medium of television claimed half the audience. The industry changed its approach and began to make "spectaculars," but these were financially high risk so projects were organized by nurturing networks of freelance employees who could be brought in on a project-by-project basis. "High-concept" blockbusters such as *Star Wars* with their sequel structure possibilities and spin-off merchandise, allowed clusters of numerous smaller service companies to proliferate.

The present horizontal, flattened out structure of Hollywood corporations has fewer employees at the studio who now subcontract to share the risk in production with smaller independent companies, who themselves outsource much of the work. Built around the blockbuster, a new economy of special-effects and digital visual-effects firms along with numerous service companies has grown up in the Los Angeles region.[4] These are flexibly specialized firms that can compete in an unstable and uncertain market (Christopherson and Storper 1987). In that sense, the Hollywood organizational model reflects a more general capitalist reorientation around the notions of flexibility and temporality rather than that of material acquisition. As Rifkin has noted:

> The culture industries—including the recording industry, theatre, television and radio—commodify, package and market experiences as opposed to physical products or services. Their stock and trade is selling short-term access to simulated worlds and altered states of consciousness. The fact is they are an ideal organizational model for a global economy that is metamorphosing from commodifying goods and services to commodifying cultural experience itself. . . . the movie industry is the front-runner in a new era in which each consumer's life experience will be commodified and transformed into an unending series of theatrical moments, dramatic events, and personal transformations (Rifkin 2005: 365)

De Filippi and Arthur further explain that:

> Hollywood historically has taken maximum advantage of the entertainment community's critical mass in Los Angeles to leverage and perpetuate the tacit knowledge vital to its art. More recently, it has responded to changing conditions by transforming from vertical structures owning the expertise to loose, temporary project groups that draw from a central talent pool. (De Fillippi and Arthur 1998: 131)

One result, however, of this looser structure is that production is no longer tied as firmly to particular centers. Hence in recent years, so-called "runaway production" has been causing an increasing unemployment problem in the Los Angeles film industry. Producers find it cheaper to exploit tax breaks and shoot in Canada, Mexico, Australia, or Eastern Europe where experienced crews can be found near the newly refurbished Barandov studios in Prague or Babelsberg in Berlin.[5]

Nonetheless, this dispersal has not entirely undermined the continued organizing importance of particular centers of production. The creative industries, including film, are part of the New Labour government strategy for marketing London's status as a global center of creativity and cultural production.[6] London is a major production and studio base, but with only a small home industry, it now serves as a satellite of Los Angeles in that many American productions use British studios and technicians. Clusters of service companies flourish in the center while western London provides proximity to the larger studios and Heathrow airport. Successful cinematographers with a home in the UK can afford to live where they choose, but they often need to attend meetings in London so they may still opt to live in London. At lower echelons of the film industry, it is most advantageous for individuals to live in London if regular work in the film industry is to be maintained. A foreign cinematographer may be able to bring in key people, such as the gaffer (chief electrician) and focus puller, but many other crew members will be hired locally through the recommendations of hire houses and other local sources. Keeping in touch with industry events, trade shows, and union, guild, and professional society events is essential to keeping in the know and being on the spot when potential jobs are offered. Agents are based in London and will send out feature scripts for cinematographers to read and coordinate their diaries, schedules, and contracts.[7]

Organizational structures of work in the contemporary film industry arise from historical implementations of technologies, production systems, and labor control. This is because the manifestation of a film is expensive and labor intensive, and requires strict concentration and timing to keep to schedule. First these requirements ensure some continuity within a strict economic and structural, if temporary, hierarchy during actual production. Second, they enable key players to produce creative work within a demanding set of technological and industrial parameters. Trust, timing, ingenuity, and improvisation, combined with talent and leadership, are deemed essential qualities of directors, cinematographers, and production designers for example. These are a matter of daily negotiation for the feature film cinematographer.

A film production is a huge undertaking. An average feature would employ sixty to one hundred crew plus the cast. On a large feature at Pinewood studios, the crew and cast would number about six hundred. On location it can be one to two hundred personnel with heavy equipment and vehicles. The work oscillates radically over the course of a day or even an hour between high excitement and excruciating monotony. To reconcile issues of health and safety with the importance of maximizing the speed and flow of work requires moment-by-moment planning, diplomacy, developed intuition, humor, and leadership to retain any creativity. There can be boredom, fear, and insecurity during the long working hours in film set environments; fourteen-hour days, six-day weeks, during a six to fifteen week shoot. But there can also be a sense of belonging and pride; doing the work together, often living twenty-four/seven abroad on location.

Film production can be viewed as a cognitively fragmented activity in which different types of knowledge are distributed across individuals, artifacts, media, and representational languages (Hutchins 1995). This knowledge of internal working processes and culture is present within the film community as a whole, but it is only contributed to actual companies during projects. Although film workers may share several jobs over many years, knowledge can be lost to the wider industry as much as it is accumulated.

In a 2004 student seminar at *Camerimage,* cinematographer Oliver Stapleton explained how easily these skills get overlooked through rapid industry changes:

> This job we do is changing at light speed. It is about manipulation of the image in post-production. Traditionally, until four or five years ago, that was very laborious, very expensive and wasn't a cannon in the arsenal of making movies. The number of guys who know their onions when it comes to the complex world of visual effects (computer generated) is relatively limited. So if you become Mister Superstar on The Day After Tomorrow you're going to get a very high salary. But I find it quite incomprehensible, that that person, who has no need of management skills whatsoever, has absolutely no need of knowing anything about actors, has no political requirement, because there's a lot of politics involved in being a DoP (director of photography, cinematographer), and doesn't need to have what you might call . . . he doesn't need to be a socially magnetic, authoritative directorial type of personality . . . so that's all that has happened. The amount you get paid and the quality or worth of what you do bears no relationship to each other.

These personality qualities and skills are often not understood to be part of the cinematographer's job description. Stapleton's account shows the leadership and strategizing needed to traverse the changing professional field. He is aware of working conditions on large and smaller budget productions in different union and national crewing contexts. Knowledge is accrued through the extreme mobility of his job as well as ability to mobilize and adapt diplomatically to different economic and organizational situations. Competency in the film industry system is gained through strategic understanding of how the industry works and how to maintain individual capital over the course of a career (Jones 1996).

The "storage" of knowledge within crews who work together often is invaluable to professional cinematographers, whose reputations depend on their individual talents as well as their ability to choose, utilize, and lead a good crew. The capacity to be able to draw upon reliable teams is a matter of survival in the industry and one reason why rumored accusations of nepotism, cronyism, and long-held loyalties leading to employment may be said to have some foundation. Such is the intensity of work that strong bonds are formed after long months on location together.

The crew and cast combined are called "the unit." During shooting, the unit receives daily "movement orders" on a "call sheet" from the first assistant director and the producer, much like an army unit would. The

Latin root of the old French word *creue,* meaning "ship's crew," is *cres-care,* meaning "to grow," "to gather forces," "recruitment," and " to accrue." Preparedness and readiness to move is a state of mind for the whole crew, but particularly for key personnel who must lead and inspire the rest in what is hard physical work carried out at considerable velocity. The impetus for "mobilization," then, must be retained whether one is then working or not.

Thus collaborations, if at all possible to maintain, become very important. Here again the tension between a dependence on teamwork and the constant recomposition of film crews is echoed by shifts within the contemporary organization of work more generally. Vera John-Steiner has argued that "[s]olo practices are insufficient to meet the demands of the new complexities of the changing workplace" (2000: 4). What she calls "collaborative dynamics" provide means for people of diverse backgrounds to complement one another in joint endeavors, making collaborative work pluralistic and interdisciplinary by nature (ibid). Along similar lines, in another 2004 joint seminar at *Camerimage,* the director Oliver Stone emphasized the level of commitment and passion needed to complete a blockbuster epic, while praising his cinematographer as collaborator:

> I do believe in teamwork. Teamwork, teamwork, teamwork. I believe in the script, the script, the script. . . . And film . . . it's a living dynamic. It's very contentious, anything can go wrong on any day. It's like an organism seeking . . . its own life, its birth. It comes into being after a year, two years. It's a long pregnancy, put it that way. And it's very fragile and a film can go wrong, even at the end it can go wrong. By the time it's over, on *Alexander* for example, maybe three thousand people will probably have been involved. Maybe one thousand, five hundred of those people worked on it a long time. This is big deal, a big crew and it's international too. Five, six different languages. So it requires above all, humility in front of the spirit of the film, because *Alexander* was a huge subject, but it requires quiet, quiet determination, which is one of Rodrigo's virtues, very quiet and very determined and we all pulled through in the end.

In contrast however, Phil Meheux provided an account of the tensions that can arise between film crews who have been moving from project to project and directors who expect an unequivocal commitment to *their* project.

> A lot of directors have been spending two years in the warmth of their hotel rooms or their homes preparing their pictures. And it's their baby and it's the one thing they really want to do. The rest of the crew have just come off another picture. . . . you go out on the new picture and the director wants you to just keep working and then not stop for lunch and things like that. It's hard on the crew. They all say a film crew marches on it's stomach. . . . if you just supply food . . . they don't have to sit down for it . . . it doesn't mean knives or forks . . . it can be sandwiches or whatever. It does keep them all amused, and . . . And after one hundred and twenty two days filming, I can tell you, you look forward to that lunch break where you can rest your feet. . . .

Relationships and Diversity

Conducting relationships and maintaining friendships is difficult in the cinematography profession, where the idea that one must be ready to travel at a moment's notice is encouraged. Filmmaking is an emotionally heightened and volatile situation, but there are no written rules for behavior, and no personnel department. Indeed, misbehavior can lead to summary dismissal and immediate removal from a project. Like their mobile counterparts in other industries, filmmakers are expected to be able to work closely with a wide variety of people drawn from different backgrounds, the kind of working cosmopolitanism that Hannerz has identified as a "matter of competence" (1996: 103).

Here's how Chris Doyle sees his role and part in this:

> What we have to do is really trust in who we are, and other people will see, yes, there's something of you in me. . . . I don't know how the United Nations Commission for Refugees actually functions, because there's people moving all the time. They're not moving with the volition we have, they're not moving because they want to, but I think that the phenomenon of this particular period of history is that this world is . . . cross-bordered.

Phil Meheux describes below the tenacity and adaptability needed to traverse this experience, and survive discontinuities in personal life. He was a nimble sixty-two years of age at the time of this interview in 2003:

> I have a brother and sister-in-law. My parents have died now and I don't have any children. . . . I love the business you know. . . . I was always the one at the BBC who volunteered to go away, because I actually enjoyed it . . . I like the camaraderie of filmmaking as well. It's your family. I get quite depressed when there's no work . . . and you've got to do mundane things like ironing shirts, making the tea, cleaning the windows. Waiting for the phone to ring and get on another picture! We always try to . . . it's so much better to have somebody you know with you. On *Round the World* . . . they wanted to use the sale and lease back agreement with England, so the crew were all British. I had my own grip, gaffer, best boy, assistant grip, operator, focus, loader, and second AC. Roger, the operator had done *Goldeneye, Entrapment* and *The Mask of Zorro with* me, and *The Saint*. He'd done a lot of films with me. . . . It depends. If you've got children at school that changes everything. No, it's a trial if you're always away. Whatever relationships you have, it's a trial. Your friends even. I mean you don't see them for six months. And you come back and they go "how was it?" You go "it was okay." And that six months of your life is reduced to three sentences.

The tension between the excitement and intensity of filming on location and the emotional toll such frequent absences can exert was also expressed by Tony Pierce-Roberts who reminisced about shooting documentaries early on in his career with the BBC:

You went away with very small groups (and) you inevitably got involved in their cultures. . . . whereas on a big feature film because there are so many of you. . . . It's easier for you to actually avoid that sort of local contact. You can take a little bit of income with you and get English caterers . . . or you can get your fish and chips or whatever. [He spent half the year shooting in Hungary prior to the interview, but calculates:] I've certainly been to more than sixty countries I would think. . . . I haven't been to Russia and I haven't been to China other than Hong Kong. You know I'm older now. I've been reining back going away all the time. It palls after a bit. It's great if I can get a job in Pinewood, frankly . . . twenty minutes from home and you can go home at night.

Spouses and families are allowed to travel with top personnel such as cinematographers, but this is not the case for most crew members and therefore the early career years working up to this position through the camera crew can be very hard on family relationships. As Slawomir Idziak explained:

We are all a victim of this love of ours, of the film industry. As a matter of fact, it's not a joke you know, it's devotion . . . it's not only . . . a sense of duty, it's an appetite. . . . It's very hard to combine both . . . the normal typical petit-bourgeois happy life and work in the business. . . . Specially if you are, as me, not in Poland any longer. .

Idziak has always lived in Warsaw, but has not worked in Poland for sixteen years over the post-Communist period. He speaks Polish, English, and German and shoots all over Western and Eastern Europe including major productions such as director Ridley Scott's *Black Hawk Down*.

Chris Doyle doesn't have children and felt being a parent would have been impossible for him, as the commitment required if you love cinema and want to be a cinematographer is "total. . . . there's no comparison. A lot of people don't know what the implication is." At the 2004 *Camerimage* festival he told a room full of students how his sister had died in Australia while he was away on set, and this circumstance was likely to be repeated with his parents too. He was very sad in noting this, but used it to illustrate the passion and belief needed to get to his current position as one of the world's most sought after cinematographers. In contrast, Nina Kellgren had just had a granddaughter born at the time of my interview with her in 2002, and she explained how she always tries to incorporate life with her work as a cinematographer: "I've always had my daughter . . . and I've spent most of my life in relationships. That kind of normality and playfulness is just fantastic compared to the madness of the film industry."

Once cinematographers reach the top of their profession, they may have more maneuverability in organizing their family life around the demands of their profession. Oliver Stapleton "made a deal" with his wife early in their marriage to spend as much time at home as away, and has managed to stick to this principle. The tenacity to maintain this level of balance requires much confidence in one's ability to get freelance work and a high salary on good films. After seven months of shooting *Casanova* in 2004 for Disney, he planned to take seven months off to be in Devon, U.K., with his family.

Rodrigo Prieto moved with his family to Los Angeles from Mexico City after the international success of the film, *Amores Perros.* He described his life in the intervening five years as "a whirlwind." He was thirty-eight at the time of interview in 2004:

> All my life I've lived in a bi-cultural environment, because my mother's American. . . . so I'm pretty used to American culture, and American way of being . . . (but it) it was still quite a culture shock . . . understanding the machine, the economy, it's bizarre. I feel I'm personally . . . the same person in one country or the other. At home I speak Spanish all the time, I have many Mexican friends, so I find myself speaking Spanish in LA at least. [On location, he hopes to take his family whenever he can, which was the case on *Alexander:*] They were able to be with me throughout the shoot. My wife did home schooling with my daughters and that was very important. Because before that, the movies I've done, *8 Mile, 25th Hour, 21 Grams* . . . my family had not been with me, except visiting, one week here and there. So I really needed . . . to have a longer connection. . . . and if they can't be physically there . . . what I take with me is their soul in my heart, in my memory. In the practical sense, I take with me music, books, something that will keep me connected to a little bit of my routine.

Network camaraderie is constantly activated in the cinematographer's working relationships, which are often collaborative and by nature pluralistic and interdisciplinary. This provides an exciting dialogue but can be tiring. Managing uncertainty and disappointment with creative and financial satisfaction is a key factor in the longevity of an individual career. Balancing this with family, partner, and friend relationships is often still harder to achieve without sacrifice of career choices or a nurturing home base. Many partners find the commitment cinematographers make to a career they love hard to understand and difficult to support for the length of time it takes to succeed (or fail) in the film industry. While employed to lead a crew and make beautiful and dramatic moving images, the cinematographer must manage a confusing array of situations and roles and develop the attributes, self-reliance, diplomacy, and readiness of the permanent traveler.

Conclusion

The necessity to combine complex logistics, speed, and mobility with ingenuity and ambition render the film industry a complex example of organization that relies on individuals' networks to maintain social order and project success. Technology and information are distributed through the power relations of linked projects and corporations encompassing many companies. However, the patterns of migration and occupational movement of individual cinematographers is also influenced by a global intensification of the movement of images and by a cross-fertilization between professional and leisure practices that continues to diversify the concepts and perceptions of places used as locations. Successful professional cinematographers are elite travelers who are able to earn high wages. As with freelance work in a variety of other sectors, maintaining this prestigious status requires a permanently mobilized state. The variety of occupational journeys and sojourns on location necessitated by the current organization of the film industry may seem glamorous to the outsider, but it requires a hard-won, accrued competence to work and live in this manner.

Notes

1. The interviews quoted from here were conducted between 2001 and 2005. The cinematographer interviewees are aged between 38 and 65. I name them here with their permission, as their knowledge is most valuable if identifiable with particular artists and their films.
2. In fact many of them also work on the production of television dramas, commercials, and documentaries. Documentary, news, and wildlife camera people may also travel widely but are generally involved with less equipment, crew, and responsibility than feature, commercials, and long-form television drama cinematographers. Commercials are the highest paid work and many feature cinematographers also try to fit these in around their work on films.
3. There are few female cinematographers shooting features. Nina is one of three women who are members of the British Society of Cinematographers
4. Mumbai and Hong Kong have substantial cluster firm economies around home-market film production in the same way as Los Angeles, but most other cities primarily host external production.
5. Successful cinematographers don't often meet, as each is involved in different productions. *Camerimage* festival has provided a rare independent opportunity for those who may know each other's work by reputation only, to discuss aesthetics and share stories of the profession as well as to explain practical philosophy, economic organization, and creative survival to the upcoming generation of would-be cinematographers.
6. Embracing this strategy, the institution where I teach has been renamed "University of the Arts" during 2004 and it publicizes its film-practice education in central London.
7. In the U.K. and U.S. a production system known as "above and below the line" operates. Above-the-line employees—actors, directors, and producers—are paid negotiable fees. Below-the-line workers are paid wages. Cinematographers are among the highest paid below-the-line employees. This divide maintains a separation between artists and technicians.

References

Christopherson, S. and M. Storper. 1987. "Flexible Specialization and Regional Industrial Agglomerations: The US film industry." *Annals of the Associations of American Geographers 77* (1): 104–117.

De Filippi, Robert J, and Michael B. Arthur.1998. "Paradox in Project-Based Enterprise: the Case of Film Making." *California Management Review* 40(2): 125–139.

Hannerz, Ulf. 2003 [1996]. *Transnational Connections: Culture, People, Places.* London and New York: Routledge.

Harrison, Julia. 2003. *Being a Tourist: Finding Meaning in Pleasure Travel.* Vancouver and Toronto: UBC Press.

Hutchins, Edwin. 1995. *Cognition in the Wild.* Cambridge, MA: MIT Press.

John-Steiner, Vera. 2000. *Creative Collaboration.* Oxford: Oxford University Press.

Jones, Candace. 1995. "Careers in Project Networks: The Case of the Film Industry." In *The Boundaryless Career: A New Employment Principle of the New Organizational Era,* eds. M. B. Arthur and D. M. Rousseau. New York and Oxford: Oxford University Press. pp. 58–75.

Rifkin, Jeremy. 2005 [2000]. "When Markets Give Way to Networks . . . Everything Is a Service." In *Creative Industries,* ed. John Hartley. Oxford: Blackwell. pp. 361–374

Sheller, Mimi and John Urry, eds. 2004. *Tourism Mobilities — Places to Play, Places in Play.* London and New York: Routledge.

6

Privileged Travelers?

Migration Narratives in Families of Middle-Class Caribbean Background

Karen Fog Olwig

Introduction

Migration studies have been criticized in recent years for focusing too narrowly on lower-class population movements in search of economic opportunities. This has led to questioning of the relevance of the conceptual framework and theoretical analysis, developed within this scholarship, for research on the movements of more privileged migrants. This chapter argues that class does not refer solely to a group of people who share a certain social and economic position in society. It is also a cultural category that concerns social as well as economic aspects of the livelihoods deemed proper within the middle layers of a society. Through an analysis of life stories related by individuals of two middle-class family networks who have engaged in extensive migratory movements to North America, Europe, and within the Caribbean, the chapter demonstrates how, in a Caribbean context, a middle-class livelihood is closely connected with a colonial European oriented attitude to education, and an associated "cultured," or respectable, lifestyle. For this reason, geographic mobility to places of learning within the Caribbean and abroad, and the maintaining of a lifestyle believed to be consummate with middle-class status, has been an integral aspect of life among migrants of Caribbean middle-class background. The migrant family members' life-story narratives therefore are not merely accounts of movements in time and space, but also foundational stories that seek to assert the rightful place in society that these people wish to establish. This points to the importance of critically examining the ways in which categories employed in migration research may attain particular meaning within the sociocultural contexts in which migration takes place.

The Notion of Class

Until the 1980s the prototypical migrants were seen to be socially and economically deprived people who left their homeland for a better life in a new land of opportunity. Migration scholars then operated with a fairly simple view of migration as a one-way movement from a place of origin to a migration destination, followed by a process of integration as immigrants and their family enjoyed upward social and economic mobility in the migration destination (Tilly 1990). In recent years, as researchers have become interested in the increasingly mobile and interconnected world that has emerged with globalization, they have realized that migrants also include relatively privileged people who travel for educational opportunities as well as career and business prospects in different parts of the world (Ong 1999; Werbner 1999; Bryceson and Vuorela 2002). These migrants are seen to enter a new country from a completely different social and economic vantage point. As noted by Nancy Foner in her study of immigration to New York, many of them are qualified for "mid- and upper level jobs in the mainstream economy," indeed, the population census from 1990 shows that "a fifth of New York City's working-age foreign-born adults had managerial or professional jobs" (2000: 89–90). Foner adds, however, that many do not succeed at obtaining the sort of positions for which they are qualified, but have to contend with lower-grade jobs. While they may earn more money in New York, they will therefore experience downward social mobility (ibid: 90–91). The risk of downward mobility is particularly strong for nonwhite immigrants. Thus, according to Mary Waters, many West Indian immigrants in New York have found that integration into American society tends to mean integration into the black, lower classes, since there is not a well-established black middle class in the United States (Waters 1999). This leads some to reject integration and to maintain strong relations with their country of origin where there is a well-developed middle class (ibid). A similar point has been made by Pnina Werbner in her study of Pakistani migrants in Britain who find that their "group is scorned and stigmatised in the wider society" and therefore prefer to cultivate a transnational, "specifically Pakistani elitist cultural tradition which sets them apart from their English professional and business counterparts" (1999: 28). They are able to do this, she maintains, because of their exposure to "an English-medium education," that has led to the development of "a hybridised set of moral and cultural assumptions and sensibilities that transcends particular national boundaries" and therefore allows them to maintain close-knit transnational networks. This is unlike the lower classes, she argues, where individuals tend to be culturally oriented toward the places where they live, whether in the site of origin or the migration destination resulting in tensions within transnational networks (Werbner 1999: 29–30). Along similar lines, Ulla Vuorela has suggested that the Western systems of education instituted in the third world has provided the basis for "transnational elites" that are at home anywhere in the world. Thus, her study of a middle class Tanzanian family showed that the emphasis on "elite school education, European language proficiency, a particular social etiquette and choice of sports, leadership skills and an engagement in local politics in addition to family and kinship networks, metaphorically 'blood ties'," had contributed to creating what she calls a "transnational *habitus*" (Vuorela 2002: 79–80).

These studies point to important new aspects of migration that have traditionally gone unnoticed in research, because of the focus on wage-labor migration in the lower classes. While there clearly are significant differences in the migration experiences of people of different class background, one should be careful not to exaggerate these differences and give the impression that there are two entirely different types of migrants. This is not warranted because the concept of class, especially that of the "middle class," is a complex one that can be defined in different ways. Thus, the term can be regarded as simply designating a segment of the population that is defined according to certain objective social and economic criteria, such as educational skills, occupation, and income that can be specified. From this point of view, different class backgrounds will refer to the fact that some persons possess better social and economic resources than others, and that they therefore may have a better vantage point from which to engage in migratory movements, as shown by Nancy Foner (2000). In common parlance, however, the notion of class does not designate a segment of the population defined exclusively by such objective criteria. It also refers to "a category of thought, a unit of division used when members of a society mentally divide up the population into status categories" (Barnes 1954). When used in this way, class tends to denote "a fluid heterogeneous socioeconomic grouping . . . having a status intermediate between the upper and the lower classes and . . . sharing common social characteristics and values" (Merriam-Webster 2000: "middle class").[1] As a cultural category, or "category of thought," the notion of class therefore is a relative term that depends on individuals' understanding of their place in society and their perception and practice of class within the context of concrete social relations.[2] When applied to the middle class this is even more the case, since this group by definition is in-between other classes.

In the modern societies of the major migration destinations, moreover, the notion of "middle class" status has become an important demarcator of belonging within the mainstream of society. As Rayna Rapp (1978: 295–96) has argued in her analysis of family and class in American society, "the middle class is a highly ideological construct which pervades American culture." For this reason, "a majority of Americans identify themselves as part of it whenever they answer questionnaires, and the category obviously carries positive connotations." Being middle class thus means being a real American and a proper member of society. Within an American context, it seems to be a relatively inclusive term, because most Americans are able to self-identify as middle class, partly because there are now modifiers of middle class status, such as "lower middle class," that allow individuals who may not quite qualify for middle-class status according to "objective" social and economical criteria to claim a place of belonging within the middle classes (see Ortner 1993: 419). Waters' study showed, however, that blacks generally have been excluded from middle-class status, and thereby mainstream American society, whether or not their social and economic background might seem to warrant this (Waters 1999).

Middle-class status therefore is not just an independent socioeconomic variable that researchers can add in their analyses of variations in population movements, modes of integration and the nature of transnational relations. The "middle class" is a rather labile term that is defined and given meaning in particular social contexts, not the least those pertaining to migration since physical movements and socioeconomic mobility are seen to be closely interrelated in many societies. Thus many, if not most, people migrate in order to improve, or at least consolidate, their social and economic position, and they are therefore quite conscious of their relative position in society in the place of origin as well as the migration destination. A good point of departure for a critical discussion of the notion of the privileged middle-class traveler, therefore, is an analysis of the social construction of class, including the role of physical mobility for people who self-identify as "middle class." In the following I will examine the close relationship between notions of class and migration. My point of departure is a study of Caribbean families that have become dispersed through migration. I will focus especially on the ways in which family members in their life stories claim a middle-class position for themselves by describing their movements within a middle-class cultural framework and compare this with the rather more complex actual movements that characterize the families.

Class and Movement in Dispersed Family Networks from the Caribbean

During the late 1990s, I undertook an ethnographic study of dispersed family networks of Caribbean origin, consisting of three groups of siblings, born in respectively Jamaica, Dominica, and Nevis, and their descendants. Since the 1940s, most of the siblings migrated. Some moved back within a number of years, others never returned, and by the end of the twentieth century, the 150 people in the three family networks were living in different parts of the United States, Canada, and Britain as well as the Caribbean. A central research method for this ethnographic research was open-ended life-story interviews. In the elder generation of siblings, born and reared in the Caribbean, individuals described in detail their Caribbean family background, including the ways in which various family members had helped give the family a name in society. On the basis of their narratives, the family networks of Jamaican and Dominican origins can be defined as "middle class" in terms of both their economic status and their social identity, as outlined above.[3] In the family of Jamaican origin, the siblings described how during the period from the 1910s to the 1950s, they grew up in one of the parish capitals of the island where their parents were involved in several commercial ventures, such as stevedore contracting, fishing, and store keeping, that gave the family a fairly stable income. The siblings in the family of Dominican origin related that from the 1920s to the 1950s, the family resided in a small village where the father was a schoolteacher, businessman, and community leader who figured as an important link between the isolated local community of peasants and the wider, upper-class colonial Dominican society. It was apparent that in both families, the childhood home represented a stage in the development of the families' middle-class status. Thus, the siblings narrated how the status enjoyed by the family when they grew up had resulted from prior physical movements in the family that had been accompanied by upward social and economic mobility within the local society, and how the families sought to further consolidate, or increase, their social status through later moves within and beyond the island society. The life stories therefore took the forms of foundational stories that accounted for the families' place in the respectable middle class. The foundational stories in the two families varied quite a bit, however, not just because the particulars of the families' middle-class background differed, but also because notions of the middle class were different in Jamaica and Dominica.

Foundational Stories

In the Jamaican family, the six siblings explained that the family name was Scottish because their great grandfather had come from Scotland to Jamaica sometime during the nineteenth century. He was a shipbuilder but had started a stevedoring business in Jamaica, when he settled in the town where they grew up and married a local woman. In the following generations, the siblings explained, the family had mixed with Jamaicans of black, Asian, and Portuguese background, and it therefore lived up to the Jamaican national motto "Out of many, one people." In their account of their own childhood, the six siblings placed great emphasis on the appearance of the family in society and the sort of people with whom it mingled. They related that their family lived in a substantial two-story home and was able to hire other people to work for them in the home as well as in the family businesses. In connection with their business ventures, which by then also included a fishing enterprise and a store, they met prominent people, such as the local professional elite of doctors and lawyers and foreign captains. Furthermore, in private life the family mixed with the better circles of society, teachers, the ward of the hospital, as well as officials in the colonial administration, and several of the siblings had attended some of the most prominent private secondary schools in Jamaica.

In the Dominican family, the ten siblings explained that their father was the first in the family to enter the teaching profession, because they were the descendants of a member of the French militia who moved during the eighteenth century to the island, where he settled and married a local person. Over the generations the family intermarried with the local black and Carib population and eventually acquired a small estate of their own. Their father opted to leave farming in order to become trained as a teacher in the local school system and he ended up as head teacher in a small village in the other end of the island. He had been an excellent educator and influential local leader, who was active in the social and economic development of the local community and in various activities in the local Catholic church. He also ran a shop and engaged in various local business ventures. The siblings rather underplayed the family's position of relative affluence in the local community and instead emphasized the significance of the father's hard work and emphasis on education. Thus, he had instilled in his children discipline and love for education and as a result, they explained, most of them had performed well in school and continued at secondary school in the island's capital, several of them on hard-earned scholarships.

In both families the siblings describe their family as the result of a blending of people from different places. They thereby adhered to the Caribbean idea that the local middle class consists of the descendants of a black-white union, historically a union between a black slave woman and a white male planter (Alexander 1973). In the accounts of these family members, however, the union is depicted as being between European men, whose occupations brought them to the Caribbean, and locally born free women of various ethnic backgrounds, a rather more benign and modern version of the Caribbean myth of the origins of the local middle class. In their accounts of their middle-class family background the two sibling groups emphasize dissimilar aspects of Caribbean middle-class culture — appearances, proper manners, and a good place in the social hierarchy of the colonial society in the case of the Jamaican family; education, leadership, and moral worth with strong roots in a rural village in the case of the Dominican family. This can be related to differences in the two island societies. Jamaica has thus been described as a highly hierarchical, plantation-based society, structured along race and class lines with a strong British colonial presence (Alexander 1973; Austin-Broos 1994; Thomas 2004). Dominica, on the other hand, has been characterized as having a weak plantation system, but a well-developed peasant society with deep roots in the French Creole and African-Caribbean populations (Trouillot 1988; Honychurch 1995). For this reason, most members of the influential middle class in the modern nation-state of Dominica grew up in peasant villages and still have strong ties with their rural communities of origin

(Honychurch n.d.). The two families' representations of their middle class background—the respectable layers of society in the British colonial town in Jamaica versus the hardworking, dedicated leadership of a French Creole village in Dominica—therefore situated the families in the most advantageous position in their respective countries of origin from the point of view of the family members' historical experience.

Movements within the Island Society

While the roots of the two families' middle-class status was found in the blending of European ancestors with various people in the Caribbean, the continued progress of the families was attributed to movements within the Caribbean islands. The Jamaican siblings noted that their mother had moved to the parish capital from a rural community in order to study for a teaching license. When she met her future husband, she gave up her career to become a wife and mother. The Dominican siblings similarly recalled that their father had moved away from his local community to train as a teacher and that he ended up as a head teacher at a village school located in another French Creole area of the island. Social mobility, in other words, was closely associated with geographical mobility. Only some physical movements, however, and related forms of social mobility, were emphasized. The Dominican siblings pointed to the family's background in another French Creole village in Dominica and described their father's move from his parents' village to the village where he became head teacher and thus obtained a prominent position in society. The Jamaican siblings, however, spoke little about their mother's rural background in a well-known village established by freed slaves after the abolishment of slavery. This black heritage was clearly not something that was celebrated in the family, and the siblings were more concerned about their mother's life in the town.

The close interrelationship between physical and social mobility was also apparent in the siblings' generation, and in their life stories the siblings placed great emphasis on the significance of their moves both within and outside their Caribbean island of origin. While many spoke with great nostalgia about the early years of their lives they spent in their childhood home and place of birth, they described their move away from home as a natural step in their personal development. For most of the siblings, this step occurred already when they were twelve to thirteen years of age and left home to attend secondary school. The siblings in the Jamaican family described their move to a secondary school as a fairly easy one where they quickly adjusted to the new school environment. The education that they received was entirely British, and patterned according to the British public school system. One of the brothers stated that he had received a "first class education" that included interesting subjects such as Latin, and he recalled being actively involved in exciting sports such as swimming, athletics, and cricket as well as boxing, where he had been captain of the team. One of the sisters described her secondary school as a finishing school as well as an academic institution and recalled being taught "elocution, drama, music appreciation" and taken to concerts and films—not just "any old film" or concert, she added, "this had to be classic, it had to be British!" While she mused at the very British atmosphere at the school, she did not experience it as a problem, "I saw it as part of life, so I just went and studied."

The Dominican siblings, who identified strongly with the village where they grew up, described their move to secondary school in the island's capital Roseau as representing a major change of environment that involved getting used to an urban way of life characterized by much greater status differences than they knew from their home village. They emphasized, however, that their father's primary school prepared them well for their secondary education—so well that most of the siblings received scholarships that paid for school fees. The secondary schools in Dominica were not as entrenched in British public school culture[4] as were the schools in Jamaica, nevertheless they taught a British curriculum and prepared the students for the Cambridge senior exams as did the Jamaican schools. The British nature of the education was not criticized in any way, on the contrary, as in the Jamaican family, one of the sons recalled with great fondness his education in Latin, stating, "those who haven't learned Latin don't know what they have missed. They don't know the roots of the English language." Some of the siblings did so well that they qualified for scholarships to study abroad. Through these siblings' excellent school performance this family therefore gained a reputation of being dedicated to education.

When the siblings in their stories talked about their youthful departure from home for secondary school and their educational experiences during their teen years, they were not just describing an important formative period of their lives. They were describing how they, in their own personal lives, were carrying on the foundational narratives that validated and confirmed their Caribbean middle-class status. Education has been described as the main avenue toward upward social mobility within Caribbean societies. In a Jamaican context Diane Austin has argued that education "became the salvation for a rural middle class unable to expand due to lack of land" which was controlled by the planter class (Austin 1983: 235). Education has been viewed as not only a means of qualifying for employment, but "the passport for most 'respectable' employment," as Shirley Gordon writes in her history of West Indian education (1963: 240). W. G. Fleming thus states that Dominicans, like other West Indians, regard secondary school "as a means of improving their status and of obtaining white collar jobs in business or government service" (Fleming 1964: 7). In a Jamaican context, Nancy Foner notes that education had become such an important mode of social mobility that "an individual's prestige in the local status system is related to his children's educational attainments" (Foner 1973: 60).

Educated persons were clearly placed in a privileged position in relation to the large population of poorly educated people during the late colonial period from the 1940s to the early 1960s,[5] when most of the siblings finished their secondary schooling. However, they did not have free access toward upward mobility within local society. Thus most of the siblings noted that the kinds of jobs that would be available to them upon their graduation from secondary schools were lower ranking positions in the banks, the colonial administration, or the private sector as well as poorly paid teaching jobs. One of the Jamaican siblings related that when he looked into the possibility of applying for a bank loan to start his own import/export business in Jamaica, the bank showed no interest in his project and that this led him to reconsider his future prospects on the island: "I felt as though I was rejected by my own country. I felt that to progress I had to go beyond Jamaica." Thus despite the position of relative privilege in their island of origin that the siblings had attained through their secondary education, they nevertheless felt the need to leave for better social and economic opportunity outside the confines of the island society. As they did so, they followed an established Caribbean middle-class tradition, begun already during the nineteenth century, of emigrating for a further education, preferably in the professions, in order to reach high positions in public life (Gordon 1963: 240; see also Kuper 1976: 121).

Movements Beyond the Island Society

When the siblings related their stories of departure for various destinations in North America, Europe, as well as other areas of the Caribbean, most of them emphasized that they wanted to go abroad to study. This reason for migrating matched the actual migration experiences of many. Thus, in the Dominican family seven of the eleven siblings studied at institutions of higher education and obtained higher degrees; in the Jamaican family four out of eight siblings received an education, although only two of them studied abroad. Nevertheless, stating that education is the main goal of migration does not constitute just a description of the factual circumstances of departure; it is also a declaration of intent that reflects a wish to further the individual's, and the family's, ambitions for social and economic improvement, as they have become defined in the Caribbean middle classes.

The ideal migratory move was a several-year sojourn at a foreign university in order to acquire a degree in the professions, followed by a return in order to practice the acquired profession in the homeland. One of the siblings in the Dominican family lived up to his ideal in the most exemplary manner because he left to study abroad on an "island scholarship." This scholarship is awarded throughout the British speaking Caribbean to the students who pass the university entrance exam with the best results so that they may pursue further education abroad.[6] While the island scholarship allows the recipients to study any field of their choice, most use it to obtain a degree in a field that will bring the social recognition and prestige that they associate with further education. This was also the case in the Dominican family that I studied. As the sibling, who had received the island scholarship, explained, "I won the island scholarship, and this allowed me to pursue any career. But those who won the scholarship usually studied law or medicine, because this was the most prestigious thing." This sibling's migration story—ten years abroad studying medicine and training in a specialized field, followed by a long career in Dominica as a highly respected professional serving his country and earning a comfortable income—became a model for the others in the family to emulate. While none of the other siblings succeeded at winning the island scholarship, six of them managed to study abroad on various kinds of scholarships and work-study programs. When I did life-story interviews with family members in Dominica in 1996, four siblings had returned to Dominica and were working within their profession. A fifth sibling had recently returned from abroad after an extraordinary career in public service at home and abroad. They therefore had become one of the most influential and respected families within the new middle class of professionals that emerged on the island after political independence in 1978.

The siblings who stayed abroad were well aware of the family's high status in Dominica, and its image as a family of well-educated professionals, and related their life stories accordingly. Those who had received a university degree felt secure in their knowledge that they had lived up to the high educational standards of the family and added that they would like to return, at some point, and contribute to the country. Those who had not received further education described their migratory move as one that, nevertheless, involved educational elements. When the eldest sister, who had receiving teacher training in Dominica, migrated to England she had to take any available employment, and this meant work in a factory and domestic service. Nevertheless, she described her move to England as one that she had enjoyed because it had made her a more knowledgeable person, stating, "I always had an urge to go out and know the other world. I knew people went to England, and I went. This was what I wanted to do, to see something, to better myself." She emphasized that she had thoroughly enjoyed living in England and visiting the "historical places" there. Furthermore, as a domestic she had made good use of her teacher's training, because she had helped the children with their home work. A younger sister, who went to Canada on a domestic scheme, emphasized that one needed a certain amount of education to be accepted on this scheme. Furthermore, she explained that she planned to study when she had finished her contract as a domestic servant: "There was not much to do in the island. I said that I wanted to be a dietician. It was a way to get in." By saying "I said that I wanted to be a dietician," however, she hinted that she might not have been so keen on studying. As it was, she ended up marrying and having children before her term as a domestic was finished, and she therefore never pursued further education. In her account of her early years in Canada, she rather emphasized that she had worked for a family who respected her: "They were dentists. And they knew that I came from a good family—they knew my background—they treated me well, and we were close." By inscribing their migration story within the narrative of a respected, educated Caribbean family these family members therefore were able to maintain a notion of themselves as part of a respectable middle class, even if their migratory moves were similar to those of the lower classes traveling for wage labor employment.

In the Jamaican family, the parents hoped that one of the sons would become a medical doctor and it therefore arranged for a close relative in New York to sponsor his immigration so that he might study in the United States. He only completed his premedical studies, however, because he married and had a family to support. He therefore decided to go into business. When I met him almost fifty years later, he was painfully aware that he had disappointed his family by not continuing his studies in medical school:

> I felt I have let them down, because I didn't achieve what I had set out to achieve by becoming a medical doctor. Quite often in later years I have had the urge to go back to medical school, but the pressure of everyday living made it too difficult.

None of the Jamaican siblings acquired one of the high-status occupations that gained entrance to the upper middle class of professionals in Jamaica. When I interviewed the siblings, only the sibling who had quit medical school had returned to Jamaica. He had had such a brilliant career in business that he was able to acquire a small hotel in Jamaica and establish himself in the upper middle class of the modern, postcolonial society. When I asked him why he opted to leave the United States, where he was doing so well career-wise, he explained that he never felt accepted in the country because of his color. He related one episode from his college days that, to him, illustrated particularly well his dislike for American attitudes to people of color:

> I remember I had a glass of beer half empty, and the [college professor] dumped it into a large vat of beer and refilled it from the same vat. He tried to make me feel there was no difference. I didn't appreciate it. I would never have done a thing like that. He was saying one for all, and all for one.

Not only did the college professor single him out as someone who was different and therefore had to be especially included, he did it in an uncouth manner. For the other siblings, a return was not so attractive, since they, or their spouses, did not have the economic means, or the professional qualifications, to establish themselves firmly in Jamaican middle-class society. When several of their children obtained the education needed to return, they were settled in the migration destination and had no desire to move to their parents' country of origin.

Education nevertheless remained an important aspect of this family's Jamaican middle-class identity, but in the broader sense of referring to the teaching of good manners, proper English, appreciation of good art and music, and the ability to feel at ease in the upper levels of society—in other words, the qualities taught at the secondary schools that the siblings attended. From this point of view, an educated person is somebody who has the sort of qualities associated with people who are of a better class. This meaning of education has played an important role in Jamaican society. Austin argues that in Jamaica education has "served as an ideology which 'established them [the educated] as qualitatively different from the poor, but without reference to color'" (Austin 1983: 235–36). This has meant that education, as Adam Kuper (Kuper 1976: 75) has pointed out, has served as "a functional alternative to 'race' in the ideological justification of Jamaican social inequality." This alternative, he argues, is "much better adapted to contemporary conditions" because it "presents itself as open to achievement, and as a channel for social mobility." According to this line of thinking, educated persons are not just qualified for respected "white collar jobs in business or government service," they are of a qualitatively different kind than the uneducated, poor, black people who comprised the vast majority of the Caribbean population.

The idea that there is a close relationship between education, human qualities, and class allowed the siblings in the Jamaican family to demarcate themselves from the huge masses of Caribbean emigrants of lower-class background who followed in their footsteps beginning with the 1960s, and made them insist on their rightful place within the mainstream, white, middle-class segment of the society where they lived. Thus the siblings purchased their own homes in white neighborhoods, as soon as they had amassed the necessary funds; they sent their children to private schools, and they sought out the company of whites or other immigrants of Caribbean middle-class background whenever possible. It was apparent to the family members, however, that the receiving societies tended not to distinguish between Caribbean migrants of different classes, but that they rather regarded the family as belonging to the same Caribbean ethnic community. When two family members attempted to move into a white suburban area in Brooklyn, for example, they found that within a few years their white neighbors moved away and sold their property to black incomers, many of them people of lower-class Caribbean background. When the family members moved away to another white neighborhood, the process repeated itself. Eventually, as American racial barriers softened and family members moved away from the traditional migration destinations in major cities, individuals succeeded in establishing themselves in primarily white middle-class areas, and when I interviewed the siblings and their descendants in North America they were firmly settled in middle-class neighborhoods.

The family members who migrated to Britain were able to capitalize on their strong background in British culture, combined with their very light colored appearance, to win acceptance in British society. One of the brothers thus settled in a small village in the southern part of England where he became part of the local community, marrying a local woman, playing on the cricket team, serving on the parochial church council. While he was fully accepted in the village, he did not win the same sort of recognition on the labor market. While he succeeded at obtaining a low-ranking civil service job, when he settled in England, he failed to become promoted, and eventually opted to take better-remunerated employment as a welder in the motor industry. He was quite conscious of the fact that he had not done as well financially as had several of his siblings in the United States, but he stated that he preferred the British to the American way of life: "I mix freely in the community, and I am not sure whether this would be the case in America. There is no type of discrimination in the local area where I live. You get that from the respect that you have gained from people." His social acceptance in the middle-class community where he lived therefore made up for the economic discrimination that he had suffered in the wider British society.

Class and Movement

A great deal of migration research is based on interviews with immigrants where they are asked to account for why they left their place of origin, how they organized their migratory move, and how they have settled abroad. Such information has provided the data for analyses of such important topics as causes of migration, choices of migration destination, and patterns of integration. There is no reason to doubt the truth-value of informants' statements, but there is good reason to analyze the context within which they give their answers and examine how this has influenced the way in which they speak about their migration. In this article I have suggested that because migration, generally speaking, is closely related to ambitions for social and economic mobility, the social construction of class may constitute an important context within which to interpret descriptions of migration experiences. This means that migrants' narratives should not be treated simply as factual accounts of moves undertaken by individuals of a particular social and economic background in order to achieve well-defined goals. They are also modes of accounting for lives within social and cultural frameworks that give meaning and purpose to the individuals involved.

For those migrants who self-identify as middle class, an important aspect of the life stories will be the validating of their middle-class background in the country of origin and their success at improving, or at least maintaining, this status through migration. If class is viewed as an objective category, defined on the basis of criteria such as educational skills, occupation, and income, it is possible to divide migrants into different classes and analyze how they have performed in the migration destination. But if it is also treated as a cultural category that involves ways of thinking about sociocultural stratification and cultural worth, which can have important concrete implications for social life, such clear-cut categories of class are not helpful. Rather, a central task becomes that of analyzing the close relation between movement and class and the ways in which individuals seek to present themselves in accordance with their understanding of their rightful place in society.

Within the Caribbean, the notions of middle-class status can be seen to revolve around a proper livelihood that became culturally constructed as based on educational achievement and the mastering of certain colonial European oriented cultural skills (Olwig 2002a). This is because the European colonial system gave high status to education by giving the educated privileged positions within the government as well as in the educational system. Education involved attending a secondary school or an institution of higher learning, which, for many Caribbean people, meant moving within as well as outside the Caribbean. Thus an institution of higher learning was not established in the British speaking Caribbean before the middle of the twentieth century when the University of the West Indies was founded. The maintaining of middle-class status and the aspiration by the lower classes for upward social mobility in society thus were dependent on geographic mobility. The notion of the middle class therefore attained its meaning within a context of extensive local, regional and international movements by people who were relatively well versed with Western culture and society.

Even though the family members were familiar with the West, when they migrated, they did not necessarily feel at home in their migration destinations. Many of the family members, who stayed abroad, experienced difficulty winning social recognition and cultural acceptance in the cosmopolitan centers where they tended to be perceived in terms of their ethnic or racial background, a categorization that places them in the lower ranks of society. The colonial societies from where they emigrated were based on a highly stratified European model of society in which education had become the key to status among the bourgeoisie, especially within the state civil service. The modern democratic British and American societies to which the family members moved, however, were based on an egalitarian national ideology. One ironic consequence of this egalitarianism is that immigrants of color were treated equally as an inferior race, instead of being differentiated into different status groups, as in the Caribbean. This study of two families of Caribbean middle-class background therefore points to the need to critically examine dominant modes of classification and representation in migration research in the light of the ethnographic understanding of the complex fields of social relations and cultural values that frame concrete migratory moves.

Notes

1. This is an abridgment of Merriam-Webster's definition (1c) of the term. The full definition is "a fluid heterogeneous socioeconomic grouping (as in the United States) having a status intermediate between the upper and the lower classes and composed principally of business and professional people, bureaucrats, and some farmers and skilled workers sharing common social characteristics and values."
2. For analyses of class as a sociocultural category in different Western societies, see Barnes 1954, Gullestad 1984, Ortner 1998.
3. Approximately fifty individuals were interviewed in each family. In the Jamaican family, I interviewed six siblings in the family, two having died before I did my research, as well as the siblings' mother. In the Dominican family, I interviewed ten out of the eleven siblings. For a further discussion of these two families, and the methods employed, see Olwig 2001, 2002a, 2002b.
4. Two of the three public schools in Roseau were run by the Catholic Church (Fleming 1964: 1).
5. Jamaica became independent in 1962, Dominica in 1978.
6. The island scholarship was introduced in Jamaica during the late nineteenth century (Gordon 1963: 240), in Dominica apparently not before the middle of the twentieth century when it became possible to take the university entrance examination at secondary schools on the island.

References

Alexander, Henry Jacob. 1973. *The Culture of Middle-Class Family Life in Kingston, Jamaica.* Ph.D. Dissertation, University of Chicago.

Austin, Diane J. 1983. "Culture and Ideology in the English-Speaking Caribbean: A view from Jamaica." *American Ethnologist* 4(3): 223–240.

Austin-Broos, Diane J. 1994 "Race/Class: Jamaica's Discourse of Heritable Identity." *Neiuwe West-Indische Gids* 68(3–4): 213–233.

Barnes, John A. 1954. "Class and Committees in a Norwegian Island Parish." *Human Relations* 7(1): 39–58.

Bryceson, Deborah Fahy and Ulla Vuorela. 2002. "Transnational Families in the Twenty-first Century." In *The Transnational Family: New European Frontier and Global Networks,* eds. Deborah Fahy and Ulla Vuorela Bryceson. Oxford: Berg. pp. 3–30.

Fleming, W.G. 1964. *Secondary and Adult Education in Dominica.* Toronto: College of Education, University of Toronto.

Foner, Nancy. 1973. *Status and Power in Rural Jamaica: A Study of Educational and Political Change.* New York: Teachers College Press, Columbia University.
———. 2000. *From Ellis Island to JFK: New York's Two Great Waves of Immigration.* New Haven: Yale University Press.
Gordon, Shirley. 1963. *A Century of West Indian Education.* London: Longmans, Green and Co.
Gullestad, Marianne. 1984. *Kitchen-Table Society.* Oslo: Universitetsforlaget.
Honychurch, Lennox. 1995. *The Dominica Story: A History of the Island.* London: Macmillan.
———. (n.d.). *Our Island Culture.* Roseau: The Dominica Cultural Council.
Kuper, Adam. 1976. *Changing Jamaica.* London: Routledge & Kegan Paul.
Merriam-Webster. 2000. *Webster's Third New International Dictionary of the English Language. Electronic Version.* Springfield, Mass.: Merriam-Webster.
Olwig, Karen Fog. 2001. "New York as a Locality in a Global Family Network." In *Islands in the City: West Indian Migration to New York.* ed. Nancy Foner. Berkeley: University of California Press. pp. 142–160.
——— (2002a) "A 'respectable' Livelihood: Mobility and Identity in a Caribbean family." In *Work and Migration: Life and Livelihood in a Globalizing World.* eds. Ninna Nyberg Sørensen and Karen Fog Olwig. London: Routledge. pp. 85–105.
——— (2002b) "The Ethnographic Field Revisited: Towards a Study of Common and Not So Common Fields of Belonging." In *Realizing Community: Concepts, Social Relationships and Sentiments,* ed. Vered Amit. London: Routledge. pp.124–45.
Ong, Aihwa. 1999. *Flexible Citizenship: The Cultural Logics of Transnationality.* Durham: Duke University Press.
Ortner, Sherry. 1993. "Ethnography among the Newark: The Class of '58 of Weequahic High School." *Michigan Quarterly Review* 32(3): 411–29.
———.1998. "Generation X: Anthropology in a Media-Saturated World." *Cultural Anthropology* 13(3): 414–40.
Rapp, Rayna. 1978. "Family and Class in Contemporary America: Notes Toward an Understanding of Ideology." *Science and Society: An Independent Journal of Marxism* 42: 278–300.
Thomas, Deborah A. 2004. *Modern Blackness: Nationalism, Globalization, and the Politics of Culture in Jamaica.* Durham: Duke University Press.
Tilly, Charles. 1990. "Transplanted Networks." In *Immigration Reconsidered: History, Sociology, and Politics,* ed. Virginia Yans-Mclaughlin. New York: Oxford University Press. pp.79–95.
Trouillot, Michael-Rolph. 1988. *Peasants and Capital: Dominica in the World Economy.* Baltimore: The Johns Hopkins University Press.
Vuorela, Ulla. 2002. "Transnational Families: Imagined and Real Communities." In *The Transnational Family,* eds. Fay Bryceson and Ulla Vuorela, *New European Frontiers and Global Networks.* Oxford: Berg. pp. 63–82.
Waters, Mary C. 1999. *Black Identities: West Indian Immigrant Dreams and American Realities.* Cambridge, MA: Harvard University Press.
Werbner, Pnina. 1999. "Global Pathways: Working Class Cosmopolitans and the Creation of Transnational Ethnic Worlds." *Social Anthropology* 7(1): 17–35.

7

How Privileged Are They?

Middle-Class Brazilian Immigrants in Lisbon

Angela Torresan

During the last two decades of the twentieth century there was an unprecedented shift in the profile of international migration from Brazil. The early influx of migrants from Europe, Asia, and the Middle East, which intensified toward the end of the nineteenth and into the first part of the twentieth century, had reversed in accordance with a worldwide change in the general postcolonial pattern of population movement. At first, in the 1970s, there was the uncelebrated but voluminous crossing of about half a million Brazilian agricultural workers back and forth across the borders of neighboring countries (Sprandel 1992). By the early 1980s, a more conspicuous movement was taking place as diverse sectors of the middle class around the country began forging the overseas paths that others would soon follow. Today, there are an estimated two million Brazilians circulating through migratory networks that reach primarily to the United States, Japan, Western Europe, and Paraguay.[1]

International migration became a strategic alternative for a widening range of Brazilians, who had repeatedly postponed their personal life projects or saw them shattered by political crisis and ever increasing economic unrest. Juxtaposing unsatisfactory living conditions, a feeling of estrangement, and a general sense of disillusionment with the allure of foreign travel and adventure, Brazilians from all walks of life embraced the idea that they could follow their dreams elsewhere. For a certain, heterogeneous, segment of the new migratory flow this involved the creation and maintenance of a middle-class status and lifestyle that could potentially reverberate in Brazil, even if this status was achieved in the country of destination. In this paper I focus on a small slice of this middle-class movement to Portugal.[2]

When I began conducting fieldwork in Lisbon in 1996 the number of permanent and temporary Brazilian residents in Portugal was 20,082. By

2002, this figure had increased to 36,237.[3] By the mid-1990s, 64 percent of the economically active Brazilian residents were liberal professionals, businessmen, and administrators, 25 percent were non-qualified laborers, and 11 percent worked in the sales and services sectors.[4] Although heterogeneous—in terms of both social origins and the accompanying social conditions in Portugal—the majority of skilled Brazilians living in Portugal between the mid-1980s and early 1990s had managed to enter the qualified job market relatively soon after their arrival. This contrasted sharply with the opportunities most middle-class Brazilians encountered in the other countries of Western Europe, the United States, and Japan. The majority of Brazilians living in London (Torresan 1994), New York (Margolis 1990 and 1994; Martes 2000; Ribeiro 1998) and Japan (Kawamura 1999; Linger 2001; Roth 2002; Tsuda 2003) often worked in unskilled jobs for many years before they could secure employment equivalent to their educational levels and some never managed to bridge the gap. As I will demonstrate shortly, the postcolonial relationship between Brazil and Portugal influenced the tendency of professional Brazilians to engage in activities associated with their credentials. Ironically, because of this colonial history and postcolonial affinity, there was a mounting resistance from Portuguese middle-class professionals, backed up by constraining immigration policies, to accept Brazilians into their midst.

After having attained some material stability, many Brazilians found themselves in a state of cultural and social limbo that seemed to impinge on their attempts to craft a sense of home in Portugal. But compliance with their social position in Portugal was not arrived at without a certain amount of dissent. Because of their privileged position, I argue, they have become the most visible and articulate portion of the Brazilian population abroad. Middle-class Brazilians have publicly campaigned for their right to live in Portugal, stressing their contribution to the country's economy and culture, both past and present.[5] Furthermore, the increased migration controls imposed on Brazilians have sparked many a public debate and fuelled diplomatic friction between the two countries.

How Privileged?

Some prominent anthropological studies on migration share with other disciplines a strong concern with the effects of the interaction between global capitalism and labor on the movement of people around the world. Such interest coincides with the general direction anthropologists have taken while analyzing this movement over the last thirty years and joins forces with our inclination in anthropology to observe the experiences of people in less favorable positions. We have concentrated much of our research efforts on the movement of unskilled labor from poorer regions of the world to the affluent economies of the Western hemisphere. Consequently, we oftentimes have disregarded other crucial aspects relating to such transit that fall outside of the perimeters outlining our interest. Even within a transnational perspective, which emphasizes the fluid nature of geopolitical borders, we find a similar tendency.

Keeping with this perspective, among the principal exponents of the transnationalist theoretical framework in anthropology, Basch, Glick Schiller, and Szanton-Blanc (1994), have stated that it is "the current moment of capitalism as a global mode of production that has *necessitated* the maintenance of family ties and political allegiances among persons spread across the globe" (1994: 24), even though they fail to explain exactly how this connection takes place. With their insightful observation that migrants create transnational social fields of action that cross national borders by maintaining their ties back home and incorporating them into their reality abroad, the authors manage to bring into the field of migration studies the kinds of concerns anthropologists have been expressing regarding the encompassing concepts of our discipline. Thus, the bounded framework of sending and receiving regions reinforced in traditional analysis gave way to flexible boundaries when migrants began participating in the "nation-building process" of two countries (ibid: 35) and found themselves in a position, for better or worse, of cultural bifocality (Rouse 1995). While such transnational social fields have presented a series of challenges to the material and ideological sovereignty of the nation-state, the relationships that formed these seemingly fixed structures keep on responding, regulating, and adapting to the increased flow across their borders (Sassen 1988; Gledhill 1998). As such, while adopting the "unbounded" concept of transnational social fields, Basch et al. could still employ the traditional macroeconomic course of investigation shared with approaches of push-pull and world-system theories while also incorporating a growing anthropological emphasis on individual agency and the plasticity of social categories. Nevertheless, the authors stress, people's motivation to engage in transnational migration, "must be analyzed within the context of global relations between capital and labor" (1994: 23).[6]

The problem is not exactly with the stress on this relationship between new capitalist structures of production and population movement, but rather with the dismissal of other critical aspects intrinsic to this relationship. The role of technological advancements, the proliferation of a globalized consumer culture with its effects on people's expectations for their future, and the hegemony of Western ideas of modernity and cultural taste, are all placed on the sidelines as if not belonging to the very fabric of this globalizing capitalist system. One of these aspects that is often neglected refers to the contrast between the various kinds of information brought to people's attention by what Appadurai (1996) has called media flows and the reality of their daily lives, creating the hope and desire for a lifestyle that is nearly impossible to achieve under their existing conditions. People's objective circumstances and their place within the intersection of global capitalism and movement are also realized through their relative perceptions of their own well-being. Images promoted by international media industries play a crucial role in structuring people's expectations of their welfare and of what they perceive as a privileged position that they should strive to achieve.

This opens up an important question in my exploration of middle-class Brazilian migration to Lisbon and to the issues discussed in this collection. Taking into account the interface between structural forces of capitalist expansion with people's agency and representations, what do we mean when we call someone a privileged migrant? Is our perception of our own well-being as middle-class anthropologists influencing our discernment of who is or is not traveling under favorable conditions? Are migrants' lives observed by the customary research on migration really that disadvantageous? Is this definition a matter of objective classification, of degree, or of positioning? These questions are even more pressing when we observe people associated with the very broad and ambiguous category of middle class who, in contrast with elite groups, are not in control of any significant means of production. Why would I describe middle-class Brazilians living in Lisbon as privileged migrants?

As a number of sociological and economic analyses have noted voluntary migrants usually possess more resources and capital than the majority of their country's population (Beenstock 1996; Chiswick 2000; Tidrick 1971). In accordance, Portes and Rumbaut (1990) note that the general idea that immigrants are poor and uneducated people escaping from penury in their also poor countries can be quite misleading. While critiquing modernization theories of push-pull factors, the authors explain that "[t]he very poor and unemployed seldom migrate, either legally or illegally; and unauthorized immigrants tend to have above-average levels of education and occupational skills in comparison with their homeland population." (1990: 10–11). The authors go on to add that poorer people usually lack the resources to finance such a move, while those who have attained a higher standard of living not only possess the material means to travel, but also harbor expectations that cannot be fulfilled by the opportunities presented in their countries. Urban professionals from developing regions for example, Portes and Rumbaut argue, choose to depart in order to resolve the contradiction between their lived realities and their aspirations, a contradiction that has some of its roots in the effects of the media flows I invoked above. This also holds true for the middle-class Brazilians I observed in Lisbon.

If this is so, if migrants are usually (but not always) better equipped with social, cultural and financial capital than the majority of the national population in their county, then what defines a privileged migrant? The material and cultural conditions that set people apart in terms of class and social status are never rigidly defined. They are not independent from the ideas of wealth and poverty that gain meaning in situations when those involved compare their conditions with that of others they perceive as being above or below themselves. The term middle class, which Brazilian immigrants in Lisbon often used to define their social and economic status, is in itself highly ambiguous. I refer to McCallum's work (1996) as an example of how this ambiguity can operate in Brazil. McCallum discovered that low-income residents of Baixa a poor neighborhood in Salvador, Bahia identified themselves as middle class. McCallum noted that from her position as a middle-class English intellectual, they were situated in a lower-strata of society and by most accounts were actually poor. These people were in fact using the term middle class to distinguish their situation from that of other residents of Baixa whom they considered poorer than themselves. One of the effects of such self-identification, as McCallum indicated, was the fact that people from Baixa would depict what she would normally consider the local middle class as part of a exceedingly affluent elite. She explained this ambivalence by the idea that middle class in these terms constitutes a 'positional metaphor' used by the people at Baixa to locate themselves "in an intermediate social position between wealth and dire poverty" (1996: 214).

Another good example is O'Dougherty's study of middle-class Brazilians from São Paulo (2002). She showed how people after a series of economic and political crisis that assailed Brazil in the 1980s and 1990s, dealt with the deterioration of the material basis through which they had constructed their sense of belonging to the middle class. As houses, cars, and yearly vacation travels became unaffordable, many Brazilians began placing their resources in smaller and less expensive imported consumer goods that they would use to distinguish themselves from those they perceived as belonging to a lower class. In this case, Brazilians were not transgressing class boundaries: they remained on the edge of the abyss while the concept of middle class shifted. The notion of middle class was reshaped according to a person's strategy in times of crisis and as to how they perceived themselves in comparison to others. It was during this period that, apart from intensifying their consumption practices of imported goods (O'Dougherty 2002), many middle-class Brazilians who believed they had nothing to lose by leaving the country transformed international migration into a viable alternative to keep their status.

How then can we define privileged movement when people's perceptions of who they are cannot be easily classified by the global structural causes and functions of international migration, or by their location within the capitalist division between those who own the modes of production and those who sell their labor? The "context of global relations between capital and labor" (Basch et al 1994) helps us analyze general trends of population movement, but it is within people's daily relationships and perception of who they are in reference to others and to their migratory experiences that we, as anthropologists, are able to explore the meanings such global contexts take on in the everyday practices of being a migrant, and more specifically, a relatively privileged one. We must consider how migrants compare their own situations with the circumstances of those, whom they identify as middle and upper class at their point of destination, and in turn how those they are thus identifying view the position of the relatively prosperous foreigners within their ranks. I propose this focus because in my comparison of the experiences of young middle-class Brazilians living in London to that of Brazilians in Lisbon, I realized that the enactment of their status varied considerably not so much at their point of origin, but at their destination. For most Brazilians in Lisbon, the achievement of middle-class status had to be recognized both at "home" and in Lisbon in order for their goal to become truly transnational. London was yet another story. The sheer fact of being in London already constituted a form of success independent from the type of work one would perform and the social status one would achieve there. The discrepancy between the experiences of those in London and those in Lisbon had to do with the global and historical hierarchies through which they envisioned England and Portugal and, concomitantly, with the kinds of work and lifestyle they were respectively willing to embrace in these countries. Brazilian immigrants in London blended into an overarching category of Latin American immigrants. Invisible to most English, their privileged position in London was recognized only by fellow Brazilians. But in Portugal, Brazilians were generally viewed as middle-class skilled immigrants. In Portugal, the efforts of Brazilians to establish themselves relied on the intensive exchange of perceptions and stereotypes between the host population and the immigrants.

Reasons for Going to and Staying in Lisbon: Work, Adventure, and Social Mobility

Most of the immigrants I interviewed in London (Torresan 1994) associated their middle-class identity almost exclusively with their previous status in Brazil even when this did not necessarily accord with their subsequent job situation in London. Although they engaged in employment that was below their qualifications, they were managing to reproduce and even improve their quality of life through increased earnings or simply by attaining a desired amount of independence (financial and/or emotional) from their families back home. Eventually, after long-term residence and adjustment of their immigrant status, a percentage of Brazilians in London would enter the qualified job market and would come to use their situation as a source of transnational status in Brazil.

In Portugal the situation was usually very different. The jobs held by most Brazilian immigrants working in Lisbon were closely related to their self-identification as middle class, a factor significantly shaping their decision to stay. Before the major flow of Brazilian immigrants to Portugal was initiated as well as over the course of the first wave of their immigration, a receptive Portuguese market had been experiencing the introduction of Brazilian capital, commodities, ideas, information, marketing concepts, business approaches, and cultural symbols. Although a common language was a crucial component in the immigrant's entry into the Portuguese job market, it was not the only one.[7] In fact, Brazilians arrived with serviceable personal and cultural assets at a period in Portugal when such qualities were welcomed by a society that had been exposed to a great deal of information about contemporary Brazil (mostly through Brazilian soap operas widely broadcasted on Portuguese television). Between 1989 and 1990, Portugal went through a period of economic boom during which Brazilian companies and business profited from partnerships with Portuguese businesses and financial institutions. Brazil became the fifth largest foreign investor in Portugal and the first among non-Europeans.

One of the oldest Brazilian enterprises to invest heavily in Portugal was the supermarket corporation *Pão de Açúcar*. Some twenty years ago this group opened its first supermarkets in Portugal and by the 1990s it controlled an enormous national chain, with stores throughout the country. As the first supermarket chain in Portugal, *Pão de Açúcar* was also responsible for changing some local patterns of commercialization and consumption. It also introduced a number of Brazilian products into local markets. Many immigrants told me they had no reason to miss their local dishes for they could find all the ingredients in any *Pão de Açúcar* supermarket. Another lucrative enterprise established as a joint venture was the planning, construction, and management of a large shopping center in Caiscais, a wealthy tourist beach resort near Lisbon built by a partnership between a Brazilian architectural firm and a Portuguese contractor. Brazilian participation in expanding and catering to a new Portuguese consumer culture went hand in hand with the country's developing infrastructure such as the construction of a highway connecting Caiscais to Lisbon, which coincided with the opening of the shopping centre.

With the flow of Brazilian capital into Portugal came small entrepreneurs and qualified people who opened up new professional fields in the mid 1980s and into the 1990s. A number of Brazilians opened small businesses, seizing the opportunity to introduce new products to Portugal. A surfer from the south of Brazil, for instance, established a surfboard manufacturing company in Lisbon, which he later expanded into a surf apparel and accessories business; and a Brazilian fitness trainer started one of the first fitness clubs to offer aerobic classes. Others even invented a new professional career for themselves, as was the case of a Brazilian math teacher who moved to Lisbon and became a physical therapist or an agriculturist who became a Brazilian martial arts *(capoeira)* instructor.[8]

Although certain professional fields became associated with the presence of Brazilians, I am not arguing for the emergence of a Brazilian (ethnic) economic enclave (Low 1997). Unlike case studies that have portrayed immigrants who had cornered and retained control of particular sectors in a receiving economy, the situation in this case is that Brazilian immigrants' professional activities were not restricted to specific niches in the economy. Rather, the activities of Brazilians extended into the mainstream and sometimes quite influential sectors of Portuguese economy. As Pessar (1995) has shown in her research into *Latinos* in Washington D.C., when immigrants participate in "mainstream social and economic institutions" there seems to be no urgent need for the emergence of an economic ethnic enclave (1995: 391). Throughout my fieldwork in Lisbon I met and interviewed engineers, lawyers, computer specialists, journalists, therapists, aerobics teachers, secretaries, real estate agents, surfers, waiters, entertainers, musicians, and dancers. There were also a number of immigrants who worked in fields related to Brazilian culture, as in the case of musicians who made their living playing Samba and Bossa Nova in the bars and restaurants around Lisbon. In addition to the qualified professionals, there were also Brazilians from middle-class backgrounds who had not attended university or had only partially completed their studies and who were working in Lisbon in service jobs similar to those they had held in Brazil: as bartenders, shop assistants, salespersons, real-estate agents, waiters and waitresses. A great majority shared a similar view about the situations they were willing to endure in Portugal. In contrast to what Margolis (1994), Sales (1999) and Martes (2000) have observed of Brazilians in the United States, and contrary also to my own research on Brazilians in London, middle-class immigrants in Lisbon would not forgo for long the social status associated with their previous occupation (or education) in Brazil. This contrast becomes clear when we read what Martes discovered about the subjectivity of Brazilian migration to Boston. She says:

> In the United States, Brazilians are not looking for prestige in the traditional sense; when they exchange occupations they had in Brazil for those they will acquire in Massachusetts, prestige is forbade in the name of new values that are not only those related to an increase of consumer power, but are also related to a new lifestyle and [an idea of] citizenship (more equality). (2000: 72)

For most middle-class Brazilian professionals in Portugal, the thought of being a cleaner, dishwasher or shoe-shiner would be as much out of the question as engaging in these same unskilled occupations in Brazil. Like the Brazilians I met in London, those in Lisbon described their experiences as an adventure but this adventure, also had to be supported by some kind of social mobility in the job market.

One Brazilian man I met in Lisbon explained the difference in very clear terms. He had lived in London for two years with a student visa and for another year without official papers. Because he had overstayed his visa, he did not regain entry into England on his return from a family visit to Brazil. Portugal was a second alternative with which he was not very happy. Although he told me he had not found a job in Lisbon yet and had very little money left, he did not hesitate to say that "in London I worked as a dishwasher, but I would never do that in Portugal." When I asked him why not, he told me "I wouldn't submit myself to washing dishes for Portuguese people and to work with people who have no education nor manners [meaning lower-income Portuguese workers]."

What was the difference between a middle-class Brazilian "submitting" himself to washing dishes in restaurants in England as compared to Portugal? Portugal did not seem to offer middle-class Brazilians any real financial or cultural compensation for unskilled jobs in the same ways that countries viewed of as modern, or "First World" nations did. There was a sense among some Brazilians that Portugal stood in a somewhat subordinate position in comparison to Brazil, or at best shared a peripheral, albeit different, position in the world.[9] Thus, without compensation in terms of a cultural learning experience—for instance a new language and or living in what they perceived as an important part of the developed world—working at an unskilled job in Portugal would have the same or worse connotations as doing similar work at home. It would mean downward mobility in every sense of the word. If the people Martes (2000) spoke with considered living in the United States "chic," regardless of their occupation, only social mobility in terms of job status could make living in Portugal an appropriate middle-class choice, and even that mostly because Portugal was now part of the EU.

A Reverse (Cultural) Colonialism

Although I have argued that Brazilians were not occupied in building an economic enclave in Portugal, careers in advertising and television, architecture, dentistry, and football became part of an early public rhetoric about their presence in the job market. These occupations had a special visibility because they were closely related to the modernization process that was taking place in Portugal in such sectors as advertising and marketing. However, before such an influence was felt, the long-term exposure to the soap operas and other TV programs produced by the Brazilian media conglomerate *Globo* played a crucial role in facilitating the subsequent incorporation of Brazilian products and labor into Portuguese society. In contrast to Brazilians, whose knowledge of Portugal came mostly from school textbooks and from the stories told by Portuguese immigrants, people in Portugal were informed about life in Brazil though the mass media. Shortly after the Carnation revolution of 1974, the national Portuguese TV channel purchased the first of many *Globo* soap operas that were broadcast until 1993. In that year *Globo* became a major partner in one of the new television channels (*SIC*) that emerged in the early 1990s. During a five-year period, *SIC* aired thirty-five *Globo* soap operas, often reaching record-breaking viewing audiences. The programs helped transform a certain notion of "Brazilianness" into an object of consumption from the various portraits they painted of modern middle-class lifestyles or colonial-era living replete with rustic, folkloric period pieces. (Key indicators employed included styles of dress, colloquialisms used by the actors, and such images as beach culture in Rio de Janeiro.) This conspicuous presence in the commercial mass media and the creation of spaces and products for middle-class consumption showed evidence of Brazilian participation in the production of a new consumer sensibility, which also influenced the emergence of a new Portuguese middle-class identity.

The irony for Brazilians living in Portugal was that participating in the process of creating public spaces, practices, and objects for Portuguese middle-class consumption did not automatically guarantee them a place within that middle class. Brazilians presented models showing how to transform spaces and objects of consumption into effective strategies of class distinction, but ultimately the appropriation of these and of other transnational commodities and the moral values of middle-class respectability transferred onto consumption practices were still Portuguese. These values were also put to use by many Portuguese as a strategy for establishing a separation from this Brazilian modernity, and thus protecting their own class position from a foreign "invasion." While Brazilian capital and know-how were welcomed, the Portuguese public in general viewed this cultural influence with vigilance.

For instance, complaints about Brazilian influence in the media and advertising sectors came not only from Portuguese professionals trying to protect their job market, as was the case with the Portuguese dentists' reaction to the success of their Brazilian counterparts in Portugal, but also from the wider public. One incident discussed in the Portuguese press offers an interesting example of the perception of this Brazilian professional expertise as a menace to Portuguese identity. In 1999, a Brazilian advertising agency created a media campaign for the Portuguese association of wine makers, Viniportugal, which was shown on television, in the press and on billboards for a period of three months. The ads showed close-up photos of couples starting to kiss or embrace, supplemented with the words: "Wine is good for the heart, especially for single people" and "Wine should only be consumed before, during and after something special." According to one news article,[10] after receiving numerous complaints from the public outraged by the ads, the Institute of Consumer Affairs (*Instituto do Consumidor*) determined that the ad campaign had infringed the regulation for the marketing of alcoholic drinks: the words "wine is good for the heart . . ." attributed therapeutic properties to wine that could mislead consumers and lead to abuse.

In addition to the initial concern of the Institute of Consumer Affairs, the incident also touched upon the general preoccupation with the internationalization (and more specifically "Brazilianization") of Portugal.

Standing as a symbol of a Portuguese uniqueness that can be exported and consumed by the foreign market but whose essence should remain untouched, the traditional image of wine was being tampered with. In the same article the creators of the ad campaign professed that they had attempted to "eroticize" the consumption of wine in order to reach a younger generation, depicting it "as a pleasant and seductive drink." Their goal was to "disassociate it from the stuffy conservative image related to an older generation and encourage a more widespread consumption in face of other alcoholic drinks." [11]

At stake was the nostalgic image that wine held as a component of the Portuguese bucolic family tradition, passed down through generations, and thus of the Portuguese national identity itself. The practice of making and drinking wine has been part of a collective imaginary of the Portuguese household in which wine and bread at the table symbolize the simple delights of an unassuming home and represent the virtues of being Portuguese. This image of a simple lifestyle in a modest rural Portugal encapsulates the moral values important to the middle class. As a shared family tradition, wine was linked to a small corner of peace and moderation, a time when everything slows down within the context of the greater empire and now of modernity. By the same token, wine was commonly associated with the daily habits of an older male generation sitting in the neighborhood plaza or cafes idly playing cards in the late afternoon. In order to expand the market, the ad campaign pulled the practice of drinking Portuguese wine out of the masculine domain of this picturesque domestic world toward images of out of wedlock youthful sexuality, introducing another time, place, and morality for its enjoyment, thus widening the possible scope of its consumption. By using sexuality and non-kin relationships, the ads stirred the imagination toward the kind of freedom and aspirations young people would be looking for in this modern day and age, which in turn not only disrupted its nostalgic image, but also offended middle-class sexual morality.

It seems quite significant that an industry designed to mold the tastes of the very (middle-class) subjects who will consume these products, has been almost exclusively dominated by Brazilian professional ideas during the late 1980s and early 1990s. These advertising professionals were not only more experienced in the new innovative approaches to marketing, but they also understood the Portuguese language and came from a culture that was somewhat familiar to the Portuguese public. The more successful advertising campaigns, however, were those that played with the symbols significant to the articulation of Portuguese identity, intertwining local content with other, more transnational, messages. The more efficient the message, the more pervasive the change would be. Hence this new media approach became a target for protest by groups who were concerned with the impact this new form of advertising was having upon traditional Portuguese values. The problem was not one of miscommunication, but the effective communication of a message that would change the way things were done in Portugal.

The feelings expressed toward this Brazilian cultural influence were at times very ambiguous. A sense of nationalistic pride resonated from those Portuguese who spoke of Brazil's achievements as a former colony that rose to become an influential player in the South America political sphere and in the world at large. It was, however, this same pride that caused many to perceive the cultural influence of the Brazilian presence in Portugal as a reverse process of (cultural) colonization.[12] This was a process of colonization not only by a former colony but also by a country, which was still struggling with significant social economic and political problems. As one Portuguese man told me, this seemed "perfectly absurd."

Cultural Competence and Privileged Migration

What the Viniportugal ad campaign demonstrated in a very public way was part of a pervasive discourse on the Brazilian immigrant's insensitivity to Portuguese traditions and national identity. The modernity Brazilians were bringing to Portugal was not viewed as equivalent to cultivated European taste. It was a hybrid, third world kind of modernity and hence could be distrusted and even perceived as threatening. It was also volatile and unpredictable, for Brazil was seen as a young country lacking strong cultural and moral traditions to counteract the cultural excesses of modernization. There was a symbolic hierarchy repeatedly being played out in public debates and in the daily encounters between Brazilians and Portuguese.

A generalized concept of "the Brazilian" seemed to be quite ingrained in the Portuguese imaginary, for it referenced Portugal's own postcolonial national discourse. In its colonial imaginary Brazil was "a land of temptation that heightened sensuality and bred immorality" (Caulfield 2000: 5), a Tropical Paradise where men went to make their fortune or find their financial ruin. There was no middle ground, for even those who succeeded would eventually succumb to the moral lenience provoked by local corruption, the tropical climate, and the beautiful exotic women. On the other hand, Brazil was also Portugal's finest colony, a product of its humanitarian and administrative genius. Such colonial connections between Brazil and Portugal, and the modern notion of the community of affection, the sharing of a common language and culture, all part of a postcolonial diplomatic rhetoric, did not necessarily grant middle-class Brazilian immigrants the "cultural competence" (Stoler 2000) to be received on the same terms as the local urban Portuguese middle-class. The situation was often aggravated by the stereotypical images many Brazilians held of Portuguese people, which were, in turn, related not only to the idea of an exploitative and inept Portuguese colonialism, but also to the millions of poor and unskilled Portuguese immigrants who arrived in Brazil at the turn of the nineteenth and twentieth centuries. Such images solidified Brazilians' own national identity as autonomous from that of their former colonizers. Consequently, Brazilian immigrants and Portuguese people struggled to find a balance between proximity and distance, by seeking to define certain cultural boundaries that would give them the authority to mark differences while allowing for certain avenues of communication. This balance, however, was not always easy to achieve.

In her work on the "affective grid of colonial politics" in the organization of domestic life in the Dutch Indies (2002: 7), and in her reading of Foucault's 1976 lectures (2000), Laura Ann Stoler shows how discourses of race, sexuality, and nation specified the particular and contingent "internal traits, psychological dispositions, and moral essence" (2000: 134) used to mark theories of difference and social membership at different times. What really mattered in colonial contexts, and, I argue, in the context of recent Brazilian migration to Portugal, was not the existence of clear boundaries between race, gender, colonizer/colonized, or national/non-national, nor the cultural contents essentialized in rhetorics of identity and difference. Rather, what mattered most was the need to establish distinction in terms of moral and cultural superiority. Hence, Stoler remarks, the idea of "cultural competence" (2002: 84)—found in the right gestures, education, dress, language, moral codes, etc.—often had a stronger grip on acceptance than did that of skin color or origin because of its flexibility to accommodate the selected criteria of moral superiority at each given time. The main issue in colonial rule was to sustain the assumption that Europeans were superior to the people they colonized and that this superiority remains intact over the postcolonial migrant population.

At times, Brazilians were viewed as not only lacking such a Europeanized cultural competence, but the one they did embody was often perceived as inappropriate for being "too Brazilian." The same cultural qualities ascribed to them—innovation, creativity, sympathy, informality, spontaneity, ability to work under precarious conditions, jack of all trades disposition—which would give immigrants an advantage in occupying certain positions in the emerging job market, were also associated with qualities viewed negatively by many as being irresponsible, irreverent, intrusive, imprudent, untrustworthy, and extravagant. In the midst of this encounter, Brazilians realized that their gestures and attitudes, expressions and tastes were not simply part of a personal choice or style that seemed so natural. All such prosaic elements of daily life were, in contrast, made evident as culture, as Brazilian culture. Some Portuguese would point out that Brazilian immigrants were too loud in public places, the women's fashion was too revealing and their gestures too sensual, and that they were too friendly and touchy on first contacts.

The image of a culture that embraces sexuality in a freer manner than that of the Portuguese would not impinge on the image Brazilian men usually had of themselves, but it could at times prove detrimental to middle-class professional immigrant women, especially if they were on their own, without a husband or other family member. Many times they were greeted with a mixture of suspicion and admiration. The preconceived notion that a middle-class professional Brazilian woman would base her sexual identity upon a relaxed Brazilian morality could be explained in at least two different ways. Her conduct could be seen as either a reflection of Brazil's recent process of modernization to be emulated or as a result of deep-rooted ideas about promiscuous colonial women's sexuality and European male domination. Elsewhere, I explore in greater detail the negotiations of gender and sexuality with which most Brazilian women have had to engage while in Portugal (Torresan 2004). For now, it suffices to say that for many professional Brazilian women who lived in Lisbon, this liminal position between modernity and patriarchal sexual morality was not easy to manage. They had tried to evade it by leaving Brazil and found another version of it in Portugal. In the next section, however, I will show how Brazilians and Portuguese disputed their respective cultural competence through contrasting ideas of modernity expressed in their different concepts of work and work ethics. Although these had strong gender configurations, Brazilians and Portuguese alike also discussed them in a very encompassing manner.

Modernity at Work

When they arrived in Lisbon, most Brazilians I worked with told me they had no fixed plans for their sojourn. Most told me that they stayed because they had managed to find jobs in their professional fields and realized they could try to build a future for themselves there. As I mentioned above, their skills were welcomed in the booming Portuguese economy of the time. However, middle-class Brazilians arrived in Portugal with work ethics and attitudes incongruent with the Portuguese work environment. Their views on work were related to the systems they had previously experienced in Brazil. These systems were usually more flexible than those of the Portuguese market, and often proved to be an important asset in a period when the market was going through structural changes that clashed with established traditions. On another occasion, I met with Adriana, a Portuguese friend I knew from Brazil, and a Portuguese couple who were her friends. When the subject of my research came up in our conversation, the man, a graphic designer, told me that in spite of himself, he began disliking Brazilians a few years ago when they first started arriving:

> *Paulo:* "They'd always tell you they know everything, even when in fact they don't. Not only that but they know it better than you. How can you tell me you know how to do something and I give you a job and realize that you were lying? How can someone do that?"

Angela: "Maybe because they thought they could learn before you noticed . . ."

Paulo: "This makes no sense."

Angela: "I guess it doesn't."

Paulo: "Then again it's a Brazilian absurdity. Don't you agree?"

Angela: "Not really, but I don't know what to tell you."

Adriana (who had previously lived in Brazil). "Brazilians have a tremendous capacity for work, they're not afraid of working. I never saw in Brazil this laziness I see here in Portugal. If they tell you they know something and they don't, it's not that they're trying to deceive you. When they honestly think they can learn something they will do whatever it takes to learn it. They are ambitious."

Paulo: "They are arrogant, that's what they are."

This kind of attitude, which Paulo had witnessed on two separate occasions, had irritated him profoundly. He could not understand why most Brazilians lacked the "humility to acknowledge their limitations." Paulo's opinion and that of many with whom I talked, presented Brazilians as good workers, but unreliable as people. Brazilians were represented as moving in the spirit of competition according to their opportunities, cutting a better deal, taking verbal agreements too lightly, abusing other people's faith in them, and frustrating their employers, who had learned by experience that Brazilians were committed only as long as it interested them. Brazilians' response to this critique depended upon a series of factors that ranged from their length of stay in Portugal, to the kind of professional acceptance and integration they had achieved, the type of personal relationships they had established with their Portuguese coworkers, along with issues of gender, race, social background, and education. In most cases, they tended to attribute disapproval of their work ethics to the formality and inflexibility of Portuguese work relationship which curbed people's ambitions and potentials, a legacy of the dictatorship.[13] Heliana, a Brazilian woman who had lived in Portugal for eight years, explained the differences in this way:

In Brazil you have to fight to hold your job. There, most jobs offer little or no stability. Here people are complacent. They do exactly what they are told to do on their first day on the job. They rarely deviate from the norm or do anything outside of their specific job requirements. But today the motto is flexibility. Portuguese people don't change. It requires too much work. Besides they don't like to work. Work relationships are too ingrained in the hierarchy and bureaucracy of the country. Everyone is afraid of stepping on each other's toes, which makes it all the more slow and difficult. This is a result of forty years of Salazar dictatorship, and the society will continue to project this attitude in the generations to come. In Brazil, outside of the civil service, this doesn't happen and it won't happen because you could lose your job to one of the forty or more people waiting outside for their chance to get in the door. Competition is fierce. This is the Brazilian way and often Portuguese people may think we intrude into other people's business, but it's only because in Brazil you have to be prepared for everything that comes your way. This is also the reason why some businesses here prefer to employ Brazilians. We are more flexible and more resourceful.

What seemed to many Brazilians attitudes that were proper and becoming to any competitive job market, had turned into negative qualities in Portugal. In other words, many of the changes in work relationships, which had also been a result of the new neo-liberal politics of opening and therefore restructuring the Portuguese market to compete in the EU, were at first associated with the arrogance of these Brazilians' style of work. Middle-class Brazilian professionals had become both the models and the scapegoats of a process of modernization that brought with it higher instability. The notions of worker elaborated in Heliana's narrative were also part of a larger debate on the measures of Portuguese and Brazilian modernities. Brazilians related their job experiences in Brazil to economic flexibility, which they saw as an outgrowth of modern global capitalism. This job flexibility entailed a requirement to take on multiple and sometimes unpredictable tasks, establishing a nonlinear work routine in terms of time and location, obtaining multidisciplinary training, and cultivating a versatile orientation toward work. It also translated into precarious short-term contracts without benefits or vacation, long hours without paid overtime, and an absolute readiness to work at any time. This approach seemed typical of a neo-liberal, post-Fordist, model of a flexible labor organization, privatizations, self-regulating markets, and an increase in corporate power. In fact, the first civilian governments following the military regime in Brazil also used a neo-liberal rhetoric of modernization. Paradoxically, this discourse transformed work practices that had long been the effect of economic instability and social inequality in Brazil into a new vision of hybrid modernity. As Heliana said, job relations in Brazil are considered more modern because Brazilians had to fight for a place, "had to do everything" to keep their jobs in an economy that has high levels of unemployment. In this view, inequality, underdevelopment and instability equated with neo-liberal modernity.

Accordingly, the Portuguese model of economic organization was a residue of the Salazarian dictatorship that was too heavily based on bureaucratization, centralization and hierarchical work relationships, and too reliant on the state as a major regulator and provider. Such correlation between the present-day Portuguese dilemmas and the legacy of the Salazar dictatorship was another recurrent theme, to which both Portuguese people and Brazilian immigrants often alluded.

A reverse perspective pointed to another kind of economy in the workplace, according to which modernity was embedded in a general European social democratic tradition and civilization that valued job stability. The emphasis here was placed on respect for a hierarchical ordering of people's personal and professional space, reliability, trust, and a regard for social conventions of civility. In this version, the Brazilian style was viewed not so much as a practice that meshed with the demands of the new global economies, but rather as an impolite and untrustworthy "intrusion into other people's business," and as unbecoming for a middle-class professional. It translated into a lack of proper manners.

Those immigrants who had gained insight into the Portuguese work ethic and practices and who then tried to readapt their conduct were mostly seen as exceptions to the rule. Some realized that imposing their views would only jeopardize their chances of advancement. Flavia, a Brazilian architect who lived in Lisbon for nine years, explained to me how she now understood Portuguese bafflement with the apparent hypocrisy of Brazilian workers maneuvering smoothly in a cut-throat job market while still offering a pat on the back and a smile on their faces.

> At first, I was taken by the Portuguese's formalism. They are very serious, but I came to understand it as the years went by, and after I lived with a Portuguese person. The Brazilian way is too sympathetic and the phrase "hey friend, can you do me a favor?" (*amigo, dá para fazer aquilo?*) just doesn't cut it in Portugal. In "Portuguese" a friend is a friend. They don't throw these words around the way we do: "My little brother" (*meu irmaõzinho*) is a real brother. This is deeply annoying to them because they would never smile to you if they don't know you well. But Brazilians who have just arrived here are very disrespectful, really. I'm not saying that this is bad. It's just different.

To some, this understanding would come with a reluctance to change something immigrants believed was important to their definition of who they are as Brazilians. Carlos, a video producer who had also been in Lisbon for almost a decade put it this way:

> You shouldn't be too impulsive, too spontaneous at work. I always thought of myself as a very spontaneous person, but I've cooled that down. Now I think twice before I act. I now understand that it's better to listen first before you give your opinion, wait and proceed with caution like they do. I believe I've learned a lot here and I had to adapt my behavior to fit in. At the same time I wished certain things were a bit different.

Cultural competence required not only time, but also a willingness to accommodate, adapt, and appropriate ways of being that sometimes contradicted how Brazilians conceive themselves. Moreover, it would also require a shift away from general Portuguese perceptions of Brazilians as transient workers who will invariably return home toward accepting them as people who are engaged in making a home in Portugal, even if they maintain a sense of belonging to Brazil, or might one day return to their country.

For some Portuguese, maintaining a certain amount of control over foreign, especially Brazilian influences on Portuguese traditions, was crucial.

It was up to them, the immigrants, to earn the right to be incorporated into the society. For others, it was precisely this nostalgia for a Portugal past that served to support the presence of Brazilians, and to denounce the rigid controls on Brazilian immigration. Such discourses usually acknowledged gratitude toward Brazil for accepting large numbers of Portuguese immigrants over the years and also pointed to the fact that Brazil was the most successful example of humanitarianism in Portugal's colonial empire. In other words, it was the colonial myth of compassion and tolerance, reinforced earlier by the Salazarian ideology, which mostly supported this narrative of acceptance and tolerance toward Brazilian immigrants.

From this perspective there could be no reverse cultural colonization, for anything Brazilians produced would have ultimately originated from Portugal. This included the "sensualization" of Portuguese wine. Others viewed the critiques of Brazilian immigration and its cultural influence on Portugal as a relic of an antiquated Salazarian protectionism that also hindered Portugal's modernization. In this view, the recent presence of Brazilians in Portugal was a result of Portugal's modernization, which consequently attracted migration. The assertion of a common heritage and destiny went hand in hand with the proclamations of a cultural and historical distance intended to produce market protection and suspend political accords of reciprocity between Brazil and Portugal. The construction of middle-class Brazilians as privileged immigrants entitled to special treatment coexisted with that of a colonial idea of Brazilianness, which was seen as both an attraction and a threat to Portugal.

Conclusion

What became significant to Brazilians who strove for some kind of intermediary position between their Brazilian identity and their status as middle-class immigrants in Lisbon, was achieving equilibrium between what one relinquished and what one embraced. Personal change was desired but was also influenced by ideals that were beyond a person's immediate control. In this encounter, agency, choice, and accomplishment, all of which were important concepts for most Brazilians' middle-class sense of identity and transnational experiences, came face to face with the highly contingent process of boundary making. During the late 1980s to mid-1990s, Brazilians arrived in Portugal believing that their professional skills and cultural knowledge would benefit their immigration and acceptance into the society. They had not anticipated that their presence would also provoke resistance and resentment. At play here were people's subjective experiences of identity and belonging as well as externally ascribed notions of who they should be. The messy negotiations between agency and structures, whether cultural, economic, social, or political can be better understood when people try to explain who they are by defining themselves through their relationships with others, as enemies and friends, as competitors in the marketplace or as colleagues at work. In the case of the Brazilian immigrants and Portuguese people with whom I worked in Lisbon, the interaction produced a clash of representations that could only happen because there were already too many expectations on either side based on the previous knowledge each possessed of the other. Whether as familiar foreigners or privileged exotics, Brazilians were indeed privileged immigrants because their ability to reproduce a desired middle-class status rested on their well-integrated economic position in the receiving society and also because they were not totally reliant on their complete acceptance by the Portuguese. What really mattered here was the mutual recognition and the intense exchange between the Portuguese and Brazilians, which led to so many public and private debates. Professional Brazilians may not have completely become part of Portugal's own middle class as they had expected, for to their surprise they were always going to be seen as foreigners. Brazilians themselves realized they did not want to integrate to the extent of losing their own sense of being who they thought they were. Nevertheless, they did achieve their very own position as middle-class Brazilians living in Portugal and many managed to feel at home in Lisbon precisely because, unlike most of those who went to London and the U.S., they are not an invisible minority. Their sense of worth in relation to the Portuguese manifested itself in proud declarations of Brazil's contribution to Portugal both past and present. Being a privileged migrant, in this case, had its roots not only in the resources they brought with them to Portugal but also in the very special historical connections between the two nations and their people.

Notes

1. The Brazilian Foreign Ministry gives a 2002 estimate of 1,964,489 Brazilians living abroad, based on surveys of its local consulates throughout the world (Azvedo 2004). However significant this number is, it is still quite conservative. Much of this population is undocumented, which makes its members all but disappear from official numbers. Moreover, they are fairly mobile within the host countries and frequently cross other international borders, including circular returns to Brazil.
2. In the last decade, a number of studies have observed different configurations of Brazilian international migration. Some of them are Fleischer (2000), Margolis (1994), Martes (2000), Ribeiro (1998), and Sales (1999), for the United States; Kawamura (1999), Linger (2001), Roth (2002), and Tsuda (2003) for Japan; Daltro Santos (1996, 2001), Gnaccarini (1994), Machado (1999, 2003), and Torresan (1994) for Europe. See also the two collections of articles edited by Martes, Reis, and Sales (1999), Patarra (1996), and Lesser (2003).
3. This number includes both permanent residents and those holding a temporary visa or a temporary resident permit. According to an article in the

Portuguese monthly magazine *Grandes Reportagens* ("Brasil-Portugal, 500 anos de desencontros," no 109, 2000), there were about 10,000 Brazilians of Portuguese descent who held a Portuguese passport, and 1,000 holding other European passports.

4. See SEF statistics from 1992 to 1996 and also Malheiros (1996).

5. Portugal and Brazil celebrated a series of international accords throughout the twentieth century, while under the light of cultural and/or economic exchanges, they concentrated on the reciprocal rights and special treatment of the citizens of one country who were residents or visitors in the other (1922 Treaty on Military Service Exemption and Dual Nationality; 1922 Convention of Emigration and Work; 1948 Accord on Intellectual Collaboration; 1953 Treaty on Consultation and Friendship; 1960 Accord on Visas and Passports; 1966 Cultural Accord; 1971 Convention on Equal Rights and Duties; 1971 Additional Protocol to the 1966 Cultural Accord).

6. Many recent migration studies have observed international movement through a historical-structural approach of world-system analysis that dismisses the neo-classic focus on economic and developmental variables in push-pull forces (unemployment, poverty, overpopulation, and labor demand) and concentrates on the structural inequalities of global capitalism. See Briggs (1975), Lamm and Imhoff (1985), Teitelbaum (1980), for a classical view according to which people migrate to escape conditions of dire poverty in their country. Proponents, such as Castles and Kosack (1973), Portes and Walton (1981), and Piore (1979), offer arguments supporting the importance of developmental and structural imbalances and the asymmetric expansion of capitalism in developed and developing countries to the contemporary flow of labor migration. Sassen (1981) and Morokvasic (1983) observe how local structures of production and labor are disrupted by that expansion, resulting in the redistribution of labor in the global economy. These studies generally show a combination of macro- and micro-structural factors working simultaneously to affect the layout of international migration. On the one hand, the process of de-industrialization of developed countries, which relocated large-scale industries to less-developed ones, has resulted in the decrease of blue-collar jobs at the point of origin. An inevitable outcome of this change was also a decrease of jobs for nonskilled immigrants (Sassen, 1981, 1988).

7. Language is indeed a crucial issue in the course of adaptation to the new country. Many Brazilians in London associated unskilled jobs with a poor knowledge of English. But language proficiency is also akin to the symbolic capital attached to certain dialects and accents. While a Brazilian accent in Portugal may be positively valued in the job market, Cape Verdean or Angolan accents, for example, were often associated with unskilled labor.

8. *Capoeira* is often described as an Afro-Brazilian martial art/dance that is fought/performed to the rhythm of drums and other percussion instruments and has become very popular with younger people in Portugal.

9. Portuguese sociologist Santos (1994) argues that the peculiarity of the Brazil/Portugal relationship hinges on the fact that Brazil holds a central role in a marginal area of the world, while Portugal retains a peripheral position in a central region. Many other Brazilians I spoke with in Lisbon also shared this perspective.

10. "Queixas à campanha Viniportugal, *Expresso* 11/9/99.

11. *Idem.*
12. Of course Brazil was not the only, or even the major, player in this Portuguese process of modernization, which was in fact heavily financed by European subsidies. Portugal has also consumed many European and North American cultural products.
13. Portugal lived under the dictatorship of António Oliveria Salazar from 1933 to 1974.

References

Appadurai, Arjun. 1996. *Modernity at Large: Cultural Dimensions of Globalization.* Minneapolis and London: University of Minnesota Press.

Azvedo, Débora Bithiah de. 2004. *Brasileiros no Exterior.* Relatório da Consultoria Legislativa da Área XVIII. Câmara dos Deputados, Brasília.

Basch, Linda, Nina Glick Schiller, and Cristina Szanton-Blanc. 1994. *Nations Unbound: Transnational Projects, Postcolonial Predicaments and Deterritorialized Nation-States.* Berkshire: Gordon & Breach.

Beenstock, Michael. 1996. "Failure to Absorb: Remigration by Immigrants into Israel." *International Migration Review* 30: 950–78

Briggs, Vernon. 1975. "The Need for a More Restrictive Border Policy." *Social Science Quarterly* 56: 477–484.

Caulfield, Sueann. 2000. *In Defence of Honor: Sexuality, Modernity, and Nation in Early Twentieth-Century Brazil.* Durham and London: Duke University Press.

Castles, S. and Kosak, G. 1973. *Immigrant Workers and Class Structure in Western Europe.* London: Oxford University Press.

Chiswick, Barry R. 2000. "Are Immigrants Favourably Self-Selected?" In *Migration Theory: Talking Across Disciplines,* eds. Caroline Brettell and James Hollifield. London and New York: Routledge. pp.61–75.

Daltro Santos, Gustavo Adolfo Pedrosa. 1996. *Sabiá em Portugal: Imigrantes Brasileiros e a Imaginação da Nação na Diáspora.* Undergraduate monograph, UNICAMP, Capinas, S.P.

———. 2001. *Relações Interétnicas em Lisboa: Imigrantes Brasileiros e Africanos no Contexto da Lusofonia.* M.Phil dissertation, UNICAMP, Campinas, S.P.

Fleischer, Soraya. 2000. "O Trabalho de Emigrantes Brasileiras: Conflitos entre Housecleaners Brasileiras e suas Clientes." In *Em Busca da Experiência Mundana e seus Significados: Georg Simmel, Alfred Schutz e a Antropologia,* ed. Carla C. Teixeira. Rio de Janeiro: Relume Dumará. pp.167 99.

Gledhill, John. 1998. «Thinking About States, Subalterns and Power Relations in a World of Flows.» Paper presented at the *ICCCR International Conference on Transnationalism,* Manchester, 16–18 May.

Gnaccarini, Isabel. 1994. *Réseau d'Information, Interaction Sociale et Stratégies de d'Adaptation: Le Cas des Brésiliens en France.* Paris: D.E.A de l'École des Hautes Études en Sciences Sociales.

Herman, Harry Vjekoslav. 1979. "Dishwashers and Proprietors: Macedonians in Toronto's Restaurant Trade." In *Ethnicity at Work,* ed. Sandra Wallman. London: Macmillan. pp. 71–92.

Kawamura, Lili. 1999. *Para Onde Vão os Brasileiros?* Campinas: Unicamp.

Lamm, Richard and Imhoff, Gary. 1985. *The Immigration Time Bomb: The Fragmentation of America.* New York: Dutton.

Lesser, Jeffrey, ed. 2003. *Searching for Home Abroad.* Durham and London: Duke University Press.

Linger, Daniel T. 2001. *No One Home: Brazilian Selves Remade in Japan.* Stanford: Stanford University Press.

Low, Setha M. 1997. "Theorizing the City: Ethnicity, Gender, and Globalization." *Critique of Anthropology* 17: 403–09.

Machado, Igor. 1999. "A invenção do Brasil exótico entre imigrantes brasileiros no Porto, Portugal." Presented at the XXIII *Anpocs Meetings*, Caxambu.

———. 2003. *Cárcere Público: Processos de Exotização entre Imigrantes Brasileiros no Porto, Portugal.* Ph.D. dissertation in Social Sciences. Universidade Estadual de Campinas.

Malheiros, Jose Macaísta. 1996. *Imigrantes na Região de Lisboa: Os Anos da Mudança.* Lisboa: Colibri.

Margolis, Maxime. 1994. *Little Brazil: An Ethnography of Brazilian Immigrants in New York City.* Princeton: Princeton University Press.

———. 1990. "From Mistress to Servants: Downward Mobility among Brazilians in New York City." *Urban Anthropology* 19(3): 215–231.

Martes, Ana C. B. 2000. *Brasileiros nos Estados Unidos: Um Estudo Sobre Imigrantes em Massachusetts.* Rio de Janeiro: Paz e Terra.

Martes, Ana C. B., Reis, Rossana R. and Sales, Teresa, eds. 1999. *Cenas do Brasil Migrante.* São Paulo: Bomtempo.

McCallum, Cecilia. 1996. «Resisting Brazil: Perspectives on Local Nationalisms in Salvador da Bahia.» *Ethos* 61 (3–4): 207–229.

Morokvasic, Mirjana. 1983. "Women and Migration: Beyond a Reductionist Outlook." In *One Way Ticket: Migration and Female,* ed. Annie Phizacklea. London and New York: Routledge. pp.13–31.

O'Dougherty, Maureen. 2002. *Consumption Intensified: The Politics of Middle-Class Daily Life in Brazil.* Durham and London: Duke University Press.

Ong, Aihwa. 1999. *Flexible Citizenship: The Cultural Logics of Transnationalism.* Durham and London: Duke University Press.

Patarra, Neide. 1996. *Migrações Internacionais: Herança XX, Agenda XXI.* São Paulo: FNUAP.

Pessar, Patricia R. 1995. "The Elusive Enclave: Ethnicity, Class, and Nationality among Latino Entrepreneurs in Greater Washington, D.C." *Human Organization* 53: 383–92.

Piore, Michael. 1979. *Birds of Passage: Migrant Labor and Industrial Societies.* Cambridge: Cambridge University Press.

Portes, Alejandro, and Rumbaut, Rubén. 1990. *Immigrant America: A Portrait.* Los Angeles: University of California Press.

Portes, Alexandro and Walton, John. 1981. *Labor, Class, and the International System.* Berkeley: University of California Press.

Ribeiro, Gustavo Lins. 1998. "Goniânia, Califórnia. Vulnerabilidade, Ambiguidade e Cidadania Transnacional." *Série Antropologia.* vol. 235. Brasília: UNB.

Roth, Joshua Hotaka. 2002. *Brokered Homeland: Japanese Brazilian Migrants in Japan.* New York: Cornell University Press.

Rouse, Roger. 1995. "Questions of Identity: Personhood and Collectivity in Transnational Migration to the United Stated." *Critique of Anthropology* 15(4): 351–80.

Sales, Teresa. 1999. *Brasileiros Longe de Casa.* São Paulo: Cortez Editora.

Santos, Boaventura. 1994. *Pela Mão de Alice: o Social e o Politico na Pós-Modernidade.* Porto: Edições Afrontamento.

Sassen, Saskia. 1981. «Labor Migration and the New Industrial Division of Labor.» In *Women, Men, and the International Division of Labor,* eds. June Nash and M. Patricia Fernandes Kelly. Albany: State University of New York Press. pp.175–204.

———. 1988. *The Mobility of Labor and Capital: A Study in International Investment and Labor Flow.* New York: Cambridge University Press.

SEF. Serviço de Estrangeiros e Fronteiras. 1992–2003, *Relatório Estatístico Anual.* Lisboa: SEF.

Sprandel, Marcia Anita. 1992. *Brasiguaios: Conflito e Identidade em Fronteira Internacionais.* Masters dissertation, Museu Nacional, Universidade Federal do Rio de Janeiro.

Stoler, Laura Ann. 2000. *Race and the Education of Desire: Foucault's* History of Sexuality *and the Colonial Order of Things.* Durham and London: Duke University Press.

———. 2002. *Carnal Knowledge and Imperial Power: Race and the Intimate in Colonial Rule.* Berkeley and Los Angeles: University of California Press.

Teitelbaum, Michael. 1980. "Right Versus Right: Immigration and Refugee Policy in the United States." *Foreign Affairs* 59: 21–59.

Torresan, Angela. 1994. *Quem parte, quem fica: uma ethnografia sobre imigrantes brasileiros em Londres.* Masters dissertation, Museu Nacional, Universidade Federal do Rio de Janeiro.

———. 2004. *Loud and Proud: Immigration and Identity in a Brazilian/Portuguese Postcolonial Encounter in Lisbon, Portugal.* Doctoral dissertation, Manchester University.

Tidrick, Katrhyn. 1971. "Need for Achievement, Social Class and Intention to Emigrate in Jamaican Students." *Social and Economic Studies* 20:52–60.

Tsuda, Takeyuki. 2003. *Strangers in the Ethnic Homeland: Japanese Brazilian Return Migration in Transnational Perspective.* New York: Columbia University Press.

Werbner, Pnina. 1990. *The Migration Process: Capital, Gifts and Offerings among British Pakistanis.* New York: Berg.

8

Imagined Communitas
Older Migrants and Aspirational Mobility

Caroline Oliver

Introduction

My husband didn't die out here, it was the one thing he wanted just to get back home. Anyhow when he went back . . . he said to the doctor at the beginning of September "when can I go back to Spain?" They said sorry I don't think you can go back. At the crematorium we didn't have hymns, I had "Viva España." It played all the way through, "take me back to sunny Spain." He wasn't a religious person to the extent that he would have wanted to sing "Jerusalem" and all those things that make you cry. So, when "take me back to sunny Spain" started everyone just looked at me, and I felt happy about it . . . well, he would have thought, "Reenie, it's only you who would have thought of that." I had really also wanted to drive our car right back [from Spain] to the crematorium [in the U.K.], because I wanted *our* car up there, and its Spanish number plate—we used to drive it down from Bilbao, through Madrid, stop at a Parador at about 2:00 and the next morning we'd be down here by 12:00—but my son went "oh no mother, this is one time when you can't."

Doreen, an eighty-one year old Scottish woman told me this account while sitting outside drinking coffee in Easter time in the pleasant surroundings of a town on the Costa del Sol. Having retired to Spain some thirteen years earlier with her husband, and now five years after his death, she was on the verge of moving "home"—to the south of England to be near her family. Her children were pleased she was returning and her young granddaughter was particularly excited at the prospect of having "Nannie Spain" back, the one who "kisses on two cheeks." However, Doreen's children had known better than to interfere in or influence her decision, more accustomed as they were to looking in their diaries to find out where on the globe their parents were at that moment. The year Doreen's husband died, the couple had only shortly returned from a cruise around Alaska, and at the time of our conversation she was excitedly planning a cruise in Australia. For Doreen's part, her arrival in Spain those years ago "seems like yesterday," and she described her time there as filled with exciting experiences of travel and discovery. Although she was happy to be returning to the U.K., she still maintained that she would keep traveling back and forth from Spain: "oh no, no no . . . I'm not going back in that sense," she insisted in her rolling Scottish accent. For Doreen, traveling to Spain was the key, she felt, to what kept her alive.

Doreen's story represents a common aspiration in the Western world: to "up stakes" and move abroad following a lifetime of work. The promise to "live the dream" is alluringly displayed in property developers' brochures and estate agents' windows, which tantalizingly offer a passport to a new life through migration. However, as this volume points out, the means by which we can analyze the aspirational movement demonstrated in Doreen's story is limited. Existing accounts of labor migration are inappropriate to understand movement pursued for motivations more readily associated with tourism, in which retiring in Spain is chosen for the better way of living on pensions in one's latter years (see King, Warnes, and Williams 2000). But analyses of tourism are not entirely appropriate either. The permanence (or at least long-term nature) of aspirational movement disrupts the definition of tourism in sociological and anthropological accounts as a temporary "break from the norm," an "away" distinct from "home" (Urry 1990) and the sharp demarcations between tourist/migrant and host/guest blur (Williams and Hall 2000; O'Reilly 2000a; Gustafson 2002; Oliver 2006). How are we to analyze movement undertaken as another migrant told me: "because it's sunny and the fruit is nice"?

The difficulty of analysis is somewhat surprising given that the anthropology of the twenty-first century increasingly posits travel and displacement as central in ethnography (Clifford 1992). Yet these developments are tempered by a concern to avoid "overemphasis[ing] the global and transient character of human life on the loose" (Olwig 1997: 17). Anthropologists have thus explored how people create "place" for one's self and group (Gray 2002) emphasizing the regrounding of identity as a countervailing process to the instability of migrancy (Ahmed, Castañeda, Fortier, and Sheller 2003). This is understandable—after all, what good an anthropology of precarious and transient relationships? On the other hand, as this chapter demonstrates, anthropologists should not lean too far in the other direction, because there are some circumstances in which transience, liminality, and interstitiality themselves -and their negotiation- are key to understanding the construction of social identities. Some of these conditions have been documented already, for example, Amit-Talai's depiction of expatriates' lives in the Cayman Islands (1998) and Linger's (2001) analysis of the predicament of Nikkeis in Japan explore the precarious nature of post-migration life. Yet there remain alternative situations in which liminality is experienced less as a side-effect of structural work arrangements and more as a beneficial condition. This is the case in the aspirational migration explored here, in which individualistic travelers take advantage of leisure spaces to experiment with and reflexively interrogate their identities, hoping to disgard their baggage and "be who they want to be" [1] through their engagement in an imagined communitas of long-term leisure.

On one level, this chapter is concerned therefore with how age-old mythologies of tourism and travel around the scope and possibility for renewal and reinvention feed into migrant narratives. Exploring how geographical mobility is made significant with migrants' own "life journeys" entails an attention to how physical travel–and the freedoms afforded in liminal, disembedded "non-places"- informs personal journeys of fulfilment of desired life projects and age-based aspirations. Explorations of this kind are more readily done with younger people; numerous studies for example document the transformative potential of adventurous backpacking trips for younger people describing for example, "that what lies at the core of backpackers' stories, though often covert, is these youths' selves and identities, rather than the exciting activities and accomplishments which constitute the overt topic of narration" (Noy 2004: 79). Yet until now, little attention rests on how travel in later life informs processes of self-renewal, despite Urry's (2002) recent call to understand the "tourist gaze" as corporeal and embodied, consumed by specific individuals of particular ages, gender, class, and more.

Themes of liminal travel are, however, particularly apt for the identity-making of older people. As Cohen (1994) points out, ethnographies of ageing in clubs and institutions document older people's struggle to maintain or reassert identities contra an assignation of the categorical identity of "old." In the context explored here, retirement and leisured travel provides an opportune platform for a "new start." with travel offering a source for self-definition. In fact, the mythological transformative potentials of travel aid proclamations of self, contributing to age-appropriate narratives of self-development and autonomy (Oliver 2006). Not that these mythologies of travel found in aspirational migrants' accounts are new; Rojek (1993) argues that escape through travel has long been imagined as inherently rehabilitative, offering tantalizing opportunities for "self-actualisation" unachievable in the humdrum of a routinized work existence. This is seen through the noble associations of Grand Tour travel (and contemporary "gap year" experiences) with "broadening the mind" (Craik 1997: 118) as well as the imagining of Victorian tours to the Mediterranean as curative of the ills, coldness, and boredom associated with northern metropolitan life (Rojek 1993). The belief in the restorative power of "getting away from it all" is still an enduring cultural myth (ibid). Moreover, it particularly persists in an era of the "myth of me," a moral stance that endorses detachment from others in the pursuit of self-actualization (Lawson and Samson 1988, cited in Urry 2002). And these putative benefits of travel echo key aspects seen in the recently emerging motif of "successful" or "positive" ageing in the West, which is linked to notions of "the third age" as a sphere of personal achievement and education (Laslett 1989).

On another level however, and even more importantly, this chapter is concerned with interrogating the implications and consequences of these aspirations for self-fulfilment envisaged in travel. Can one really "be who one wants to be" through aspirational migration, particularly after a lifetime of being what one is? And what are the necessary outcomes of this maxim for social relationships and self-identities? Although the enormity of such questions cannot be answered in one small chapter, the ethnographic analysis given here suggests a number of potential difficulties arise. These particularly manifest in social relationships, because the imagined communitas generates limitless potential intimate friendships yet gives no means of assessing their trustworthiness. This–and other related consequences- emerge, I suggest, from a contradiction at the heart of the aspirational migration process in the Western world, between the freedom, sociability, and egalitarian possibilities imagined and emerging out of liminal travel and the strong individualism espoused by those engaging in exactly that practice.

The fieldwork on which this analysis is based was carried out in two sites, a coastal town ("Tocina") located in the East part of the Costa del Sol and a prettified *pueblo blanco* (white village), "Freila," [2] perched high up the hill overlooking the coast. It is worth pointing out from the outset there is much about these field sites and the "community" (as articulated by migrants) that depart from any conventional notions of the field. The "natural" congruency between place and culture (Gupta and Ferguson 1997) unravels in a fluid scene of Spanish, expatriate, and tourist networks. Even within these networks, there is little homogeneity, particularly among the expatriates who fragment according to nationality, age, interests, and tastes. Stability within the "community" is subject to disruption by the regular transience of short-stay and longer-stay tourists and migrants coming and going as well as the presence of casual workers and those on sabbaticals, etc. Particularly in summer the population swells. Before turning toward an analysis of the implications of this mixed "field" for social relationships, I shall situate how and why retirement migration has occurred in this area.

The Context and Scope of Movement

Older travelers represent the changing expectations associated with retirement in the contemporary Western world. In addition to the increasing longevity and better health through developments in medical technology in recent years, there is an increased affluence for some older people[3] (King et al 2000). This reconstitutes retirement as a sphere of new opportunities, increasingly exploited through travel, marking a de-differentiation of tourism into retirement (Rojek 1993). Urry observes that "for many reasonably wealthy retired people, life may indeed be akin to a continuous nomadic existence" (2002: 32). Evidence of this is seen in Counts and Counts' (1996) ethnographic study of "RV-ers": itinerant seniors who travel around the U.S. in recreational vehicles identifying positively with the freedom of their mobile life passed, "spending their children's inheritance." Their outlooks are evidence of the development of a "new morality" of ageing (Blaikie 1999: 74) reflected for example through popular culture's newly emerging labels of older people such as "recycled teenagers" or "SAGA-louts."[4]

The growth of retirement travel has also involved a circumscription of particular spaces as appropriate sites for ageing well. Blaikie points out with reference to the U.K. how there has been a "conflation of positive ageing and seaside living" (Blaikie 1997: 629). This relates to the metaphorical association of good old age with warmth and leisure, evidenced in the use of "sunshine" buses (Fennell et al. 1988: 138), the naming of units in residential homes after vistas of nature, such as "rivers, gardens, trees, villages" (Oliver 1999) or the "Sun-city" phenomenon in the U.S. Chaney shows how tourism agencies, keen to exploit this congruence, target the grey market by specific marketing strategies that represent the novelty of holidaying "within the reassurance of tradition" (Chaney 1995: 211). Similarly the popularity of Spain, imagined as a "home from home" (O'Reilly 2000a) rests on its simultaneous foreign yet familiar appeal, known before migration through prior holiday experiences (Rodríguez et al. 1998; King et al 2000). Retiring to Spain seems to appeal as a new rendition of an old classic of "retiring to the sea."

The popularity of Spain as a tourist destination began in earnest in the 1950s and 1960s, evidenced in the rapid development of the costas. Spain's little discovered corners were also proving attractive for a number of self-described "pioneers," often writers and artists, seeking respite from modern life in and around the simple *pueblo blancos* of the hills beyond the coast. It was in the 1980s when the potential of Spain as a destination for seasonal or permanent migration exploded (King et al 2000). Many migrants live in Spain full-time, at least until ill health comes about (Oliver 2004), although some (known as "snowbirds" or "swallows") stay for only the winter months, returning to their native country for the summer (for a typology of migrants, see O'Reilly 2000a: 52–59). The expatriate "community" has a varied composition; among those I spent time with were former social workers and teachers, retired ex-servicemen, a model, an actress, a former spy, but also expatriate workers and ex-colonials who, weary after a lifetime globetrotting had retired, as Bob described, to "their bolthole in the sun."[5] Like the expatriates in the Cayman Islands explored by Amit-Talai, a number of financial, political, and emotional constraints operate on expatriates' ability or desire to return "home" following the end of contracts or retirement (1998: 56). Bob, for example, had spent thirty-five years abroad, was accustomed to the warm climate of Dubai and felt no attachment to England. His criteria for a retirement destination included good weather and the need to be "somewhere with European facilities." Leah on the other hand complained that:

> I'd go home [to the U.K.] straightaway if Len wanted to go. I miss my family too much, but then we've always been "in transit." It was on and off from Nigeria, with the U.K. in between. It was my husband's idea to be here—he still works in the mornings, in insurance.

The particular town and village considered in this ethnography is little different to numerous similar settlements in the South of Spain, varying only in terms of the number of foreigners and concentration of different nationalities in each location. Development is a matter of concern among migrants (Oliver 2002) especially in villages further inland that were previously chosen by migrants for their seclusion, "Spanishness" and lack of development. These are now increasingly marketed to replicate the economic successes of other villages, provoking protest at the spread of the coastal sprawl. In Tocina recently there has been a growing entrenchment of an English-speaking social infrastructure oriented to foreign visitors, at times modelled on a seaside carnivalesque theme. There are a number of English bars (such as Pie Inn the Sky), restaurants (such as the new fish and chip venture, the Codfather), a healthy production of magazines and newspapers (the *Marketplace,* the *Coastal Gazette*), a number of expatriate radio stations (Coastline Radio and Radio Sol Almijara), and shops (including the bookshop WHSmiths), which sell a gamut of products including traditional English sweets, Cornish pasties, and Marmite.

Living in Liminality

Migrant experiences have previously been interpreted through the lens of liminality, and this is certainly apt to understand the identities of older migrants in Spain. I have referred previously to Amit-Talai's exploration of how global economic restructuring manifests a feeling of perpetual limbo for expatriate workers in the Cayman Islands (1998). Malkki's work on Hutu refugees in Tanzania also argues how they are a structurally invisible "abomination" produced, made meaningful by and excluded by the categorical order of the hegemonic nation-state (Malkki 1995). And closer to home, O'Reilly's ethnography of the British on the Costa del Sol (2000a) show expatriates inhabiting a marginal status betwixt and between Spain and the U.K., which, coupled with the tourist orientation of the zone as a space apart compounds the liminality (Graburn 1978; and see Shields 1991 on Brighton in the U.K.). It perhaps also explains the contemporary disdain often leveled at the Costa-del-Sol expatriate (O'Reilly 2000a).

Yet the liminality of older migrants is not purely borne out of the place. Hockey and James (2003) remind us that the inhabitation of age-based identities comes through the rites of passage, and within Western societies retirement is widely understood as a liminal phase, a life course moment "betwixt and between" a categorical working identity and mortality. Indeed, although anthropologists have paid little explicit attention to ageing, of the few ethnographies of clubs or institutions for older people conducted, including those by Hazan (1980), Myerhoff (1986), Hockey (1990), Okely (1990), Jerrome (1992), Huby (1992), and Dawson (2002), most articulate the liminal qualities within. Despite a fragmentation of the life-course and doubts of the rigidity of the rites of passage (Hockey and James 2003), postmodern approaches to ageing continue to reinstate liminal conceptions of retirement as a "transition to a new life" (ibid: 102). Recently emerging discourses of the new old agers as "middlescents" (Blaikie 1999) reflect anti-structural principles, encapsulated in the popular anthem to "grow old disgracefully."

Transforming Self through Travel

Ever noticed how most foreigners you come across here seem to have had two lives. There's their life "before" and their life "after" . . . the opportunities for reinvention are endless. . . . It's liberating, this freedom to become someone else, to leave behind lives that never, frankly, quite fitted us. And amazing how quickly and completely those lives are shed. When you ask people here about what they did before, they often blink in confusion as if that side of their lives belongs in the distant past, or to someone else entirely. . . . Most of us seize the chance to reinvent ourselves. (Article from *Marketplace* magazine, 2005).

The liminal qualities of both site and people manifest repeatedly in migrants' stories, a small number of which I consider here. Willie provides an initial example. He was a man in his fifties who retired early and could be regularly found propping up Bar Antonio in the village, striking up conversation with expatriates and tourists alike. (His limited Spanish meant his communication was limited on that front.) On our first meeting, Willie explained that he used to work in computer technology, although moved because he had got "sick of England":

You know, I got sick of the whole treadmill . . . all the people talked about how much they had, what cars they drive. Whereas here, nobody cares. No one gives a shit who you are. . . . You can have fifty million pesetas in your pocket or nothing at all.

He was keen to learn the Spanish language so that he could take himself off for days at a time to Córdoba and Sevilla: "you know, it's so friendly there, you can go into a bar and get talking. It's like, hey, I'm home!" From the vantage point of his bar stool, he recommended the experience of living in

Spain. "Being with so many nationalities broadens your mind—they can tell you all about Belgium and Germany, etc." At this point, Willy lowers his voice and draws me in closer: "watch out for Doug, though, keep your distance from him. With him," he explained, "everything is *más más más* [more, more, more]. If your wife has two breasts, his has three, you know what I mean?"

Rose, on the other hand, was a retired social worker who had come to Spain following a period of depression not long before I arrived. When we met for tea and a chat at Joy's house, she told me excitedly of how she had felt transformed by the move and said, "home is where I lay my hat. All my most precious things are here. There's nothing left for me in England, I'm settled here and I could never go back as I am a different person now." During the course of our acquaintance, her appearance, hair, clothes, and makeup changed constantly beyond her initially more conservative style. Initially she had come to Spain with her reluctant partner David, but he had expected her to follow him to France the year after, although during my fieldwork she had decided not to go. At a social gathering at the British Legion, she confided to me,

> The thing is, I think he was surprised. He came here last year following me and I think he expected some little woman to follow him if he went back to France. But being here has changed me . . . I think especially as you get older, you reach a point where you think to yourself that you don't want to please everybody else. You do what you want to do. I think it's to do with age.

By contrast, when I first met Margaret, it was in the cool surroundings of the *ambulatorio* (clinic) where she was seated behind a desk to help out as a voluntary translator. Having lived in Spain for some time following a later-life marriage, and following her husband's death, she was constantly busy. Her various commitments included researching her retirement hobby of local Spanish history for her lectures on the Phoenicians to the SAGA holidaymakers at a nearby town. "People ask me what I do all day," she told me, "but I just don't know where the time goes. I used to joke with my husband that I needed another day in the week so that we could have a day off!" (echoing comments made by interviewees in King et al's 2000 study). I tried to keep up with her, including during many Saturday mornings where we called in briefly at the International Club, before walking uphill through the busy, noisy streets of Tocina to a bar where members of the American Club met. On regular occasions I met Julian there, who came to the group following his morning swim. Over an early afternoon beer one afternoon, he told fellow listeners and me how although "he burns the candles at both ends," he doesn't fear getting old: "trick is, Caroline, is to spread yourself around," he explained:

> . . . one month at one place, then you move on, a month next with my son, a couple of months here. . . . 'Course England will always be my home and my

roots will be there, but I didn't want to grow old or stay there—they're all a bunch of fuddy duddies.

A number of themes recur in these stories, which help explain the renewing invigoration that migrants such as Doreen have in wishing to return time and again to Spain. Willy and Rose's story initially suggest that the migration process acts as a new beginning or catalyst for change. Other migrants even used the familiar language of the rites of passage to describe themselves as "a blank slate" by virtue of their travel to Spain or as starting a new chapter of their life. The move becomes a definitive moment of migrants' lives, a point of reference that alters the orientation to life beyond it .[6] As Rose signifies, this fact is compounded by the ageing of migrants and consequent awareness of "time ticking" that makes imperative a need to seize the day.

The presentation of self-growth and independence invested in the travel experience also reconciles with common assertions of individualism made by migrants to me at the beginning of numerous introductions. I was regularly told, "well, I don't know how useful I will be, as I am not a typical migrant" or "not the norm" or "a bit different." Bob, the expatriate from Dubai, for example, saw himself as "a lone operator" and told me, "pick me up and put me anywhere and I'll survive." Likewise, Rachel lived in the village passing her time sewing, weaving, and taking the bus alone to explore destinations such as Córdoba, Cádiz, and Barcelona. She also told me how she kept her distance from the social circle, claiming, "I'm an independent person, not an easy person." For others, these claims are reinforced by reference to their journey and adaptation as a struggle, as Rose explained to me, "You have to be tough to survive it here." The movement process is understood to trigger a strong individualism, self-sufficiency and independence, as Robin demonstrates:

> It wasn't a problem when we came to Tocina. We'd been expats [in Central Africa] for twenty-five years, away from our roots in other countries where they didn't speak the language. We had cut our roots with England. . . . I could be plonked in the Sahara and it wouldn't be a problem. We are extroverts, but also by nature very solitary, and wary of being involved in a clique. I think you carry yourself with you, don't you?

Despite the claims to independence of migrants–and its enhancement through travel- there is, on the other hand, evidence of an egalitarian communitas. David, Rose's partner, surprised himself when he came to enjoy life in Spain despite his initial rejection. He was attracted by the spirit of cooperation, as he put it:

> It's easy to make friends here, much easier. People are very friendly, you know when you go around to someone's house you are greeted like an old friend. I suppose I find that shallow a lot of the time, but there's good sides to it . . . people are really willing to pass on information and show a willingness to help you out.

The absence of economic ties and paid work commitments mean that relationships are made through periods of socializing at each other's houses, clubs, and bars or through voluntary work. Moreover, as my fieldnotes suggest, the looseness of holiday relations infect sociability:

> On the way down to the British Legion, I see people I've never seen before walking along, and I say hello. That's what you do in a holiday place isn't it? It's so easy to make friends here, almost too easy. I think about the countless times that I have been involved in long conversations with strangers here that began absolutely out of the blue. And then I think about the friends I have here, and realize that I have got friends, but in this context, it's the people that you have the least differences with rather than those that you could have the most in common with.

Certainly "the scene" is very welcoming to newcomers, and acquaintances are easily and quickly formed (O'Reilly 2000b). These may be surprisingly intimate; sometimes migrants' friends are described using the idiom of kinship (Bell and Coleman 1999: 7), as "like a sister or brother." Yet these relationships emerge quite spontaneously and are sometimes made on rather arbitrary grounds. One night I met a close-knit "breakaway" faction of members of the American club who met for video nights together on Wednesdays. A man walked into the *tapas* bar where the group met. He had been told to come there by a member who had, quite by chance, heard him speaking in an American accent in a supermarket and invited him along. On the basis of this tenuous link, the members greeted him like a long-lost friend and accepted him with enthusiasm, inviting him to share their *tapas*.

Being Who You Want to Be?

> But it's also disconcerting when everyone you meet is shiny new, seemingly without history or continuity. So much has now to be taken on trust. . . . And as the past becomes literally a foreign country, so some elements of truth can be lost in translation. Back home, my children were naturally child geniuses, our last home palatial, and my career a glittering, award-studded success. And who's to say any different? (Article from *Marketplace,* 2005: 53).

Early into my fieldwork, I was visiting Joy for a cup of tea and biscuits at her house in an *urbanisation* in the town. The room was strewn with pieces of embroidery, paintings, and cards discarded from her artwork, and while I was enjoying the view of the blurry distant haze of the sea through the patio windows, she told me ominously, "everyone here is running away from something. Oh yes, she said, "dig deep enough and you'll find it." Similarly, at a dinner with the American club, Bradley asked about my study and told me, "well, I heard the Brits come here to reinvent themselves," which prompted David to join in. "It's more that there's suspicion about other people's backgrounds. . . . It's strange, I thought I'd be asked a lot more what I did for a job, but I don't get asked at all or hardly," he expressed. Meanwhile, contradicting David's statement entirely was Terri's observation: "people here ask a lot about your past, why you came and what brought you here. That galls me a bit."

These observations, although fundamentally different in content, all share a common concern in articulating myths of reinvention that trigger suspicion and concerns about trust and privacy. These myths, I suggest, reflect a conflict at the heart of aspirational movement. The conflict emerges, on one hand, from the embrace of the looseness and freedom governing social expectations, in which liminal travel gives rise to possibilities for starting afresh and forging positive social relationships in the here and now. On the other hand, however, there are contrasting individualistic drives to know more securely of self and others in the finite period of active old age. Indeed, the self-reliance and independence that is fostered through the travel experience can be potentially read by others as a claim of exclusivity and superiority (see Bailey 1971), causing tensions in social relationships. There are inconsistencies and contrasting messages in the ethos of migrants as both preserving and desiring an egalitarian social basis and being strongly individualistic, which potentially undermines it.

Cohen points out how in Whalsay, Shetland, similar ideals of self-sufficiency, independence, and individual distinctiveness conflict with an espoused egalitarianism (Cohen 1978). In Spain, it occurs because the strength of individual character forged through travel risks disrupting the level playing field of egalitarian communitas, particularly given the backdrop of face-to-face relations in village life. For instance, following my discussions with Willy, I was surprised when Nigel, a mild-mannered and bohemian character who drank in the same village bar as Willy, unexpectedly told me forcefully, "I'm not one to talk about people," he said, "but there's only so much of Willy I can take. We're just such different personalities." The cause of the problem was theorized in the expatriate society, as Bierta, a German woman expressed at one of my social visits to her house:

> All the people who come here come with different sets of values. I asked one American woman what class she was and she told me her father earned £60,000. We're all differently educated, we have different manners, money, ways of talking. Before there was a smaller group of foreigners and they all knew you. Now there's cliques and nastiness. I get classed as the German one—I'm known for being outspoken . . . I've tried to moderate it.

In Whalsay, different orientations of egalitarianism and individual distinctiveness are overcome through allocations of varying and distinctive characteristics in which villagers present a front of cultural integrity (ibid). In this case, the transience and fluidity disrupts an enduring sense of cultural integrity. In fact, different tactics that utilize the excuse of regular comings and goings are themselves developed to limit the potentially infinite number of social bonds. For example, when Beth, an American woman arrived in the village, she described how Elizabeth, the longest-standing foreign resident in the village, literally ignored her friendly overtures and turned her head the other way as she passed. Elizabeth justified this by recourse to her seniority and longevity and explained, "I came here to escape people like that!" Original migrants claim a "local absolutism" not based on any sense of primordialism, but manifested by a "morality of stasis" (Rapport 1997: 75) against newcomers invading their home. It is therefore common for distinctions to be made using a claim of nostalgia for the "interesting people" that used to live in Spain, while expressing dismay at those moving en masse now. One couple of migrants who had been in the area for fifteen years even named them "the lottery winners," alluding to their money but lack of class and taste.

The major concern in the egalitarian lifestyle of leisured sociability is the suspicion that people can potentially manage their self-presentation in order to "deliberately attempt to mislead others by signalling an attitude to which they don't subscribe" (Bailey 1971: 113). The perceived irrelevance of what one did before means in effect, "no-one knows who you really are" (observed by O'Reilly 2000a: 112). This is heightened by the sociable informality of exchanges, in which people's surnames are not widely known; rather, nicknames (such as "Cod'n'Chips"), current job roles ("the woman who is the secretary of the fine art club"), and stereotypes ("the music lady") are used as references. Even Margaret, who was a key member of the associative life, confessed that she found it difficult to remember regular members' names. The consequence of this is the harboring of suspicions, summed up by Kate, a woman in her sixties in the village who observed, "You'll never know the true person. Everyone puts it on. They'll tell you something, and you're sure that its porkie-pies." O'Reilly suggests, "There are problems of mistrust and doubt in a situation where personal histories are not shared and futures are ambiguous" (2000b: 246).

The pride in migrants' individuality and autonomy preceding and developed by migration also strengthens the urge to keep oneself guarded. People regularly told me that although they were content to engage in social niceties, they "kept themselves to themselves." As Elizabeth, in a letter, remarked, "I find it very difficult to reveal anything private." Another friend told me about her new landlady: "She's okay, at least I think she is. I mean I don't really know her that well, and you know, you shouldn't judge a book by its cover." And on various occasions I was warned not to "be sucked in" by seemingly innocent people. This, however, makes one prone to insularity, as Mary, a younger woman pointed out:

> You can't confide in people here. I wouldn't let personal things away, because you don't know how others take it. For you, it could be really serious, but another person could read it lightly. You all take things in different ways don't you?

Ironically however, as Bok suggests, "gossip increases whenever information is both scarce and desirable—whenever people want to find out more about others than they are able to" (1984: 91). John, for instance was known as a recluse from the start of his time in Spain, when he and his wife were among the first (and small) set of cosmopolitan migrants. He explained how there was a lot of "infighting" among early migrants. "Our opinions just did not meet," he told me, "and anyway, my wife and I just came here to retire to ourselves, grow things in the garden, that sort of thing." In a rare chat with him, I was told, "I keep myself a closed book, I won't let too much of myself away." However, his unwillingness to engage with others simply made him all the more interesting. When I told Elizabeth that I was to visit John that afternoon, I was told, "oh him, yes, well I'd be keen to know all about him; I know nothing about him, even though he's been here for years. He's a mystery, that one" The extent to which such guarding occurs is revealed by Marge, the disc jockey on the local expatriate radio. She told me after my publicity slot in which I had assured confidentiality to the people with whom I spoke:

> That's a good thing you said. . . . People all know each other here, you see. I find it difficult to get people to even come on the radio; they won't come on and say anything in case people recognize their voice. We call this place Rumorsville.

These tendencies are indeed confirmed by the mawkish titles of the regional sections of one of the ubiquitous expatriate magazines, the *Coastal Gazette,* including "Herradura Whispers" (by "Adam Hearsay"), "Almuñecar Echoes" (by "Sir Veil Lance"), "Torre twitterings," the "Axarquia briefs," and "Tocina Noises" (by "The Moles"). Many stories circulating in the expatriate scene cast extreme aspersions on people, portraying them as alcoholics, crooks, mentally ill, or involved in dubious activities. Nor was I immune: during my time in Spain I found myself, for example, apparently involved in a number of improbable affairs, having no idea of the source of the fictions. The over-the-top stories confirm Rapport's observations of village life in the U.K., in which he found "individuals guided as if by a dramatic sense, writing themselves into 'reel life melodramas' with related machinations of character and plot" (1997: 162).

It seems to me, however, that given the precariousness of expatriate society, extreme stories also function to provoke refutations of the stories and evidence of what one really is. For instance, I talked to Terri, a woman in her late sixties who provoked suspicion by regular trips from her house with a couple of men. She told me of some stories circulating and explained:

> Oh, don't worry . . . they had me down as a prostitute. . . . When I lived on the coast, I had some Jehovah's Witnesses as friends. They have to travel around in pairs, so these two men used to come around every week. It was even worse when we went to functions together. They'd come and pick us up in really nice cars, you know, as they do. Well, of course I was seen as a high-class prostitute. It was even funnier when you consider that neither of us groups drank, and that we were actually discussing the Bible when we were supposed to be . . . well!

The extreme aspersion of this allegation succeeded in soliciting other vital information to establish what Terri was doing, if not engaging in prostitution. The stories strip away any potential masquerade created in self-presentation and reduce the person under discussion to his/her naked individuality. In response to the allegation, individuals are forced to depart from the anonymity that the egalitarian nature of society fosters in "being who one wants to be." Rather, migrants must state more explicitly who they are, preferably revealing some evidence to refute the false story.

Despite the less-than-desirable consequences of suspicions arising from the simultaneously liberating possibilities of the liminal space, Jerrome points out how older people remain particularly in need of social validation in one form or another (Jerrome 1990). In fact, friendships in the expatriate context are perhaps even more important given the absence or limited extent of kin and work relationships. As Rapport reminds us, "[t]he denser the relations, the more the evidence of one's own existence, the greater the significance of that existence, the more exact the nature of that existence is made" (1993:151). But even Elizabeth, a woman now growing older in the village she moved to some forty years previously, felt uncomfortable in negotiating the tensions around relationships in the liminal environment. Reflecting fears both of trusting in the community and the consequences of individual self-sufficiency, she told me that even after all her time there:

> I don't know who to trust. Maybe I've made a mistake coming out here? Sometimes, I feel like turning away all my visitors as I need to be alone. Sometimes I do and it doesn't worry me at all. Yet, I try not to do it too much, as I'm frightened that nobody would come at all and I'd die alone.

Conclusion

> Anyway, almost nobody here is who they say they are at first. They aren't even who someone else thinks they are. In this place you get at least three versions of everything, and if you're lucky one of them is true. That's if you're lucky. (Atwood 1996: 149)

Doreen's opening explanation of the lure of Spain highlights the immense range of possibilities for personal renewal through new friendships, a social life to please and the space and autonomy to find oneself in aspirational migration. The liminal characteristics of both the cultural geography and cultural construction of older people outside the working life encourage this transformative potential of travel and the opportunities for self-discovery. The disparate body of migrants unite through their common investment in the site as a space for the realization of life projects in an "imagined communitas" where, the maxim has it, the past is less important than the present. This chapter demonstrates the consequences–both positive and negative- of this liminality in terms of the personal identities and social relationships of older migrants embarking on their dream new lives in Spain.

First, the analysis reveals how myths of travel are articulated that present the move as offering space and freedom for the conclusion of migrants' personal life projects. Yet, second, it also demonstrates how the management of social relations is difficult in the transient and liminal context where there is an almost infinite number of potential friendships and no means of assessing who is trustworthy or not. This is particularly heightened by the tension between the imagined communitas and a current of self-sufficiency and individualism that underpins the very migration process to the site. The same dynamic that drives older persons to migrate is ultimately counterproductive to the desired characteristics of the society as fundamentally egalitarian. Resulting dynamics work to ensure that in this migrant context, the consequences of being in a condition in which "you can be who you want to be" work against that very possibility.

In considering the consequences of liminality and transience in privileged movement, I end with some observations relevant to the wider study of migrancy in anthropology. The strength of anthropological engagement with globalization and cultural complexity to date lies in its attention to the maintenance and reconfiguration of cultural identities beyond place (Hastrup and Olwig 1997), with research commonly taking on a trans- or multilocal dimension (Hannerz 2003). Analyses tend to explore how "community" in its myriad forms is transformed by creolizing and hybridizing processes, with individuals reproducing a sense of place in the process. Not only does the "community" remain intact, but there is a sense that it does so *despite* transience. A focus on community in globalization need not, however, limit itself to this remit. Because attention to transience and an interrogation of the consequences of social negotiations in fleeting encounters on the move do not reduce the anthropologist's job to a meaningless pursuit. In fact, a consideration of attempts at constructing meaningful social relationships and identities formed in travel is vital, particularly in analyses of privileged travel. Much can be gained in considering individuals' negotiation of precarious face-to-face but historically shallow communities as well as analyses of the problematics of these (Amit and Rapport 2002). Moreover, in recognizing that these different and new constitutions of attempted community exist, and analyzing their associated dynamics through ethnographic accounts, forces a realization that some are formed not despite transience but—partly at least—because of it.

Notes

1. An observation noted by O'Reilly (2000a) and repeated by several people in this study.

2. All names of people and places are pseudonyms.
3. For instance, two-thirds of migrants in King et al's study of British retirement migration to the Mediterranean were from social classes 1 and 2 (2000: 76).
4. A term described to me by a recently retired woman, which is an ironic play on both SAGA, a U.K.-based company that caters to the over-fifty crowd, and "lager louts," a term applied to hedonistic drinkers.
5. In King et al's study, there was a significant representation of, "people who have not lived in Britain very much, who have had mobile international careers and who have biographical backgrounds in the former British colonies" (ibid: 124).
6. The discontinuity of the movement is represented as something like a "career break" (Humphrey 1993: 166) in the narrative life stories.

References

Ahmed, Sara, Claudia Castañeda, Anne-Marie Fortier and Mimi Sheller. 2003. "Introduction: Uprootings/Regroundings: Questions of Home and Migration." In *Uprootings/Regroundings: Questions of Home and Migration*, eds. S. Ahmed , et al. Oxford: Berg.

Amit, Vered and Nigel Rapport. 2002. *The Trouble with Community: Anthropological Reflections on Movement, Identity and Collectivity.* London and Sterling, VA: Pluto Press.

Amit-Talai, Vered. 1998. "Risky Hiatuses and the Limits of the Social Imagination: Expatriacy in the Cayman Islands." In *Migrants of Identity: Perceptions of Home in a World of Movement*, eds. N. Rapport and A. Dawson. London: Berg.

Atwood, Margaret. 1996. *Bodily Harm.* London: Vintage Books.

Bailey, Frederick G. 1971. *Gifts and Poison: The Politics of Reputation.* Oxford: Basil Blackwell.

Bell, Sandra and Simon Coleman. 1999. "The Anthropology of Friendship: Enduring Themes and Future Possibilities." In *The Anthropology of Friendship,* eds. S. Bell and S. Coleman. Oxford: Berg.

Blaikie, Andrew. 1999. *Ageing and Popular Culture.* Cambridge: Cambridge University Press.

———. 1997. "Beside the Sea: Visual Imagery, Ageing and Heritage." *Ageing and Society* 17(6): 629–648.

Bok, Sissela. 1984. *On the Ethics of Concealment and Revelation.* Oxford: Oxford University Press.

Chaney, David. 1995 "Creating Memories: Some Images of Aging in Mass Tourism." In *Images of Ageing: Cultural Representations of Later Life,* eds. M. Featherstone and A. Wernick. London: Routledge.

Clifford, James. 1992. "Traveling Cultures." In *Cultural Studies,* eds. L. Grossberg, C. Nelson and P. Treichler . London: Routledge.

Cohen, Anthony. P. 1978. "'The Same-but Different'": The Allocation of Identity in Whalsay, Shetland." *Sociological Review* 26(3): 449–470.

———. 1994. *Self Consciousness: An Alternative Anthropology of Identity.* London: Routledge.

Cohen, Tammy. 2005. "Life after Spain." *The Marketplace* 54:52.

Counts, Dorothy Ayers and David Counts. 1996. *Over the Next Hill: An Ethnography of RVing Seniors in North America.* Peterborough, Ontario: Broadview Press.

Craik, Jennifer. 1997. "The Culture of Tourism." IN *Touring Cultures: Transformations of Travel and Theory,* eds. C. Rojek and J. Urry. London: Routledge.

Dawson, Andrew. 2002. "The Mining Community and the Ageing Body: Towards a Phenomenology of Community?" In *Realizing Community: Concepts, Social Relationships and Sentiments,* ed. V. Amit. London: Routledge.

Fennell, Graham, Chris Philippson and Helen Evers. 1988. *The Sociology of Old Age.* Milton Keynes: Open University Press.

Graburn, Nelson. 1978. "Tourism: The Sacred Journey" In *Hosts and Guests: The Anthropology of Tourism,* ed. Valene L. Smith. Pennsylvania: University of Pennsylvania Press.

Gray, John. 2002. "Community as Place-Making: Ram Auctions in the Scottish Borderlands." In *Realizing Community: Concepts, Social Relationships and Sentiments,* ed. V. Amit. London: Routledge.

Gupta, Akhil and James Ferguson. 1997. "Introduction." To *Culture, Power, Place: Explorations in Critical Anthropology,* eds. A. Gupta and J. Ferguson. Durham: Duke University Press.

Gustafson, Per. 2002. "Tourism and Seasonal Retirement Migration." *Annals of Tourism Research* 29 (4): 899–918.

Hannerz, Ulf. 2003. "Several Sites in One." In *Globalisation: Studies in Anthropology,* ed. T. H. Eriksen. London: Pluto Press.

Hastrup, Kirsten and Karen. F. Olwig. 1997. "Introduction." To *Siting Culture: The Shifting Anthropological Object,* eds. K. F. Olwig and K. Hastrup. London: Routledge.

Hazan, Haim. 1980. *The Limbo People: A Study of the Constitution of the Time Universe among the Aged.* London: Routledge.

Hockey, Jennifer. 1990. *Experiences of Death: An Anthropological Account.* Edinburgh: Edinburgh University Press.

Hockey, Jennifer and Allison James. 2003. *Social Identities across the Life Course.* Hampshire: Palgrave.

Huby, Guro. 1992. "Trapped in the Present: The Past, Present and Future of a Group of Old People in East London." In *Contemporary Futures: Perspectives from Social Anthropology,* ed. S. Wallman. London: Routledge.

Humphrey, Robin. 1993. "Life Stories and Social Careers: Ageing and Social Life in an Ex-Mining Town." *Sociology* 27(1): 166–178.

Jerrome, Dorothy. 1992. *Good Company: An Anthropological Study of Old People in Groups.* Edinburgh: Edinburgh University Press.

———. 1990. "Intimate Relations." In *Ageing in Society,* eds. J. Bond and P. Coleman. London: Sage.

King, Russell, Tony Warnes and Allan Williams. 2000. *Sunset Lives: British Retirement Migration to the Mediterranean.* Oxford and New York: Berg.

Laslett, Peter. 1989. *A Fresh Map of Life: The Emergence of the Third Age.* Basingstoke: Macmillan.

Linger, Daniel. T. 2001. *No One Home: Brazilian Selves Remade in Japan.* Stanford: Stanford University Press.

Malkki, Liisa. 1995. *Purity and Exile: Violence, Memory and National Cosmology among Hutu Refugees in Tanzania.* Chicago: University of Chicago Press.

Myerhoff, Barbara. 1986. "Life Not Death in Venice: Its Second Life." In *The Anthropology of Experience,* eds. V. Turner and E. M. Bruner. Urbana: University of Illinois Press.

Noy, Chaim. 2004. "This Trip Really Changed Me: Backpackers' Narratives of Self Change." *Annals of Tourism Research* 31(1).

Okely, Judith. 1990. "Clubs for the le troisième âge: 'Communitas' or Conflict?" In *Anthropology and the Riddle of the Sphinx: Paradoxes of Change in the Life Course,* ed. P. Spencer. London: Routledge.

Oliver, Caroline. 2006. "More Than a Tourist: Distinction, Old Age and the Selective Consumption of Tourist-Space." In *Narratives of Place and Self: Consumption and Representation in Tourism,* eds. K. Meethan, A. Anderson and S. Miles. CAB International.

———. 2004. "Cultural influence in migrants' negotiations of death: The case of retired migrants in Spain." *Mortality* 9(3):235–253.

———. 2002. "Killing the Golden Goose? Debates About Tradition in an Andalucian Village." *Journal of Mediterranean Studies* 12(1): 169–189.

———. 1999. "Ordering the Disorderly," *Education and Ageing* 14(2): 171–185.

O'Reilly, Karen. 2000a. *The British on the Costa-Del-Sol: Transnational Identities and Local Communities.* London: Routledge.

———. 2000b. "Trading Intimacy for Liberty: Women on the Costa-Del-Sol." In *Gender and Migration in Southern Europe,* eds. F. Anthias and G. Lazaridis. Oxford: Berg.

Olwig, Karen Fog. 1997. "Cultural sites: sustaining a home in a deterritorialized world" In *Sitting Culture: The Shifting Anthropological Object,* eds. Kirsten Hastrup and Karen Fog Olwig. London and New York: Routledge.

Rapport, Nigel. 1993. *Diverse World Views in an English Village.* Edinburgh: Edinburgh University Press.

Rapport, Nigel. 1997. "The Morality of Locality: On the Absolutism of Land-Ownership in an English Village." In *The Ethnography of Moralities,* ed. S. Howell. London: Routledge.

Rodriguez, Vicente, Gloria Fernández-Mayoralas and Fermina Rojo. 1998. "European Retirees on the Costa del Sol: A Cross National Comparison." *International Journal of Population Geography* 4: 183–200.

Rojek, Chris. 1993. *Ways of Escape: Modern Transformations in Leisure and Travel.* London: Macmillan.

Shields, Rob. 1991. *Places on the Margins: Alternative Geographies of Modernity.* London: Routledge.

Urry, John. 1990. "The 'Consumption' of Tourism." *Sociology* 24(1) 23–35.

———. 2002. *The Tourist Gaze: Leisure and Travel in Contemporary Societies.* London: Sage.

Williams, Allan M. and C. Michael Hall. 2000. "Tourism and Migration: New Relationships between Production and Consumption." *Tourism Geographies* 2(5): 5–27.

9

Privileged Time

Volunteers' Experiences At a Spiritual Educational Retreat Center in Hawai'i

Margaret C. Rodman

Kalani Oceanside Retreat is "an educational nonprofit organization that celebrates Hawaii, nature, culture and wellness."[1] Located in a rural area on the big island of Hawaii, it is about an hour's drive from the town of Hilo. Molten lava flows into the sea at the end of the road to Kalani, and Hawaii Volcanoes National Park is a half-day adventure away. *Kalani Honua* means "harmony of heaven and earth" in Hawaiian. This is a powerful place of bare rocks, starry nights, and big surf on black-sand beaches. A tropical sensorium softens the hard edges: scarlet hibiscus, fragrant plumeria, misty rains, sweet pineapples. Hawaii is synonymous with paradise, and travel to such a destination is easily equated with privilege.

Vered Amit has organized this volume around the scope and implications of the privileged circumstances that accompany certain forms of contemporary mobility. This chapter explores privileged travel to a privileged place. The focus is neither on guests nor staff at Kalani, but on people who are in between those categories. "Resident volunteers" pay a maximum of $500 a month and work thirty hours a week for at least a three-month period at Kalani. How is time a privileged resource in this form of travel? How does travel in the context of volunteering at Kalani foster and yet limit community? What relationships manifest here between time, space, community, and capitalism? What links do volunteers posit between Hawaii as a place and their personal transformation? How do volunteers' inner journeys intersect with their real-world trips to Kalani and to similar destinations on a circuit of retreat centers?

Kalani's Privileged Travelers

Kalani looks like a summer camp crossed with a tourist resort. Guests and staff occupy rooms in two-story, quasi-Polynesian buildings, as well as smaller cottages and a camping area. There is no air conditioning; screened bedroom walls let breezes in and give a sense of living outdoors. Life centers on the swimming pool and adjacent hot tubs, as well as on the *lanai*, which is an open-walled, cafeteria-style restaurant.

The use of space is a bit unconventional in that the pool area is clothing optional after 3:00 p.m. The public beach down the road from Kalani is always clothing optional. Areas that would be lounges in other resorts are yoga, meditation, and dance spaces at Kalani. There are also two large Quonset-type structures for workshops ranging from contra dance to yoga teacher training to Body Electric, which is a workshop that focuses on men giving pleasure to men. Kalani attracts gay men through its marketing, and its gay-positive environment encourages a sense of the place as both safe and edgy, physical and spiritual. Kalani is, one volunteer told me, "somewhere between an ashram and a whore house."

Except for a handful of Hawaiian employees, everyone at Kalani is a traveler in that they came there from somewhere else. Not all are recent arrivals. The founder and director has been there for more than thirty years. Guests come for short stays of a few days to a few weeks, mainly to participate in workshops. They are, in a sense, the most privileged travelers in that their visits to Kalani require the most money.

There is another category, however, between guest and paid staff, that of resident volunteer. These are the people on whom my research focused. The privilege that volunteers bring to Kalani is time. They are expected to stay for at least three months and many stay longer and/or return regularly to volunteer at Kalani. A few had been there for as long as six years.

In 2005, resident volunteers went through an application process to work and live at Kalani. Some questions on the application addressed people's familiarity with group living situations and their "relationship to work," including their ability to give and receive direction. Applicants were also asked to share "insights about themselves," including: "Where are you in your personal journey?" When volunteers arrived at Kalani, the website promised, they would receive a journal: Your journal "can be a way of capturing your journey into our community and memorializing its lessons so that you can maximize its value after you have left." Volunteers received the same meals as the guests. They had access to all facilities, and accommodation in staff quarters—shared rooms or private 64 sq. ft. A-frames—in exchange for paying $1,500 for the first three months and working thirty hours a week. (Guests paid between $105 and $240 per night). Most resident volunteers worked in the kitchen, housekeeping, or maintenance departments, but some with particular skills worked on construction, landscaping, or other special projects. The fee structure has changed over the years. Initially volunteers paid nothing, working in exchange for room and board. As recently as 1997, volunteers paid just $100 per month for the first three months, and nothing more if they stayed longer. The fees steadily increased as management sought to recover costs and to attract volunteers who were more focused and older. As someone with long-term experience at Kalani put it:

> Back when it was only $300 [for three months], the types of applicants or volunteers tended to be a little bit more of a younger crowd because I think it was more accessible for students and those with lower incomes. And I think there was also a little bit more of an earthy, hippie, alternative culture . . . crowd that came through. Although right now it's almost a little bit more like the new-age, earth-conscious person who has money, who is coming here.

When I conducted research at Kalani in 2005, many different financial arrangements were in play, with the most senior volunteers paying nothing and new arrivals paying $1,500 for three months. Some regarded Kalani as a bargain even at the higher fee levels, but others felt the fees affected people's attitudes toward work: "if I'm already paying 500 bucks a month to be here and then I have to work four days a week . . . I don't know how excited I am about going the extra mile for somebody, you know what I mean?" Some of those shouldering the higher fees were well aware that they were paying guests as well as workers and sometimes expressed a sense of entitlement or privilege as guests.

The spatial boundaries between guests and staff were blurred. Guests, volunteers, and staff used the same spaces—for example, the dining area, and the pool—at the same time. Nobody wore name tags, uniforms, or anything that marked a difference between guests, paid staff, or volunteers. They participated in the same yoga classes and activities such as volleyball and hula classes. In fact, it could be hard for new arrivals to tell who was a Kalani guest and who was working there. Some who came as guests went on to become resident volunteers and then paid staff; former staff and volunteers have returned to visit as guests.

Resident volunteers were not the only kind of volunteers at Kalani. Additional categories further blurred the boundaries between tourists who visited Kalani as paying guests and staff who worked there for wages. Volunteer scholars applied to come for one month, paid $1,000, and worked twenty hours a week. In 2005, Kalani introduced a third volunteer category, volunteer guest. No application was required; volunteer guests could come for a variable period of two weeks to three months, stay in whatever level of guest accommodation they choose, and receive a discount in exchange for working six hours per week.[3] A fourth category, artist-in-residence, offered writers and artists who wished to stay at Kalani for two weeks to three months the opportunity to apply for a stipend to reduce the cost of guest accommodation by as much as $1,600 per month.

This chapter focuses on resident volunteers (hereafter called "volunteers"). It explores how volunteers at Kalani manifest a particular kind of contemporary mobility in which (1) time can be as significant a resource in privileged travel as money, credentials, or skills; (2) self-styled loners produce an ever-shifting community that critiques yet operates within capitalism; and (3) Hawaii as a travel destination is attributed with the power to change lives. The conclusion ties up these threads in terms of the volunteer experience as both an inner and an outer journey with destinations on circuits that include but also extend far beyond Kalani.

Privileged Time

In contrast to other forms of mobility described in this volume, time is the key privilege that Kalani volunteers enjoy. For North Americans in the workforce, time often seems in shorter supply than money; but volunteers at Kalani often have more time than money and their privilege is to be able to spend months or even years in a place most could visit only for a few days or weeks. How did people get the time they need to be resident volunteers at Kalani? The key was to trust one's gut feelings and to see time as very precious. A variety of paths led people to this twofold realization.

I interviewed forty-two resident volunteers and paid staff at Kalani in the winter of 2005.[2] These men and women ranged in age from young people who had just finished college to retirees in their sixties. They were nearly all white, of seemingly middle-class backgrounds. Most were North American, including a handful of Canadians, but volunteers at that time also came from Germany and the United Kingdom. Sexual orientation added variety to the straight majority, with a transgendered volunteer, a few lesbians, and many who identified as gay men.

The first question I asked was, "How did you come to volunteer at Kalani?" The responses emphasized the importance of following one's intuition as well as acting decisively to break old patterns and step into an experiential space that opened people to new possibilities. Larry was going through a marital breakup. He visited with his "energy worker," who introduced him to Kalani:

> I just thought I would like to be here, it would be a good place for a transformation, which is the key word of this place. And so we visited here and I thought it was really beautiful and I met the person who was in charge of personnel at the time, and I just had an amazing feeling about her, and I thought, well, if everyone here's like this, this is where I'd like to be.

An affordable working vacation was important to Amy, a woman in her thirties who first came to Kalani when it cost $300 for three months:

I was just randomly searching [the Internet] for a vacation. I found the Web page and the three-month resident volunteer program. It sounded perfect, because I was experiencing some heavy job burnout and I just knew I had to get something different. I was doing solar electric stuff—installation and sales, working for a small company . . . I really liked my job, but I had done it for two and a half years and I was just ready for a change. So Kalani sounded perfect when I saw a way to have a working vacation, because I don't have a lot of money.

Finding the time to get away for three months was easiest for young people. Some volunteers, especially during the summer, were as young as eighteen, but most came to Kalani after college, like Jacqueline who wanted more hands-on, experiential learning when she finished her B.A. in philosophy in the U.S. She moved into a tree house in a friend's backyard and worked six part-time jobs in order to make the necessary money. Interested in permaculture, she was attracted to Hawaii because of its diverse ecosystems. She decided "just to take a leap of faith and come to Hawaii . . . just get the ticket and see what happens . . . not really knowing what was going to happen. What's to lose? [I feel that] I'm taken care of, I'll be alright." She ended up at Kalani by a chain of apparent misadventures that she came to see as putting her in exactly the right place at the right time.

For Neil, Kalani seemed like a dream summer job:

I first heard about Kalani during my junior year of college, I was twenty-one and I was looking for a summer experience that I would enjoy and remember for the rest of my life before I moved into the workforce. I had recently come out of the closet and I was getting used to gay culture and feeling comfortable with that, and I'd explored just a very little bit. And so in my mind I thought, well, if I could go anywhere in the world and have any summer job, where would I want to go? And I decided that I would really like to experience some gay cultures and I was looking for a gay resort in Hawaii. That was my criteria for my dream summer job.

Neil found an ad for Kalani in a gay magazine, volunteered for three summers in a row, then moved to Hawaii.

Making the time to volunteer at Kalani was also relatively easy for retired people. One straight couple had retired from working for the Federal Emergency Management Agency in Washington, D.C. She had some interest in yoga, and he in the "Power of Now" evening sessions at Kalani, but they really volunteered because it was in Hawaii and something different. Ironically, they found Kalani when they were looking on the Internet for a coffee called Kalani that they had enjoyed.

For many, however, making the time to volunteer at Kalani meant a major lifestyle change and financial sacrifice. A Canadian woman who had worked as a legal secretary told me that her job had become more stressful and she increasingly disliked life in a polluted, crowded city. She reached a turning point five years ago when she decided to leave what she called "crazy life." She was willing to live with much less money and fewer material things in exchange for free time, clean air, a connection with nature, the opportunity to live in community, and the chance to develop her yoga practice:

> I had been to a yoga retreat for a weekend. . . . They often attract a lot of needy people. But that one was very different. Every person seemed to be totally empowered and by the end of the weekend, after talking to these people, I realized that they had all quit "crazy life" and were doing what they wanted to do. One was a doctor and he was now running a horse farm or something. But they were all doing what they wanted to do.
>
> So I went home that Sunday night—that weekend changed my life. I went to work Monday and all day at work something was churning inside me. And at the end of the workday, I walked home. It was about two hours, and when I got home I had made the decision. I was going to quit working in a law office and that meant I would have to sell my house and move out of [the city] because I couldn't afford one without the other. If one went, they both went. So that was it! I'd made the decision and never looked back.

Some volunteers had no career or permanent work when they came to Kalani. But many others left or sold their businesses to free up not only the cash but also the time to volunteer. Fred sold his catering business. Alex sold his construction business. Mina left a high power job in New York's fashion industry. Dale's dot-com business was thriving, so he got out and came to Kalani as a volunteer just before the tech stocks crashed. Maria sold the health-food business she ran with her husband when their marriage broke up. She followed her daughter's suggestion and came to Kalani to begin her journey into a new life. Francis was an officer with the Royal Canadian Mounted Police (RCMP). He told me:

> In 1990, about halfway through my career, I had reached the pinnacle of what I wanted to do with the RCMP, which was to be an instructor at the academy; I had just got a promotion and I had a girlfriend, so on the outside everything looked like I had "made it," yet inside there was a deep sense of dissatisfaction of not being fully myself, of not having arrived . . . not being happy, basically. I left my girlfriend; I took a fifteen-month sabbatical from the RCMP—leave without pay—and I went to live at . . . Kripalu Centre. That's when my spiritual search started.

Volunteers in all age groups sometimes first arrived as guests. Alex told me he visited Kalani as a guest for a yoga workshop for two weeks: "As soon as I came here, the question that kept occurring to me over and over was "Why do I live where I live? . . . Why do I live in [a big mid-Atlantic city]"? He had lived there for fifteen years, but when he came back from visiting Kalani the question would not go away. He concluded, "I need to go back to [Kalani] and live there for a while and let it be less of a vacation and see if I still feel that way." When I interviewed him, he had been a resident volunteer for several months and he did still feel that way. He was considering selling his house and business and moving permanently to Hawaii.

Sandy was transitioning from male to female when she came to Kalani as a guest:

> I stayed a week and went through [changes] in that I would just sit here and cry and laugh, and it was fun and hard and hard (laughs), and I decided I needed another week! So I stayed another week. [Then] I realized I had to live here. I wasn't really sure why, or what was up with that. [But] I went home [to San Francisco] where I had a three-bedroom home I lived alone in, packed with all the usuals—guest room, office, and a shop.

Sandy sold her house and shop, and got rid of most of her possessions in the San Francisco area. She came back to Kalani as a volunteer. For her, and for many of the others I spoke with, Kalani provides a place and a community that encourages self-transformation. Ironically, time is the key resource that makes it possible to volunteer at Kalani, but volunteering there also buys people time. As Alex put it, he has the luxury of time at Kalani to allow what he should do next to unfold:

> I would say definitely the common thread is that people here are in some kind of transition. . . . Some people are in a state of limbo where they're trying to find a new career, but they don't know what that is; so rather than just sit at home and watch TV, they wanted to do something. Or maybe they don't have the money, so they come here—they could afford this, just to hang out and wait for something to happen. . . . [Many volunteers] are here to have fun, but also to "figure it out," whatever it is they have to figure out. You know, what do I want to do for work? That's a big question in my mind. I have a lot of different ideas, but nothing really has gripped me yet. I have the luxury of staying here or traveling for a while until it does, which is great. I feel very fortunate to have that luxury, to not have to keep going.

Personal transformation, then, arises partly from making the time to step out of "normal" life. Traveling, as a temporary state, seems a low risk way to do this because one can keep traveling, return home, or find a new place to live. But travel to Kalani opens volunteers to new possibilities, including more permanent lifestyle changes that critique the normalcy of capitalism. For example, for Amy, who left the solar panel business, being at Kalani changed her attitude toward work and possessions:

> I just felt really free. It felt really good to be away from the usual rigors and responsibilities of life, like having a car and having the electric bill and having to cook your food. It was just really freeing to not have to deal with all those responsibilities any more, and I've been on a quest ever since. I guess what it really showed me was like—wow—I don't have to live my life at all the way that I've been living it before and I'm not going to do that anymore. It really hit it right home for me. I met so many other people that were doing cool things

and were living outside the normal ways of life—when I say "normal," I mean having your nine-to-five job, having the stresses built into that, commuting to work and back, and living in your apartment, and paying rent, and all those little bits that you have to get together that almost everyone does—live in a town and have a life. I just wanted to do it another way. . . . So then I met a lot of people here who were doing it in different ways and it was very inspirational—well, if they can do it, I can do it—so it was a really big deal.

Community, Capitalism, And Travel

Another of the new possibilities that volunteers experienced at Kalani was a greater sense of community. For example, Daniel, who had a B.A. in anthropology, was looking for community as an alternative to the nuclear family when he volunteered at Kalani.

I was in my late twenties and a lot of my friends were getting married or coupling off. They weren't available to do things and that left a big void in my life—more loneliness. Also, I was working in a mental health hospital psych unit with adolescents, a lock-up unit—chemical dependency, mental health. I was realizing that so many of their problems came from the family dynamic—- single family—and realizing that even my family, as great as it looked from the outside, was pretty dysfunctional. Believing that nuclear families were not a good way to live started me thinking about a more tribal and communal kind of life.

At Kalani, with its metaphor of *ohana*, or Hawaiian extended family, Daniel found some of the support and accountability that was missing for him in nuclear-family living. People's openness in conversations at shared meals took up "the lack of friendship void." Many volunteers described themselves as loners in search of community. Kalani was "where Frosty the Snowman came to life," the "home for broken toys," a place for "everyone who used to sit alone for lunch at school." The gay-positive environment at Kalani, *ohana*, and the emphasis on one's personal journey made it a much more inclusive environment than many volunteers were used to, encouraging openness and conscious communication.

As these examples suggest, Kalani offers a kind of community that many find missing in capitalist society. Kalani is a nonprofit enterprise, but it is very much a part of the larger system. Miranda Joseph (2002: 73) argues that nonprofits "do not merely complement the market and the state but rather mark the absent center of capitalism"; they make that absence present and call it "community." So while volunteers explore paths toward alternative lifestyles at Kalani, participation in a capitalist economy is a necessary step on their journey. Moreover, the desire for community at Kalani articulates with capitalist desire in the spaces between work and tourism: volunteers purchase the opportunity for community with their time, their $500 a month, and their air ticket to Hawaii. But they achieve a sense of participation in that community through their trips to the volcanoes or the beach as well as through their work with team members, their shared spiritual practice such as yoga or ecstatic dance, and the particular skills they share, ranging from astronomy to body work.

A sense of community for volunteers at Kalani—and, I suspect, at other retreat centers—arises in spaces that capitalism produces but does not fill, spaces that fill through working, playing, and living together. A retired woman spoke of how she bonded with a young man through training and working together in housekeeping:

> We have a wonderful relationship. I've already organized to go to Philadelphia to visit him and to see Evita with him. [Work] is a way of getting to know people—when you're making beds with them, when you're cleaning the floor with them. Some of these people are a little bit—what do I say—they look different from my friends back home, and they might have seemed a little bit scary to me—maybe not scary, but "Oh my god, I don't want to talk to him! He's got tattoos all over him and rings in every orifice"; but that is not the case once you have worked with them. You live with them and love with them and work with them and it just changes everything.

The interplay between Anderson's (1983) imagined community and the "actual and limited social relations and practices through which it is realized" produce the affective, emotive power of community (Amit 2002: 18). This interplay was evident in the ways volunteers spoke about travel and community. While travel was important to the production of community, it also was responsible for some of Kalani's limitations as a community. Volunteers described these limitations in two ways: on the one hand, there was too much turnover as volunteers moved through Kalani and, on the other, volunteers who stayed longer than three months could have difficulties leaving.

On the one hand, the constant turnover that brought together such unlikely friends as the retired woman and the young man was something that volunteers valued, yet it was also a source of stress and a limitation on participation in the community. People spoke of burning out, of not having the energy to keep making new friends only to have them leave in a few months.

> Jacqueline: I would say a hard thing for me . . . is loving people and letting them go. I've made great friends and really loved them and gotten attached to them and then they leave. [It makes me feel] overwhelmed here socially . . . the constant turnover of people—guests, volunteers . . . It's really hard to continue to put out the same type of energy to everyone. I'd like to think I can meet every person and be present with every single person and give everybody everything, but it just can't happen. . . . [So] I'm not always sitting next to the new person saying "How are you? Where are you from?" I don't like to be [like this], because I've always been the compassionate person, the friend of the new kid . . . I know what it feels like to be "new" and I don't want to have to

go through that alone, but at the same time, I have to take care of myself, too and every day—every meal—there's a new person here that I'm sure could use a friend. I used to be somebody who would sit down next to them and say "Hi, how are you? Where are you from?" But every day, I can't do that.

On the other hand, volunteers can have difficulty moving on. Daniel, the anthropology graduate who sought and found community at Kalani, observed that:

[Kalani] becomes an easy life, too . . . all your meals are cooked for you, if you want to do something for fun, you don't have to go somewhere because there's stuff going on here. [One effect is that] when you leave at the end of the year, it is like your whole life is pulled out from under you, all your friends, everything, you know? And unless you have something to go to that you're really into, it can be like your heart being pulled out: all my friends are gone, my life is gone. It's a lot different out there in the real world. Did you ever see *Dances With Wolves?* It's like when he's leaving at the end and it's such a heart-rending thing. You probably know more about this than me, but in a lot of tribal communities, worse than putting somebody to death was to kick them out of the community, to be on their own.

Although it could be hard to leave after a year, very few volunteers stayed longer. I was told that burnout set in after a couple of years, especially for people in managerial positions. Living where you work can make it feel like you are working "twenty-four/seven." Just as it was hard to tell who was working at Kalani, it was hard to tell who was *not* working. Guests waylaid volunteers on their days off with work-related concerns. Issues from work could be hard to leave behind at meal times or in the staff quarters. Although some volunteers had been at Kalani for six years in 2005, most felt the urge to move on long before then. Those who stayed longest generally lived off the property or on its fringes.

Hawaii Rocks

In 1985, Bellah and his collaborators wrote about consciousness, culture, and the daily practices of life as reflexive, critical "habits of the heart" through which subjects, including what could be called privileged travelers, situate themselves between faith and doubt, self-reliance and engaged citizenship. In *Sources of the Self,* philosopher Charles Taylor draws on this work but notes that the authors elide two crucial areas of modern concern: the loss of meaning in our culture, and the need for commitment to a greater whole. What is obscured, Taylor says, is "personal resonance," namely "the search for moral sources *outside* the subject through languages which resonate *within* him or her, the grasping of an order which is inseparably indexed to a personal vision" (1989: 510). Personal resonance articulates "our farther, stronger intuitions [that] the world is not simply an ensemble of objects for our use, but makes a further claim on us. [This demand is one] of attention, of careful scrutiny, of respect for what is there. [It] . . . is not simply one of self-fulfillment. It emanates from the world" (ibid: 513).

At Kalani, people describe this resonance of the self with the world as arising from both a sense of community and a sense of place.[4] We have seen how people found community at Kalani. They also identified powerful, and challenging connections to Hawaii as a place. Volunteers did not regard Kalani itself as remarkable; it was equated with Hawaii in their descriptions of how nature resonated for them. Not surprisingly, when I visited in January, almost everyone told me how the fact that Kalani was in Hawaii had influenced their decision to volunteer. "Being in nature," as many put it, was important and the kind of nature Hawaii offers was nourishing. Devon, a man in his late twenties told me:

> Well, Hawaii is Hawaii. It's a beautiful state . . . and it's a tropical paradise, so initially there was a pull, but coming here opened my eyes to the big island in particular and to this area of the big island. Just being in Hawaii in general changed my life, on top of Kalani—this place is incredibly powerful, being close to the ocean. My relationship with the ocean developed. I'd never really spent much time with the ocean [but] I'm a very strong water person, so I spent a lot of time swimming and snorkeling and being connected to the ocean. Hawaii and Kalani really nourish my being, really encourage me to be physical—swimming or surfing, doing yoga—just being outside in this warm environment is so nourishing.

Francis, the former RCMP officer, observed that an appreciation of nature, of living in a tropical paradise, is one thing that links the otherwise diverse members of the Kalani community:

> There are [volunteers] who are yogis that are on the path. There are party people . . . There is a commonality around connection to nature though . . . because we're surrounded by such beauty. I think most people here, if not everybody, takes time out of their day and, because we have that luxury here, we only work thirty hours a week, [we are] able to commune with nature, whether it's taking a walk, going to the beach, or going on little adventures; but there's such richness here to be in communion with nature that it's part of the experience here, it's a big part of it.

More than Hawaii's climate attracted volunteers. Much of Hawaii's resonance arose, in volunteers' experience, from the harsh power of the volcanic island as well as from the lush tropical landscape that covers the lava rock. To contextualize his point about nature, Francis described his trip to the Kilauea caldera as part of one of the guest "adventures" that Kalani allows volunteers to join:

> We left in the afternoon and walked to the volcano, to the lava flow. Then, in the evening, it was dark and then we could see the lava at our feet—earth being

created at our feet—it was so powerful. I'd never seen anything like it. Hot, red, molten lava at my feet. You can feel the heat emanating, and anywhere you walk, at any moment, the earth might give way. So very powerful and, well, dangerous—a little bit. There's an element of danger [so] you have to be very present. And [it's] powerful, very powerful. I can't explain it other than to say it's earth being created in front of your eyes.

Pele, the fire goddess, transforms matter, including people. Clare told me: "Being on the big island has the energy of transformation and support. I feel like this island in particular . . . [gives you the] feeling of being welcomed and sort of hugged, even though it brings up a lot—because Pele's here and there's a lot of transformation—but if feels like it's a safe place to have it [happen. The island's energy] will hold you while you go through it. In Mina's words, "You just become a complete conduit and clear channel for all these things to happen. A lot of it has to do with the lava. We're walking on seismic ground constantly, so . . . it churns fire in you. That can be destructive, but you can use it for growing."

The big island of Hawaii is associated with the first or root chakra. Volunteers told me, that people are drawn to Hawaii to work on "first chakra" issues. Even those who have done a lot of spiritual work may come there to work on their first chakra if they still have "blockages" around core issues like survival or sense of belonging. Clearly Hawaii becomes a practiced place in de Certeau's (1984) sense, where a way of living, including varieties of spiritual practice, creates dynamic, meaning-filled space. The experience of place is multilocal in that it is different for everyone yet finds expression in shared cultural terms, such as Pele (Marcus 1995; Rodman 1992).

Conclusion: Inner And Outer Journeys

Emotions stirred by the power attributed to Hawaii resonate in volunteers' descriptions of the personal, often spiritual journeys that led them to Kalani, that evolve there, and that link their Kalani experiences with their volunteer work at other retreat centers.

Particular kinds of intuitive knowledge seem both to constitute and be constituted by the praxis of privileged travel itself. There are two dialogical aspects to this: a metaphorical travel that is an "inner journey" of self-discovery, and the real-world travel to spend time at Kalani. Volunteers who consider themselves to be on a spiritual path talk about how they came to Kalani in terms of gut feelings, of being drawn there, of inevitability or something that was meant to be. The inner journey intuitively encourages their travel to Hawaii and to Kalani. And being there opens people to further personal transformation that values intuitive knowledge.

The outward journey enables the inner one, and the inner journey encourages more travel. Many of those who worked as resident volunteers at Kalani have also volunteered at other retreat centers or plan to do so. At the time of my research, their informal circuit included the Omega Institute in New York state, where some regular winter Kalani volunteers worked during the summer. Kripalu, a yoga retreat in Massachusetts that offered a three-month Spiritual Lifestyle Program, gave many Kalani volunteers their start. Other retreat centers that Kalani volunteers frequented included Findhorn in Scotland, Breitenbush Hot Springs in Oregon, and Mount Madonna Center in California as well as its sister community, the Salt Spring Centre of Yoga in the Gulf Islands of British Columbia. Comparison of Kalani with other retreat centers was a frequent topic of conversations in the lanai. One volunteer told me that Kalani was the "least spiritual community" she had visited, and others regarded it as a good place to "work through stuff" in a vacation-like atmosphere. The circuit also included nonspiritual destinations that volunteers favored when they needed to earn money, notably employment during the summer tourist season in Scagway, Alaska.

A reflective, inner journey is not necessary for guests, staff, and volunteers to enjoy the time spent at Kalani, but the Web site's emphasis on renewal, the gift of a journal to each new volunteer, opportunities for daily yoga, and an atmosphere in which spirituality is talked about a lot, all encourage such a journey to enrich the playfulness and sensuality of a Hawaiian holiday in an open, tolerant community. While people's transformative paths are recognized as individual and unique, they have many common cultural dimensions. These include a focus on personal development as well as consciousness of connections with place and community. Intuitive, experiential learning is basic to this process and volunteers speak in those terms when they describe the process of coming to Kalani—"I knew I was taken care of"—and the changes they experienced while volunteering there.

Both the metaphorical and the physical journeys can be round-trips. They seem to arise from the stresses of contemporary, Western life and they return people to face those stresses with new, inner resources that make them and the world "better." But, as we have seen, the journey can be open-ended. Many volunteers return to Kalani, continue their journey at other spiritual retreat centers, or find other ways to opt out of "crazy life permanently." The contemplative life has a long history of connection to organized religion and to poverty. But Kalani offers an alternative space that can be filled with diverse combinations of spiritualities, sexualities, and other activities; moreover, it makes this space available to mainly middle-class, secular people whose immersion in capitalist circuits seemingly devalues such a way of being. These include people who choose to step out of that world, at least for a while, even if the nonprofit center to which they travel remains structured by capitalism. As we have seen, finding the time to exit the rat race of such a workaday world and volunteer at Kalani can be crucial to personal transformation, to finding a particular kind of community, and to connection with the power of place.

Travelers vitalize the community at Kalani, bringing together people whose paths would be unlikely to cross elsewhere. Yet travel also strains community, as people lose the energy to make new friends who will soon leave and, conversely, as they feel devastated when they themselves have to move on. The power of the volcano makes Hawaii far more than just a tropical holiday destination for volunteers, although they acknowledge that attraction, too. Nature resonates with self, supporting the personal transformation that draws volunteers to the big island and to Kalani.

Notes

1. Quoted from the Web site for Kalani Honua, also known as Kalani Oceanside Retreat. The source for this and all other material cited here from the Kalani Web site is http://www.kalani.com/index.asp, 1 September 2005.
2. Interviews at Kalani were part of a larger research project for which I am grateful for funding from the Social Sciences and Humanities Research Council of Canada. Pseudonyms are used for all the people interviewed.
3. Volunteer guests paid between $560 and $1,050 per person per week for double accommodation, compared to the $840 and $1,260 that guests paid, but the guest package included two bodywork sessions and a half-day adventure that were not included in the pricing for volunteer guests.
4. Personal resonance, notably, did *not* arise from a sense of political engagement at Kalani. A few volunteers told me that feeling detached from political activism was important to them and that they had engaged in such activities in their lives in Canada and in the U.S. outside Hawaii. In my brief period of fieldwork, I could find no connection between volunteers and local politics or native Hawaiian issues.

References

Amit, Vered. 2002. "Reconceptualizing Community." In *Realizing Community: Concepts, Social Relationships and Sentiments,* ed. V. Amit. New York: Routledge. pp. 1-20.

Anderson, Benedict. 1983. *Imagined Communities: Reflections on the Origin and Spread of Nationalism.* New York: Verso.

Bellah, Robert, et al. 1985. *Habits of the Heart: Individualism and Commitment in American Life.* Berkeley: University of California.

de Certeau, Michel. 1984. *The Practice of Everyday Life.* Berkeley: University of California.

Joseph, Miranda. 2002. *Against the Romance of Community.* Minneapolis: University of Minnesota.

Marcus, George. 1995. "Ethnography In/Of the World System: The Emergence of Multi-sited Ethnography." *Annual Review of Anthropology* 24: 95-117.

Rodman, Margaret. 1992. "Empowering Place: Multilocality and Multivocality." *American Anthropologist* 94: 640–656.
Taylor, Charles. 1989. *Sources of the Self: The Making of Modern Identity.* Cambridge: Harvard University Press.

Notes on Contributors

Vered Amit is Professor of Anthropology at Concordia University in Montreal. She has conducted fieldwork in the U.K., Canada, and the Cayman Islands. Her research interests include youth cultures, the politics of ethnicity, transnational mobility, elites, and community. Recent books include *The Biographical Dictionary of Social and Cultural Anthropology* (2004*), The Trouble with Community* (2002) (with Nigel Rapport), *Realizing Community: Concepts, Social Relationships, and Sentiments* (2002), and *Constructing the Field: Ethnographic Fieldwork in the Contemporary World* (2000).

Anne-Meike Fechter is Lecturer in Anthropology at the University of Sussex. Her doctoral thesis analyzes Euro American expatriates working in Jakarta within a framework of transnationalism and globalization. Anne-Meike Fechter's research interests include transnationalism and migration, the anthropology of gender, the body, and space, with a regional emphasis on Southeast Asia. She is currently preparing a monograph based on her Ph.D. research, entitled "Transnational Lives: Expatriates in Indonesia."

Cathy Greenhalgh is Principal Lecturer in Film and Television at the University of the Arts London, originally working as a cinematographer in the film industry. She is the author of "Shooting from the Heart: Cinematographers and their Medium" in *Making Pictures: A Century of European Cinematography* (2003), and is writing *Cinematography,* a book for Wallflower Press (due 2007). She is conducting ethnographic research with feature-film cinematographers. Her research interests include collaborative and interdisciplinary creativity, filmmaking practices, cinematographic phenomena, performativity, and narrative.

Sawa Kurotani is currently Assistant Professor of Anthropology at the University of Redlands. She received a Ph.D. in anthropology in 1999 from the University of Colorado, Boulder, and was a Rockefeller postdoctoral fellow at the University of North Carolina, Chapel Hill, in 1999–2000. Her main research and teaching interests center on globalization, Japanese national identity, and gender. Her first book, *Home Away from Home: Japanese Corporate Wives in the United States,* was published in 2005.

Caroline Oliver has recently joined the Faculty of Education at the University of Cambridge, having worked as a lecturer in the School of Geography, Politics and Sociology at the University of Newcastle upon Tyne for the last three years. She received her Ph.D. in sociology and social anthropology from the University of Hull, researching migration and ageing identities among older people retiring from Northern Europe to Southern Spain. Aspects of this research have been published in journals including *Mortality* and the *Journal of Mediterranean Studies* while the main findings are to be published as a research monograph in 2006.

Karen Fog Olwig is Professor of Anthropology at the Department of Anthropology, University of Copenhagen. Her main research interests are migration, family networks, and inter-generational relations, and the Caribbean. Recent publications include *Work and Migration: Life and Livelihood in a Globalizing World* (2002, coedited with Ninna Nyberg Sørensen); *Children's Places* (2003, coedited with Eva Gulløv), and *Caribbean Narratives of Belonging* (2005, coedited with Jean Besson).

Margaret Rodman is Professor of Anthropology at York University in Toronto, Canada. She first conducted research in Vanuatu in 1978 while a graduate student at McMaster University. Her most recent books on Vanuatu include *Houses Far From Home* (2001) and *Home in the Islands* (1997, coedited with Jan Rensel). *New Neighbours* (1992) resulted from her research with Matt Cooper on Canadian housing cooperatives. Professor Rodman's interest in meanings of place finds new expression in her research on spiritual educational retreat centers.

Angela Torresan holds a doctorate in Social and Visual Anthropology from the University of Manchester, England. She is presently a Research Fellow and Visiting Lecturer at the Universidade Federal do Rio Grande do Norte, Brazil. She has conducted research among indigenous groups in northeast Brazil and with Brazilian immigrants in England and Portugal. Her work explores the politics of emerging identities, political anthropology, postcolonial relations, middle-class migration, and ethnographic filmmaking.

Index